INSTRUCTING AND EVALUATING IN HIGHER EDUCATION

A Guidebook for Planning Learning Outcomes

Ron J. McBeath, EDITOR

Faculty and Instructional Development Office
San Jose State University

EDUCATIONAL TECHNOLOGY PUBLICATIONS
ENGLEWOOD CLIFFS, NEW JERSEY 07632

Library of Congress Cataloging-in-Publication Data

Instructing and evaluating in higher education : a guidebook for planning learning outcomes / Ron J. McBeath, editor.
p. cm.
Includes bibliographical references and index.
ISBN 0-87778-242-3
1. College teaching--United States. 2. Educational tests and measurements--United States. I. McBeath, Ron.
LB2331.I59 1992
378.1'25'0973--dc20 91-40486
CIP

Printed in the United States of America.

Library of Congress Catalog Card Number:
91-40486.

International Standard Book Number:
0-87778-242-3.

First Printing: January 1992.

TABLE OF CONTENTS

Part 1. INSTRUCTION

Part 2. TESTING AND EVALUATION

CONSTRUCTING AND SCORING ESSAY QUESTIONS

PERFORMANCE TESTING

DEVELOPING OPINION, INTEREST, AND ATTITUDE QUESTIONNAIRES

PREFACE

THE CHALLENGE . . .

One of the significant professional challenges we face in teaching and training is to identify and meet students' immediate expectations, and to encourage and guide lifelong learning, by serving short- and long-term needs. Are we ready to do this?

- ☐ **Are the skills and habits we have developed over the years suited to the educational challenges of today?**
- ☐ **Do students know what learning outcomes are expected in the course?**
- ☐ **How well do we know our own approach to teaching?**
- ☐ **What type of classroom atmosphere do we set?**
- ☐ **Are we facilitating learning to the best of our ability?**
- ☐ **Do we teach and test on the whole range of intellectual skills?**
- ☐ **Are our practices in keeping with our beliefs?**
- ☐ **Are students encouraged to participate fully in the instructional process?**

The **Self-Appraisal Form** and instructional modules in the guidebook are designed to help you answer these and similar questions. The basic purpose of the self-appraisal form is to help you identify professional areas you would like to further develop. The five areas covered in the form are: instructional strategies, tests and evaluation of learning, discussion techniques, instructor-student relationships, and course structure. Within each area four levels of activity and four levels of commitment are described, to help you identify your level of interest.

The eleven instructional modules incorporate the principles of active learning with examples and exercises included for each new concept. The materials can be used by individuals on a self-instructional basis, or by a workshop leader in a group setting. In addition to a wide range of examples and activities from different disciplines, each module concludes with a comprehensive application exercise where you apply the techniques learned in a specific course you are teaching.

Under the direction of the editor, *Ron J. McBeath*, the modules have been created by a team of developers. The developers are *Jerrold E. Kemp, Janice Lane, Jeanne Lassen, Ron J. McBeath, Philip C. Seyer, Robert J. Simas,* and *Carol R. Smith.* Other contributors are *David Cohen, Oswald B. Carleton, Fred E. Dillman, Damon G. Nalty, Donald G. Perrin, Peter Pipe,* and *Robert Rubeck. Richard B. Lewis* was editorial consultant for the first prepublication edition.

THE RATIONALE . . .

The improvement of instruction in adult learning and higher education is a complex professional challenge. This is due in large part to the fact that the individual learners and their teachers are so diverse, with different interests, backgrounds, skills and expectations. During this century educational theorists such as Dewey, Piaget, Bloom, Gagne and Maslow have developed theories which help educators to identify these differences and to create instructional programs that help students to learn in stages from the simple to the complex, from low level factual recall to higher level intellectual skills such as critical thinking.

A scheme which has helped educators identify stages of learning in students was developed by William Perry (1970) at Harvard University. Perry identified nine growth steps or transitions which he grouped into four major stages of intellectual and ethical development. The terms *dualism, multiplicity, relativism,* and *commitment* were used to describe each stage. A set of teaching styles (McBeath, 1987) which parallel the four stages of learning are also outlined in Figure 1. The *Perry* outline shows how students move from the need for certainties and a dependence on authority, to being able to accept ambiguity as they create meaning and order in their world. The *McBeath* teaching stages show how instruction becomes less teacher centered and more inquiry or learning centered as teachers' behavior becomes less dominating and more collaborative.

STAGES OF LEARNING

Dualism

The dualistic student sees the world in polar terms of right and wrong, good and bad, not better or worse. The right answer exists for each problem and the right answer is known by an authority, usually the teacher. For students, gaining knowledge and achieving goodness are both accomplished through hard work. The dualistic student avoids ambiguity and is dependent on authority figures, to the point of blind obedience.

Multiplicity

At this stage the dualistic, authority oriented structure is modified. Ambiguity is grudgingly acknowledged, but it is seen as a temporary thing because the final truth has not yet been determined. Everyone is seen as having a right to his or her own opinion, and there is a permissive attitude regarding the diversity of both options and values. Uncertainty is seen as being resolved when the authorities determine the right answer. At this stage no one needs to be wrong, and there is no pattern or system in the opinions expressed. The quantity of information held has more significance than the quality.

Figure 1. Stages in Learning and Teaching.

Learning Stages (Perry)	Teaching Stages (McBeath)
Dualism	**Teacher Dominated**
Wants the answer	Teaching is telling
Knowledge equals facts	One-way communication
Avoids ambiguity	Questions and answers
Authorities have answers	Subject matter acquisition is basic
Memorize by hard work	Tests on recall
Multiplicity	**Subject Centered**
Wants more answers	Teaching is telling plus media
Ambiguity grudgingly acknowledged	One-way communication—some ambiguity
Everyone has right to opinion	Cites multiple authorities
Permissive regarding diversity	Student expected to be active learner
No one is wrong	Evaluation on recall and applications
Relativism	**Learning Task Oriented**
Context determines inquiry	Teaching includes group and individual work
Ambiguity is fact of life	Needs assessment—alternative methods
Knowledge is constructed	Different authorities—ambiguity accepted
Reasonable people can disagree	Two-way communication for mastery
Knowledge is qualitative	Evaluate recall, applications, implications
Commitment	**Inquiry Centered**
Contextual relativism assumed	Courses based on readiness levels
Open to alternatives	Critical inquiry encouraged
Learning is enfolding and unfolding	Creativity supported
Decisions based on reasoning	Collaborative problem solving
Explores issues responsibly	Evaluation based on mastery criteria

Relativism

The student at this stage has made a shift from accumulating quantities of information where right and wrong prevail, to seeing all knowledge and values as contextual and relativistic. Ambiguity is accepted as a fact of life, and knowledge is seen as a blend of fact and opinion—the result of human interaction. Knowledge is now qualitative and some opinions are seen as important; others as not important, depending on the context.

The transformation of relativistic thinking is most significant and is precipitated by the failure of the dualistic framework in the first two stages to help students to see the interdependence of parts within the whole, to explore alternative points of view, make viable comparisons, examine assumptions, form their own opinions and make their own decisions.

Commitment

Students at the stage of commitment are accepting responsibility for their own ideas and actions. It requires courage of convictions and acceptance of one's doubts; being able to recognize one's potential as well as limitations. A strong sense of identity is developed as the students learn to explore and develop a sense of confidence in a relativistic world where reasonable people can disagree, where there are no pat answers and where new challenges continue to appear.

As in other stage theories of development (e.g., Piaget), each stage is more complex and comprehensive than the previous one, as the student perceives increased complexities in the world and uncertainties in knowledge. Progress through the stages involves not only the joy of realization, but also a loss of certainty, acceptance of ambiguity, and an altered sense of self, according to Perry.

STAGES OF TEACHING

Styles of teaching have a profound effect on how students progress through the stages of learning. The four stages of teaching are closely correlated to the four stages of learning.

Stage 1 (Teacher Dominated)

Teachers who teach predominantly in the style of Stage 1 are serving the needs of the dependent, authority centered, linear thinking students, but are not helping them to move on to other stages.

This traditional technique is a carry-over from an earlier era in education in which the acquisition and memorization of information were regarded as the main tasks for students. The mind was seen as a fish net which would catch whatever was poured into it. Naturally it was assumed that the bigger minds (nets) would catch more.

Basically, the teacher would direct students' learning through the textbook and lecture mode. Questions would be asked to check that students were memorizing the correct information. Tests were mainly used to measure the recall of information provided, on the assumption that this would help maintain the *status quo* in society.

Stage 2 (Subject Centered)

Teachers at Stage 2 are providing more information while also using a greater variety of presentation methods. Films, slides, television and other forms of media are very popular and used to add interest. Teaching at this stage is still basically one-way communication from teacher to students. However, new techniques, in addition to increasing information available, bring in some uncertainties and ambiguity. Divergent views are presented, but students are not expected to share and qualify their interpretations with other students. Tests are based on recall and applications, but seldom on examining the implications.

The student is still expected to gain high marks through the hard work of memorizing the information presented. The responsibility for learning is placed upon the student, while the teacher primarily provides opportunities for learning to take place.

Stage 3 (Learning Task Oriented)

The shift in emphasis at this stage is as significant for the teacher as it is for the student. Attention is now given to improving learning conditions and facilitating learning. There will be some large group teaching, but more time is spent on small group work, and individual studies.

A needs assessment may be conducted to determine learning requirements and instructional objectives may be written. Alternative methods and materials are provided for students who have different levels of experience and different learning styles. A conscientious effort is made to plan, design, and support a curriculum that will serve a more diverse student group.

The teacher not only provides different points of view, but also helps the students to see the implications of the various positions. Tests are expanded from recall and application questions to include questions regarding implications of the ideas being studied. At this stage, discussions involving student experiences and individual opinions become an important part of the program.

Stage 4 (Inquiry Centered)

Teachers working at this level encourage students to explore, think creatively, and take risks in their educational activities. They help students to identify problems and search for new ways of initiating inquiries. They encourage students as they expand their patterns of learning. Not only does testing include recall, applications, implications and creative explorations, but it is also used diagnostically to help open up further avenues for learning.

Courses are developed now to serve the different readiness levels of students, intellectually and ethically. Students are more likely to reach the fourth stage of commitment when an instructional program is designed to meet their diverse learning needs.

IMPROVING INSTRUCTION

Perry's research indicates that we should expect to have students in higher education classes at different intellectual stages. In a first year class the majority are generally dualistic and would probably prefer to be taught in the *teacher dominated* style in order to meet their own immediate self perceived needs. The challenge we face as professionals is not only to identify and meet students' immediate needs, but also to encourage and provide for their growth through the sequence of stages. The Self-Appraisal Form and modules in this Guidebook are designed to help you plan, implement, and evaluate instructional programs to meet these outcomes.

Research indicates that we tend to teach as we were taught. In order to change the long established habits we have developed as students and teachers, the principles and activities provided here can help you to develop effective techniques in a reflective and purposeful way.

BIBLIOGRAPHY

Banathy, Bela. **Systems Design of Education.** Englewood Cliffs, NJ: Educational Technology Publications, 1991.

Bohm, David. **Wholeness and the Implicate Order**. London: Routledge and Kegan Paul, 1980.

Davies, Ivor K. **Competency Based Learning: Technology, Management and Design**. New York: McGraw Hill Book Company, 1971.

Dewey, John. **Experience and Nature**. New York: Open Court Publishing Co., 1929.

Drucker, Peter F. **The New Realities**. New York: Harper and Row, Publishers, 1989.

Erikson, E.H. **Insight and Responsibility**. New York: Norton, 1964.

Gagné, Robert M. **The Conditions of Learning**. (4th ed.) New York: Holt, Rinehart and Winston, 1985.

Kuhn, Thomas S. **The Structure of Scientific Revolutions**. Chicago: University of Chicago Press, 1962.

Lewin, K. **A Dynamic Theory of Personality**. New York: McGraw-Hill Book Company, 1935.

Lovell-Troy, Larry and Eickmann, Paul. **Course Design for College Teachers**. Englewood Cliffs, NJ: Educational Technology Publications, 1992.

Mager, Robert F. **Developing Attitude Toward Learning**. Palo Alto, CA: Fearon, 1968.

McBeath, R.J. (Ed.) **Extending Education Through Technology**. Washington, D.C.: Association for Educational Communications and Technology, 1972.

McBeath, R.J. *Toward a Faculty Self-Appraisal and Development Program.* **Instructional Development: The State of the Art II,** Co-editors Ronald K. Bass and Charles R. Dills, Dubuque, IA: Kendall/Hunt Publishing Company, 1984.

McBeath, R.J. *Stages in Learning, Teaching and Media Support Services,* **Educational Technology**, Englewood Cliffs, NJ: Educational Technology Publications, October 1987.

McKeachie, W.J. **Teaching Tips: A Guidebook for the Beginning College Teacher**. (8th ed.) Lexington, MA: D.C. Heath and Company, 1986.

Perry, William G. **Forms of Intellectual and Ethical Development in the College Years**. New York: Holt, Rinehart and Winston, 1970.

Wilshire, Bruce. **The Moral Collapse of the University.** Albany, NY: State University of New York Press, 1990.

THE RESOURCES . . .

Self-Appraisal Form assists in identifying your interests and level of commitment for improving professional competencies.

Setting Objectives reviews the role of learning or performance objectives, in planning, implementing, and evaluating instruction. Criteria and guidelines are provided for writing and using objectives at different levels in the intellectual process.

Preparing Lectures focuses on selecting and organizing content, choosing examples and resources, selecting presentation methods, creating conditions for successful learning, and on planning to evaluate lecture effectiveness.

Conducting Discussions explores the discussion process in regard to patterns, purposes, preparing, conducting, and evaluating three types of discussions.

Improving Instructor-Student Relationships guides the participant through exercises to increase sensitivity to student perceptions of the classroom, and to build skills in communication. Instructor functions and learning styles are described with ways to alleviate negative feelings, increase positive responses, develop self-confidence, and enhance the sense of responsibility among students.

Constructing Multiple Choice Test Items gives seven rules and four tips to assist in item construction in different subject areas and at six levels of intellectual skill.

Constructing True-False Test Items describes simple, complex, and compound forms of the test. Three rules are given to guide construction and use of test items.

Constructing Matching Test Items describes the three components and two types of relationships in a matching test. Guidelines are given for constructing and using test items.

Item Analysis on Objective Tests describes procedures for determining test reliability on norm referenced tests. A detailed interpretation of item analysis from a computer printout is given and a brief statement is included on item comparison in criterion referenced tests.

Constructing and Scoring Essay Questions presents guidelines and exercises for developing and reliably scoring essay test questions using the point score and rating methods.

Performance Testing provides construction and use guidelines for several performance tests. Examples include simulations, work samples, projects, and problem solving.

Developing Opinion, Interest, and Attitude Questionnaires gives guidelines for developing and using adjective and behavioral checklists, Likert and semantic differential rating scales, ranking techniques, and open ended questions.

These materials were originally developed as part of a project for the Center for Professional Development, Office of the Chancellor, California State University and Colleges System, and funded in part through the Fund for the Improvement of Postsecondary Education, U.S. Department of Education.

SELF-APPRAISAL FORM

The basic purpose of this form is to help you identify professional areas you would like to further develop. Resources and activities to assist you in meeting the needs you identify are included in the development modules in the Guidebook.

Five major instructional areas are listed below. Please read the description under each area and circle the appropriate response(s) for each description.

A	NOT NECESSARY	I don't feel that I need help in this area.
B	LOW PRIORITY	I am interested, but for the time being this is low priority.
C	MORE INFORMATION	I'd like to find out more about this area.
D	READY FOR ACTION	I would like to develop this area as soon as possible.

INSTRUCTIONAL STRATEGIES (Lectures, Group Work, Self-Paced Learning, etc.)

A B C D — Give effective lectures with clear goals, appropriate examples, and in a well-organized manner.

A B C D — Make use of a variety of media and resources in my instruction to add interest and clarity.

A B C D — Provide opportunities for self-paced learning and interactive group work through planned modules and support resources.

A B C D — Design an instructional system in which the students are pretested and guided into alternative activities (self-paced and group) to reach desired learning outcomes.

TESTS AND EVALUATION OF LEARNING (Objective and Subjective)

A B C D — Use assessment techniques to measure the student's knowledge of the course content, based on standards from previous semesters.

A B C D — Use assessment techniques to measure the student's understanding and ability to apply knowledge.

A B C D — Use assessment techniques to measure the student's level of learning, ability to apply intellectual skills, and to explore further implications.

A B C D — Use assessment techniques to measure the student's mastery of knowledge, learning and intellectual skills for problem solving, critical inquiry, and creative applications.

DISCUSSION TECHNIQUES

A B C D Have students respond to questions I raise.

A B C D Have students develop and ask me questions related to the topic.

A B C D Have students raise questions to develop a free interaction within the group.

A B C D Have an exchange with and among the students so that both the students and I measurably benefit.

INSTRUCTOR-STUDENT RELATIONSHIPS

A B C D Establish an atmosphere in the classroom so that the students will be receptive to the instructional program.

A B C D Build good rapport with the students in order to ascertain and meet their course needs.

A B C D Develop sound interpersonal relationships with students in order to encourage their personal development, self-confidence, and ability to accept ambiguity.

A B C D Create a common ground with students in order to collaborate with them in realistic problem solving, and creative problem identification activities.

COURSE STRUCTURE

A B C D Plan the course in order to present the subject matter in a well-rounded, logical manner.

A B C D Provide flexibility in course structure by relating to the self-perceived needs of the students.

A B C D Develop the course based on a specified set of performance objectives and provide alternative means for the students to reach learning objectives.

A B C D Develop the course in a systematic way and, in addition to providing alternatives to students, obtain their feedback for course restructuring and improvement.

SETTING OBJECTIVES

Module Developers:	Jerrold E. Kemp Ron J. McBeath
Editorial Associates:	Oswald B. Carleton Fred E. Dillman Philip C. Seyer Carole R. Smith
Editorial Consultant:	Richard B. Lewis

SETTING OBJECTIVES

The development of objectives is one step in the process of planning, presenting, and evaluating instruction. By making it the first, it can then serve as a guide for the other phases of the process. When used as a guide for planning, the objectives become a means to focus on the specific requirements in a presentation or course. They also assist in the selection of the appropriate content, techniques, strategies, and evaluation procedures. To help you develop and use objectives effectively in your instructional programs this module is organized under the following headings:

I. **Course Goals and Performance Objectives**
II. **Parts of Performance Objectives**
III. **Levels of Performance Objectives**
IV. **Categories of Performance Objectives**
V. **Summary Outline**
VI. **Review Test**
VII. **Application Exercise**

I. COURSE GOALS AND PERFORMANCE OBJECTIVES

Course Goals

The best start for developing objectives is to review your course goals as stated on the course outline provided for students. Course goals are usually stated in general terms so that the students will be quickly informed about the nature of the course and the course requirements. Terms such as those below are used to introduce the goal statements and give students a general idea about the overall purposes of the course.

- ☐ gain an understanding
- ☐ become aware
- ☐ develop an appreciation

For example, *gain an understanding of the factors contributing to the Industrial Revolution* could be one of several goals listed for a history course.

In order to have students reach such a course goal, lectures, discussions, self-paced learning, and various other instructional activities and resources may be provided. The resources could include textbooks, workbooks, reading assignments, study films, videotapes, guest lecturers, and computer data bases. The decisions that lead to selection of the instructional activities and resources can be greatly facilitated by the development of a series of *objectives* for each unit or topic. These objectives can assist you, the instructor, to decide specifically what you want your students to learn. When students are informed of the specific objectives, they should know what you will require of them so that they will be able to prepare themselves for your examinations.

Performance Objectives

The expression *performance objectives* is often used to indicate that an objective is written in terms of what the student should be able to *do* as a result of instruction. This would include typical student activities such as *writing, listing, analyzing, solving, designing, producing,* and *experimenting*. Performance objectives may also be called **learning objectives.**

How well can you differentiate between *course goals* and *performance objectives*?

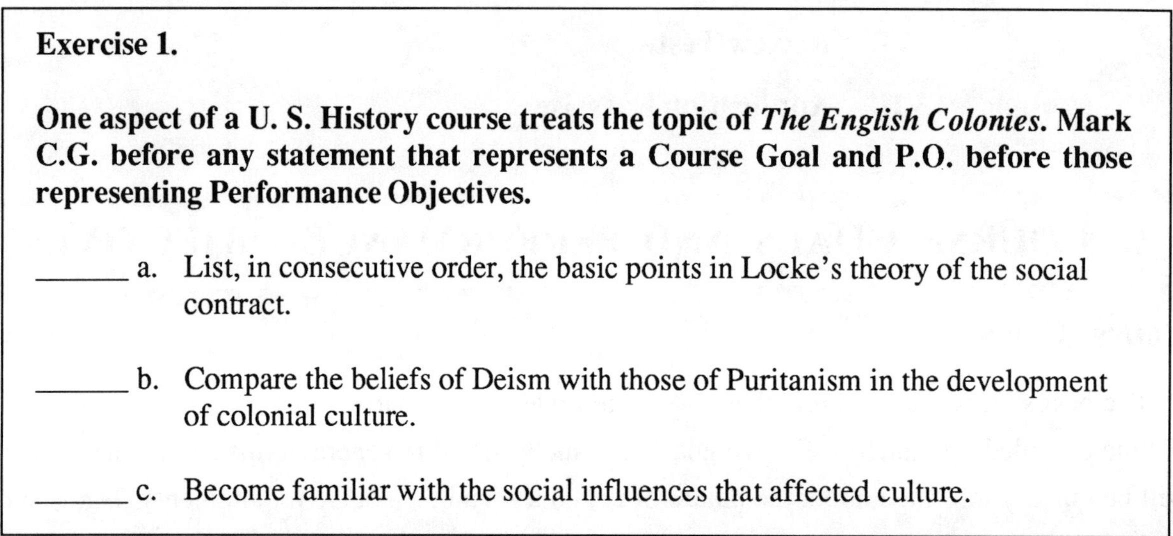

Exercise 1.

One aspect of a U. S. History course treats the topic of *The English Colonies*. Mark C.G. before any statement that represents a Course Goal and P.O. before those representing Performance Objectives.

______ a. List, in consecutive order, the basic points in Locke's theory of the social contract.

______ b. Compare the beliefs of Deism with those of Puritanism in the development of colonial culture.

______ c. Become familiar with the social influences that affected culture.

Of the three statements in Exercise 1, item **c** is the goal statement. This is what the instructor may have included in the course outline to describe in broad terms the emphasis that would be given to the topic, *The English Colonies*. The phrase, *become familiar with*, is generalized and provides an indication of one of the purposes for the course.

The other two statements are examples of performance objectives. They describe more specifically what content will be treated and what students will be expected to do. Performance objectives are distinguished from course goals by their higher degree of specificity.

Exercise 2.

Of these six statements, select those that are Performance Objectives.

______ a. Introduce a chronological framework for the evolution of style in the history of art.

______ b. Represent any number less than 1000 in the Egyptian, Roman, and Babylonian numerical systems.

______ c. Explain in words and drawings the basic structure of protein molecules.

______ d. Know the characteristics of weather frontal types.

______ e. Grasp the significance of the changes in America during the period of the Jeffersonians.

______ f. Identify three kinds of photographic lenses from photographs taken with each one.

In Exercise 2, items **b**, **c**, and **f** are specific performance objectives. The others are general statements of course goals and do not indicate what the student will be able to do as a result of learning. The course goals provide students with a general orientation and can be used as a general base from which a series of performance objectives may be constructed.

Turn to the **gray sheets** and complete items A and B on page 17.

II. PARTS OF PERFORMANCE OBJECTIVES

A performance objective has two essential parts and may include two optional parts. The essential parts are the ***action verb*** and ***content reference***. Look over the statements you have already worked with in Exercise 1. The verbs in **a** and **b**, *list* and *compare,* are action words. They direct students to a specific performance. The remainder of each statement is the content reference, relating to subject content for treatment in instruction. The optional parts are ***standard of performance***, and ***statement of conditions***.

Action Verbs

The most difficult part of writing a performance objective is the selection of an appropriate *action verb*. It should express clearly what you want your students to be able to do with the subject content, *recognize, explain, solve, construct, assess*, and so on. Such verbs indicate observable and measurable learning activity.

How well can you select verbs that express *observable* action?

Exercise 3.

Check those terms that could be useful as action verbs in performance objectives.

______ a. predict	______ h. formulate
______ b. compare	______ i. perceive
______ c. comprehend	______ j. name
______ d. define	______ k. grasp
______ e. distinguish between	______ l. select
______ f. rate	______ m. categorize
______ g. appreciate	______ n. label

The verbs that do not express observable action are, comprehend, appreciate, perceive, and grasp. They are broad, goal-oriented terms and do not describe the specific, observable types of behavior associated with performance objectives.

Verbs suitable for performance objectives include **a, b, d, e, f, h, j, l, m,** and **n.**

Content Reference

The content reference indicates the particular subject matter that the student is to learn. It is the means for enabling the student to develop a broader knowledge base for future applications and further learning.

In Exercise 2, the content references in items **b**, **c**, and **f** are: *numbers in Egyptian, Roman, and Babylonian numerical systems*, *the basic structure of protein molecules*, and *kinds of photographic lenses.*

Standard of Performance

When preparing performance objectives, in addition to the action verb and content reference, you may want to include a level of competency that indicates the standard of performance you require for satisfactory learning. Such expressions as *with 80% accuracy*, *within five minutes*, *including at least six factors*, *all in correct order*, are examples of standards that may be included as an optional part of a performance objective.

A well-constructed performance objective might be stated as follows: *identify at least six major parts of the compound microscope*. The statement informs students of what they will be expected to do and the standard of performance required. It also helps the instructor design his test to evaluate student learning.

Exercise 4.

Some of the following performance objectives are acceptable as stated. Others are either incomplete or improperly stated. Place a check mark before the acceptable ones. For the others, make appropriate corrections or additions to make them acceptable.

______ a. List, in proper sequential order, the five steps of the injection molding machine cycle.

______ b. Learn about anatomical components of the heart.

______ c. Read an article on causes of the American Revolution.

______ d. Place a work of art in its correct context with regard to the artist, title, style, date, and country.

______ e. Construct a flow chart showing the procedure a bill follows through Congress, specifying the requirements for passage at each step.

______ f. Given a number and a base, write the number in expanded notation, in the given base, for eight of ten problems.

Your answers may differ somewhat from those given here, but should agree on the general points made for each item. Item **a** is an acceptably stated objective. It contains three parts: the action verb, *list,* the content reference, *injection molding machine cycle*, and a performance standard, *proper sequential order*, which means that the five steps must all be included and in proper order.

Item **b** is poorly stated. *Learn* doesn't tell the student what performance is required. Should he be able to *identify* the parts, *list* them, or *draw* them, or what? A specific action verb is necessary, and in your correction you should have indicated a suitable one. Also, as was done in the five steps of item **a**, the number of components the student is required to include could be stated. On the other hand, if part of the objective is to have the student identify the number of key components, the phrase *all essential* might be added to *anatomical components.*

You could set a standard against which you would grade a test item by adding *according to the diagram presented in class* or *in the textbook.* The corrected item **b** might read, *to identify all essential anatomical components of the heart according to the diagram presented in class.* The decisions about requirements for any performance objective are yours, but the suggestions here may help you to state them in terms meaningful to your students.

Item **c** is worded as an activity rather than as an objective. The objective might be *to report on three causes of the American Revolution, defending or denying each in a one page paper.* This gives the student a satisfactory indication of what is required.

Item **d** is stated in acceptable form. When no performance standard is included, then the student should understand that he must strive for a 100% correct performance.

Item **e** is clearly stated in performance terms.

Item **f** is a properly stated objective.

For this exercise, you should have marked as acceptable items **a**, **d**, **e**, **f**, and made changes in **b** and **c**.

Statement of Conditions

Note that in addition to the three parts, the statement in item **f** is preceded by some information that tells the student about important parameters or conditions for the attainment of the objective.

The prefix phrase, *given a number and base*, tells the student what to work with in satisfying the objective. Other phrases such as *using a tool*, *given a procedure*, *with a calculator*, or *without a reference guide*, can be used to describe specific conditions. Such statements of conditions, while optional, clarify the performance objective.

Parts of Well-Stated Performance Objectives

Essential:	**an action verb** **a content reference**
Optional:	**a performance standard** **statement of conditions**

III. LEVELS OF PERFORMANCE OBJECTIVES

Action verbs cover different levels of intellectual activity. Some of them place the emphasis on memorization or the recall of information. Others require a higher degree of mental activity. Can you place action verbs on either of these levels?

Low and High Level Objectives

Exercise 5.

For the verbs which follow, write *low* before those action verbs that are on the lowest level of learning, requiring only remembering of information, then write *high* before the verbs that require higher levels of thinking.

______ a. predict

______ b. compare

______ c. define

______ d. distinguish between

______ e. rate

______ f. formulate

______ g. name

______ h. select

______ i. categorize

______ j. label

For Exercise 5, the verbs, define, name, and label usually require only memorization and information recall. So items **c**, **g**, and **j** are low level. Items **a**, **b**, **d**, **e**, **f**, **h**, and **i** require higher levels of intellectual activity. These verbs represent the kinds of learning that instructors often want students to experience as they use acquired knowledge. Therefore, performance objectives should include these higher order mental processes as well as the recall of factual information.

IV. CATEGORIES OF PERFORMANCE OBJECTIVES

In 1956, Benjamin Bloom headed a group of educational psychologists who developed a classification of levels of intellectual behavior important in learning. This became a taxonomy including three overlapping domains; the cognitive, psychomotor, and affective.

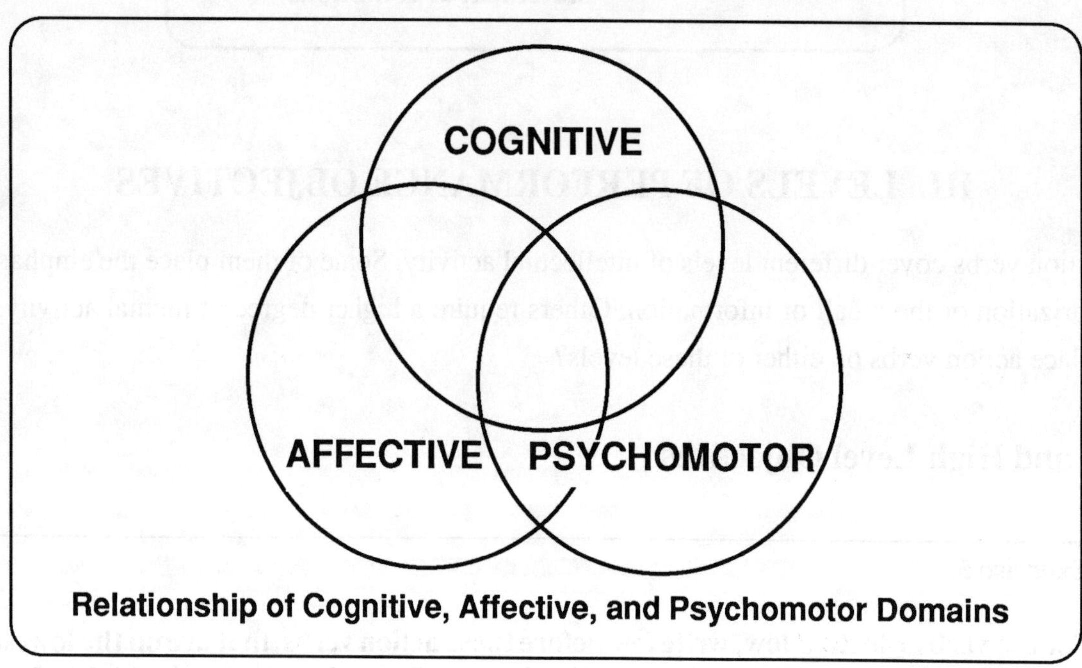

Relationship of Cognitive, Affective, and Psychomotor Domains

The Cognitive Domain

This domain on the acquisition and use of knowledge is predominant in the majority of courses. Bloom identified **six** levels within the cognitive domain, from the simple recall or recognition of facts, as the lowest level, through increasingly more complex and abstract mental levels, to the highest order which is classified as evaluation.

Examples of verbs that represent intellectual activity on each level are listed below. These verbs can help you to express performance objectives when you wish to plan specific learning requirements on any of these levels. Some verbs may apply to more than one level. Read through the classifications, and consider how you can apply the information to your course development.

Verbs Applicable to the Cognitive Domain

1. **Knowledge**		2. **Comprehension**	
arrange	order	classify	locate
define	recognize	describe	recognize
duplicate	relate	discuss	report
label	recall	explain	restate
list	repeat	express	review
memorize	reproduce	identify	select
name	state	indicate	translate

3. **Application**		4. **Analysis**	
apply	operate	analyze	differentiate
choose	practice	appraise	discriminate
demonstrate	schedule	calculate	distinguish
dramatize	sketch	categorize	examine
employ	solve	compare	experiment
illustrate	use	contrast	question
interpret	write	criticize	test

5. **Synthesis**		6. **Evaluation**	
arrange	formulate	appraise	judge
assemble	manage	argue	predict
collect	organize	assess	rate
compose	plan	attach	core
construct	prepare	choose	select
create	propose	compare	support
design	set up	defend	value
develop	write	estimate	evaluate

The Psychomotor Domain

This domain treats the skills that require use and coordination of skeletal muscles for *manipulating, constructing,* and *operating*. Many learning experiences which we classify as physical activity skills in the creative and performing arts, come within the psychomotor domain.

Verbs Applicable to the Psychomotor Domain

bend	operate	shorten	differentiate (by touch)
grasp	reach	stretch	express (facially)
handle	relax	write	perform (skillfully)

The Affective Domain

The third domain is the area of affective behavior. This domain relates to *emotions, attitudes, appreciations*, and *values,* such as *enjoying, conserving, respecting*, and *supporting*. It is often difficult to write performance objectives for the affective domain so that the outcomes are observable and measurable. Most often we do this indirectly by identifying certain behaviors that give an indication of a student's positive approach toward an attitude, appreciation, or value. For example, if you want to judge each student's attitude toward laboratory work, you might evaluate attitudes to cleanliness of his/her work area, the way he/she handles equipment, conserves supplies, and cooperates with other students. Indicator behaviors help in writing objectives for the affective domain.

Verbs Applicable to the Affective Domain

accepts	defends	judges	shares
attempts	disputes	praises	supports
challenges	joins	questions	volunteers

Exercise 6.

To which domain does each of the following performance objectives relate, Cognitive, Psychomotor, or Affective?

_______ a. List six important procedures when going for a job interview.

_______ b. Take responsibility for organizing social activities for an honorary society.

_______ c. Take blood pressure with a sphygmomanometer according to the procedures in the laboratory manual.

_______ d. Sight-read and play a given piece of organ music with no more than three mistakes.

_______ e. Compare three psychological teaching models in the literature in terms of all components of the basic model presented in class.

_______ f. Challenge given criteria for judging a work of art.

For Exercise 6, **a** is cognitive; **b** is affective; **c** is psychomotor; **d** is psychomotor; **e** is cognitive; and **f** is affective.

While each objective in this exercise best relates to the domain indicated, some of them may overlap. For example, item d is indicated to be an objective in the psychomotor domain because the main behavior is playing the organ, a physical activity. To sight-read music, a person must also master a number of cognitive skills; the ability to identify various types of notes, rhythmic patterns, and melodic movements. Thus, objectives could relate to more than a single domain.

In higher education, the majority of the objectives you develop will probably be in the cognitive domain, but there may also be some overlap. The important thing to remember is to develop objectives which:

- ☐ **Meet the purposes of your course.**
- ☐ **Reflect the ideas and principles of your discipline.**
- ☐ **Encourage a range of intellectual activity.**
- ☐ **Establish appropriate levels for evaluation.**

V. SUMMARY OUTLINE

I. COURSE GOALS AND PERFORMANCE OBJECTIVES

Course Goals

Performance Objectives

II. PARTS OF PERFORMANCE OBJECTIVES

Action Verbs

Content Reference

Standard of Performance

Statement of Conditions

III. LEVELS OF PERFORMANCE OBJECTIVES

Low and High Levels

Recall and Application

IV. CATEGORIES OF PERFORMANCE OBJECTIVES

Cognitive Domain

Psychomotor Domain

Affective Domain

VI. REVIEW TEST

A series of statements is listed relating to the topic, *The Circulatory System*, as part of a course in Human Biology. Some are in the form of performance objectives, while others are not. Refer to the list and then answer the questions that follow.

A. Trace the course of blood from the right atrium through the left ventricle by referring to a diagram similar to one used in the lecture and making reference to at least six parts of the circulatory system.

B. Name the three main structures of the circulatory system.

C. Understand the function of the circulatory system within the human body.

D. Volunteer for an exercise program to maintain a proper functioning human heart.

E. Know the role of the red blood cell in metabolism.

F. Operate a microscope in order to see blood cells on a slide.

G. Compare erythrocytes, platelets, and leukocytes according to their functions.

Questions

______ 1. Which statement is a course goal but not a performance objective?

______ 2. Which two statements contain both of the essential components only?

______ 3. Which statement selected in question 2 is lower level cognitive?

______ 4. Which statement selected in question 2 is higher level cognitive?

______ 5. Which statement includes both the essential and optional components ?

______ 6. What needs to be changed in E to make it a performance objective?

______ 7. Statement D is an example from which domain of objectives?

______ 8. Statement F is an example from which domain of objectives?

Check your answers:

1, C; 2, B & G; 3, B; 4, G; 5, A; 6, verb; 7, affective; 8, psychomotor.

Turn to the **gray sheets**, pages 17-18, and complete the application exercises.

REFERENCES AND RESOURCES

Bloom, Benjamin S. and others. **Taxonomy of Educational Objectives, Handbook I, Cognitive Domain.** New York: Longman, 1956.

Bloom, Benjamin S., George Madaus, and J. Thomas Hastings. **Evaluation to Improve Learning.** New York: McGraw-Hill Book Company, 1981.

Diamond, Robert M. **Designing and Improving Courses and Curricula in Higher Education: A Systematic Approach**. San Francisco: Jossey-Bass Inc., 1989.

Harrow, A. J. **Taxonomy of the Psychomotor Domain.** New York: Longman, 1972.

Krathwohl, David R. and others. **Taxonomy of Educational Objectives: Handbook II: Affective Domain.** New York: Longman, 1964.

Mager, Robert F. **Preparing Instructional Objectives**. (2nd ed.) Belmont, CA: Lake Publishers, 1985.

McKeachie, W. J. **Teaching Tips: A Guidebook for the Beginning College Teacher.** (8th ed.) Lexington, MA: D.C. Heath and Company, 1986.

Pipe, Peter. **Objectives—Tool for Change**. Belmont, CA: Fearon Publishers, 1975.

Popham, W. James. **Modern Educational Measurement** (2nd ed.) Englewood Cliffs, NJ: Prentice-Hall, Inc., 1990.

VII. APPLICATION EXERCISE

Complete each of the following:

A. State a topic in a course or training program you will be presenting.

B. State a course goal relating to the topic.

C. Write seven performance objectives based upon the goal.

1. A recall level, cognitive objective, that includes the two essential parts.

2. A recall level, cognitive objective, that includes the two essential parts and the two optional parts.

3. A higher level, cognitive objective, at the application level including essential parts only.

4. A higher level, cognitive objective, at the analysis level, essential parts only.

5. A higher level, cognitive objective, at the synthesis or evaluation level, essential parts only.

6. A psychomotor objective, essential parts only.

7. An affective domain objective, essential parts only.

PREPARING LECTURES

Module Developers:	Jerrold E. Kemp Ron J. McBeath
Editorial Consultants:	Oswald B. Carleton Richard B. Lewis

PREPARING LECTURES

When you prepare a lecture, several interrelated matters should receive your attention. In this module we will explore and have practice exercises in each of the following areas:

I. **Selecting the Content**

II. **Organizing the Content**

III. **Choosing Examples and Resources**

IV. **Selecting Presentation Format**

V. **Creating Conditions for Successful Learning**

VI. **Planning to Evaluate Lecture Effectiveness**

VII. **Summary Outline**

VIII. **Application Exercise**

I. SELECTING THE CONTENT

The lecture is one way to help students understand and master fundamental concepts, the modes of inquiry, and the techniques of evaluation used within a field or discipline. To ensure a close relationship of purposes and content between a course and any lecture, planning for lectures should start with course goals.

Course Goals

The course goals are broad statements which give the students a general idea of what they will learn in the course. The goals reflect the professional experience and interest of the professor, tempered somewhat by societal, institutional, and student influences.

Well-designed course goals give an indication of the breadth and depth of knowledge to be covered as well as the range of intellectual skills required. In the following examples, the goals stated for the first two courses are broad and encompass a number of units or topics in the course, while the goals for the latter two courses are much more explicit; each one refers to a single unit of the course. Both types of goal statements are commonly used.

Examples of Course Goals

Child Development

To study the qualitative as well as quantitative changes that take place in the pre-adult years of an individual.

To help students correct misconceptions they may have concerning pre- and post-natal child development.

Survey of Western Art (Renaissance to 20th Century)

To familiarize the student with the important developments and key movements in the history of Western art from the Renaissance to the present.

To interest students in the process of human creativity and its various expressions that make art a natural and familiar part of the individual's everyday life.

General Biology

To provide an understanding of the molecular foundations for cellular activity.

To become familiar with the mechanism for transmitting human traits from generation to generation and how this procedure can control the development, growth, and maturation of an organism.

United States Government

To grasp the dynamic nature of the presidency and the problems and responsibilities faced by the President.

To know the relationship among the various state courts and the procedures in the different kinds of court cases.

Turn to Exercise A on the **gray sheet**, page 55, and complete Items 1 and 2.

Topic Outline

The goals stated for a course normally lead to a topic outline which establishes the structure of the lectures. Here are examples of topics or units that relate to some of the previous course goals:

Child Development

Prenatal development
Early infancy (birth-2 years)
Pre-school period (3-5 years)
Primary grade years (6-8 years)
Middle years (9-11 years)
Teenage period (12-16 years)

Heredity and Genetics

Process of chromosomal inheritance
Nature of a gene
Mendelian inheritance
Probability
Incomplete dominance
Linkage

Art History

Art of 15th Century Flanders Classical
Humanism and the Renaissance
Leonardo da Vinci
Michelangelo
16th Century German Art
Mannerism in Italy, France, and Spain
Baroque and Renaissance Architecture

The State Courts

State Supreme Court
Superior Court
Trial Courts
Local Courts

The next logical step in organizing content for a lecture is to expand the topics into detailed outlines. Thus each topic will include several sub-topics. Here are sample outlines based upon the above examples:

Sub-topics

CHILD DEVELOPMENT

Prenatal Development

Ovum and embryo stages
Development of body structures
Major functions and reflexes

Early Infancy

Physical and motor development
Cognitive and mental development
Emotional and social development
Language development

HEREDITY & GENETICS

Chromosomal Inheritance	**Nature of a Gene**	**Mendelian Inheritance**
Sex determination	Chemical	Law of dominance
Chromosomal abnormalities	Cytological	Law of segregation
Turner's syndrome	Mutational	Law of independent assortment
Down's syndrome	Functional	Test cross

STATE COURTS

State Supreme Court	Superior Courts	Trial Courts	Local Courts
Functions	Functions	Types(5)	Types(4)
Judges	Judges	Functions	Functions
		Judges	Judges

After a topic outline is developed to meet the general goals of a course, the process continues with the selection of appropriate facts, concepts, principles, and intellectual processes that will become the basic elements of the lecture. Major guides for the selection process are:

1. **The texts, readings, and other resource materials available.**

2. **A statement of the learning outcomes you expect from the students.**

The importance of item 1, resource materials such as texts, can readily be accepted, but their value is limited since their organization is usually designed for a widely dispersed and average audience and may not be entirely appropriate for your specific class. You must be selective and choose, probably from a great wealth of materials in addition to texts, the content and processes that meet the requirements of your own instructional situation.

Item 2, the statement regarding expected learning outcomes, is the result of your own professional judgment in terms of content and student needs. By specifying final desired outcomes, the decisions regarding what to include and what to omit have a logical and psychological base. By identifying the expected outcomes as performance objectives, you can more easily select appropriate content and organize the lecture and other related activities to help students achieve a desired level of learning.

Performance Objectives

Performance objectives contain an action verb and a content reference which may be qualified by including a performance standard and statement of conditions. The objectives may be set at various levels of knowledge and for such different intellectual processes as comprehension, application, analysis, synthesis, and evaluation. Here are performance objectives for some of the topics in the previous examples. Do you recognize those objectives that are for intellectual levels higher than the recall of factual information?

Examples of Performance Objectives for Topics

Early Infancy

Identify motor coordination of which the newborn is capable.

Compare infant coordination with normative data.

Plan activities for infant crib enrichment and stimulation.

Michelangelo

List at least three works of Michelangelo that reflect the changed conditions brought on by the changed religious climate of Italy.

Describe the iconography of the Sistine ceiling including the titles of the nine major scenes.

Appraise the influence of neo-Platonism on the art of Michelangelo, citing specific works and explaining the neo-Platonic ideas implicit in each.

Heredity and Genetics

Define the concepts of dominant and recessive genes, relating them to the 3:1 ratio in Mendel's crossing experiments.

Explain the inheritance pattern of chromosomes in sex determination, including the X and Y chromosomes in humans.

Formulate in words and sketches the inheritance pattern of any of the four genetic characteristics discussed in class.

As illustrated above, a set of performance objectives for a lecture should indicate the various levels of conceptual development and range of intellectual processes you want the students to master. The first objective listed under each of the *topics* requires the recall of factual information to be presented in a lecture for each topic. This is the lowest level of learning that can take place. The other objectives direct the student to engage in higher intellectual activities; *compare, plan, describe, appraise, explain*, and *formulate* are all action verbs that are more challenging and mentally demanding than simply the memorization of specific details. Thus, performance objectives can become significantly important for selecting course content.

The procedure that has been described for selecting content can help you to plan lectures which will:

1. **Focus on the key ideas and processes you want to treat.**
2. **Include only pertinent information about topics.**
3. **Relate new information to past experience and present applications.**
4. **Demonstrate uses of the information in solving problems.**
5. **Provide a valid base for evaluating student learning.**

The use of performance objectives can also help you to plan assignments, exercises, and other activities which may be required to complete the learning cycle.

Complete Exercise A on the **gray sheet**, page 55.

II. ORGANIZING THE CONTENT

Once you have selected a series of topics and sub-topics for a lecture, you should organize the elements of content and intellectual skills for each topic. Robert Gagne, a learning psychologist, offers a framework for the sequential organization of subject content and related learning activities. The four levels he describes can help you to establish conditions for successful learning and use of knowledge. Through this approach students can be helped to:

1. **Establish a *factual* foundation.**
2. **Develop *conceptual* understandings.**
3. **Use *principles* and *rules*.**
4. **Engage in *problem-solving* and *creative* applications of the content.**

By giving attention to each of these levels through lectures and related activities, students can be guided to apply and use the knowledge and skills gained beyond the classroom. Let us examine each of the levels listed above.

Factual Foundation

Items of information like *terms, names, dates, places, methods*, or *events* are the elements of subject matter which provide basic terminology and facts relating to a topic. When you require students, through your objectives, to identify, name, list, or label, you are treating the *lower* levels of informational content. In each discipline and subject field there is a great quantity of such detail to be learned and much attention is given in lectures and texts to presenting and explaining facts, but unless details are arranged in a structured pattern, they may not be used and may be quickly forgotten.

Conceptual Understandings

Students need help in organizing and structuring facts, recognizing those that have common features and can be grouped together as concepts.

Here is an example of facts (objects) that lead to the formation of a concept.

When students discriminate among objects and events by classifying or grouping those that have similar characteristics under a generalized name, they are using their ability to conceptualize. Concept formation may be very simple, as in the above illustration, or more abstract and complex, as when many attributes must be identified and integrated to provide understanding of such higher order concepts as *democracy, kinetic energy*, or *psychosis*. Every field includes a wide range of concepts from the simple and concrete to high level abstractions.

Exercise 1.

A number of items are listed for units in *American History* and *Biology*. These items are either factual elements or concepts. For each unit, mark the items accordingly.

A. American History	**B. Biology**
(World War I)	(Blood Circulation)
______ 1. General von Hindenburg	______ 1. Blood
______ 2. The ***Lusitania***	______ 2. Food transportation
______ 3. Balance of Power	______ 3. Red blood cells
______ 4. U-boat warfare	______ 4. Anemia
______ 5. Western Front	______ 5. Pulmonary artery
______ 6. Woodrow Wilson	______ 6. Right ventricle

For the World War I unit in American History, facts are Items **1**, **2**, and **6**. Concepts are **3**, **4**, and **5**. You may feel that even some of these items designated as on the factual level should be concepts because they consist of a group of factors, behaviors, events, or whatever, that in total comprise, for instance, the person Wilson. Your reasoning may be equally correct.

There is an indefinite line of separation between a fact and a concept since a fact may carry implications of large or complex ideas, as in **6**, Woodrow Wilson, but student insight into the level of meaning implied varies according to individual experience and ability. What is important is that a foundation of factual details is used to help students develop concepts.

For the Blood and Circulation topic, we might list as facts Items **3**, **5**, and **6**, while concepts are **1**, **2**, and **4**. Again, there may be some variations in answers depending on individual interpretation of terms.

Many objectives in a course go beyond requiring the understanding or formation of concepts developed only from facts within the same group. Concepts can be derived from facts that relate to different knowledge classes. The concept *blood* in the Biology list is built upon the relationship among plasma, platelets, red blood cells, white blood cells, and other facts. The development of higher level concepts also resembles a chain in which each subsequent concept depends upon one or more previously learned concepts. The concept *echo* in physics requires an understanding of *sound waves* and *sound reflection*; whereas the concept *investment* is built upon other simpler concepts such as *stocks, bonds*, and *dividends*.

A major outcome of any lecture or other teaching-learning activity is for students to be able to generalize from the facts and concepts you present to form their own concepts on various levels.

Exercise 2.

Indicate which of the concepts, *amino acid, breakfast cereal, nutrition,* is an example of the statements below.

Concepts can be formed in three ways:	Concept
1. From members of a class having common characteristics.	__________
2. From facts that are unrelated by class, but have a relationship that leads to the concept.	__________
3. From a set of lower level concepts that lead to a higher conceptual level.	__________

As stated, concepts can be formed in three ways. First, from facts having common characteristics. The first example is breakfast cereal, derived from such items as Corn Flakes, Wheaties, or All Bran.

The second way is from facts that are unrelated by class, but that have a relationship that leads to the concept. Amino acid is the example. The separate elements, carbon, hydrogen, oxygen, and nitrogen, are combined chemically to form a particular amino acid.

And third, a concept can be formed from a set of lower level concepts that lead to a *higher* concept level. The final concept, nutrition, represents this higher, more complex level. It is generated from many other concepts, food classes, vitamins, minerals, calories, and so forth.

Complete Exercise B on the **gray sheet**, page 56. Use the three ways for forming concepts.

Were you able to select and relate facts (1) to concepts in a single class, (2) from different but related classes, and (3) from simpler concepts leading to higher level concepts? At times you may find it preferable first to select the concepts that relate to your objectives and then, list the factual and supporting conceptual information, details, and examples that you will utilize in your lecture.

Principles and Rules

The next level of organization of subject content involves statements that show the relationships among two or more concepts. Read these two statements:

A sentence starts with a capital letter.

The circumference of a circle equals 2 π r.

Each statement illustrates a principle. Each one is derived from a particular set of concepts. In the first statement *sentence, starts, capital*, and *letter* are concepts. Together they comprise an important rule in written composition. In the second statement *circumference, circle, equals, two,* π*, and radius (r)* comprise the set of concepts which makes this a principle or formula in mathematics.

Exercise 3.

Look at the statements below. Each one is an important principle in its own subject area. For each, underline the concepts that are used in deriving the rule. Before each statement, write the total number of concepts you identified for each one.

______ a. Each chemical element has an atomic number which distinguishes it from every other element.

______ b. A speech consists of three parts: the introduction, the body, and the conclusion.

______ c. An economic upturn in the business cycle stimulates growth, employment, and risk-taking.

In Exercise 3, for **a**, there are six concepts, *each, chemical element, atomic number, distinguishes, every, other*. You may indicate that the last word, *element*, is also a concept. It is probably the same concept represented by the earlier term *chemical element*. For **b**, there are seven concepts, *speech, consists, three, parts, introduction, body*, and *conclusion*. And in **c**, we find six concepts, *economic upturn, business cycle, stimulates, growth, employment, risk-taking*.

Do you see the dependence upon concepts when principles or rules are being taught? Be sure that students understand the meaning of the concepts you use when a principle or rule is being presented and explained in a lecture.

Turn to **gray sheet**, page 57, and complete Exercise C.

Exercise C is devised to emphasize the importance of recognizing how principles and rules are derived from concepts. It is essential to make sure that students have the basic foundation of facts and concepts before they can be expected to understand and use the related principles. Is there a process you can use during your own lecture preparation to accomplish this requirement?

Problem-Solving and Creative Applications

In learning principles and rules, students should understand the basic facts and concepts and also know how to use the related principle or rule in different situations. Knowing a principle means much more than just memorizing a statement. Application of the principle is an essential stage in learning. You may require the students you teach to *apply* the principle by solving problems, by explaining situations, by inferring causes, or by predicting consequences. Some of the performance objectives you specify should include creative applications of principles.

Exercise 4.

For each of the stated principles, indicate with a checkmark the one or more items that apply the principle or otherwise *use* the principle in problem-solving.

1. The prenatal development and appearance of new body structures in the human fetus follow a definite sequence.

_______ a. State the principles in your own words.

_______ b. Arrange the set of photographs of a human fetus in developmental order.

_______ c. List the order in which new body structures appear in the development of a human fetus.

_______ d. Indicate what the next step in development will be after the one described.

2. The form of haiku poetry consists of three lines. The first has 5 syllables, the second 7, and the third 5.

_______ a. Examine samples of poetry, selecting those that are haiku.

_______ b. Write a definition of haiku.

_______ c. Write a haiku selection.

_______ d. Evaluate other students' haiku in terms of following the proper form.

For Exercise 4, Items **1b** and **1d** are activities for students on the problem-solving level, while **1a** and **1c** only relate to recall of the principle itself. Items **2a**, **2c**, and **2d** cause the student to use and apply the stated principle. Again, **2b** is simply informational recall.

The organization of content for successful learning includes facts and information details, concepts, and principles or rules, all leading to problem solving or the creative application of the knowledge to new situations.

Complete Exercise D on the **gray sheet**, page 57.

III. CHOOSING EXAMPLES AND RESOURCES

While much of a presentation may include verbal information about the topic, there is the need in every lecture to employ examples so that terms and concepts are understood clearly and the topic is presented in an interesting manner. Without an adequate use of examples, illustrations, or applications, memorized information can remain vague and meaningless for students.

Where possible, select examples that have meaning for students in terms of their own background and experiences, rather than examples solely from your own particular experience. Examples should assist students to recognize, identify, compare, distinguish, evaluate, and otherwise understand and apply the facts, concepts, and principles that comprise your subject content.

Exercise 5.

For each of the performance objectives described below, cite at least one example you might use to help student understanding.

a. Assess the benefits derived by using solar energy for some heating purposes in a home.

b. Compare the *checks and balances* in our Federal Government with the British system.

c. Distinguish duties of the five crews under direction of a stage manager for a stage show.

Obviously a wide range of examples might be selected to provide an understanding of each of the situations in Exercise 5. For **a**, you might illustrate the amount of money saved over a period of time when a solar installation replaces conventional electric or gas heating. In **b**, a specific piece of legislation might be followed through the Congress, acted on by the President, and reviewed by the Supreme Court. The procedure followed for similar legislation in the British system could then be traced and the two paths compared. For **c**, the assignments for each crew during an actual play could be indicated, and thus their responsibilities distinguished. Your replies might be different but equally satisfactory.

The use of humorous anecdotes and personal experiences, when pertinent to the topic, may also help students to grasp meanings and see applications of the major ideas you are having them consider. Often students can be encouraged to suggest relevant examples, illustrations, and applications. Through these examples and by class discussion, an instructor can judge whether students understand the ideas under consideration.

In addition to using verbal examples, and in order to provide concrete illustrations of concepts and rules, one or more instructional resources may be chosen to supplement your words. Resources typically available for use in lectures include:

- ☐ guest speakers as specialists on a topic
- ☐ real materials or models and mock-ups
- ☐ displays, diagrams, or other graphic materials on the chalkboard or on suitably large charts
- ☐ audio recordings
- ☐ still pictures, slides, filmstrips, overhead transparencies
- ☐ films, videotapes, or videodiscs
- ☐ multi-image projection or computer displays

The decision to select one or more of these resources for use in a lecture should be based on your performance objectives and nature of the content to be treated. For example, an objective that requires students *to identify the sequence of steps in a process* may best be illustrated by showing the steps with a large chart or projected still pictures. Or the objective *to explain the significance of certain events leading to the formation of a principle or rule,* may be explained through the words of an expert on the topic, or possibly more clearly and dynamically by means of a film or videotape.

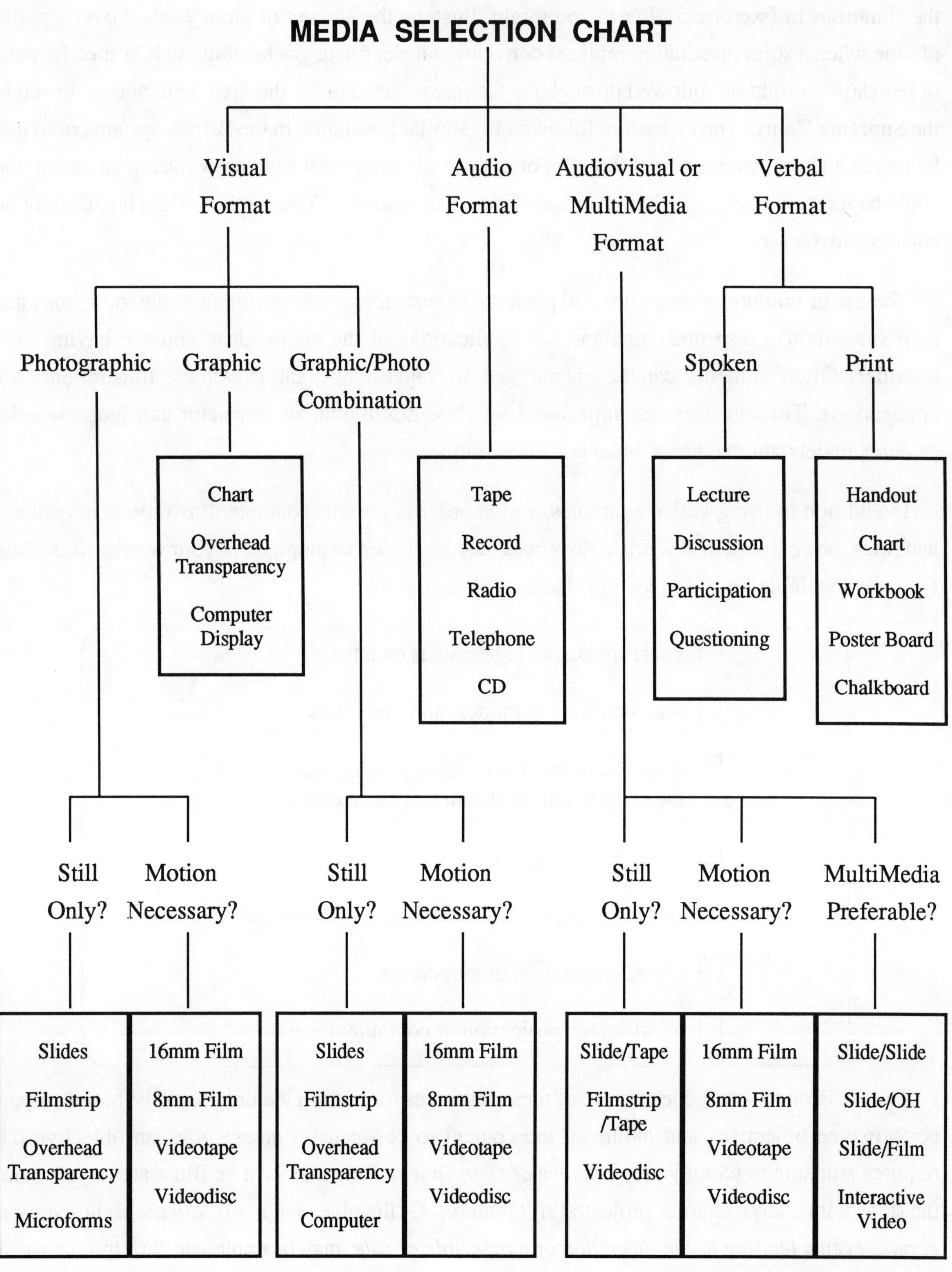
MEDIA SELECTION CHART
Visual Format
Audio Format
Audiovisual or MultiMedia Format
Verbal Format
Photographic
Graphic
Graphic/Photo Combination
Spoken
Print
Chart
Overhead Transparency
Computer Display
Tape
Record
Radio
Telephone
CD
Lecture
Discussion
Participation
Questioning
Handout
Chart
Workbook
Poster Board
Chalkboard
Still Only?
Motion Necessary?
Still Only?
Motion Necessary?
Still Only?
Motion Necessary?
MultiMedia Preferable?
Slides
Filmstrip
Overhead Transparency
Microforms
16mm Film
8mm Film
Videotape
Videodisc
Slides
Filmstrip
Overhead Transparency
Computer
16mm Film
8mm Film
Videotape
Videodisc
Slide/Tape
Filmstrip /Tape
Videodisc
16mm Film
8mm Film
Videotape
Videodisc
Slide/Slide
Slide/OH
Slide/Film
Interactive Video

Adapted from Kemp and Smellie.

The previous diagram can guide you in selecting a suitable resource for one or a series of objectives. The questions at each level can be answered in terms of your perception of the requirements for an objective or segment of content. Thus, you are led sequentially to one or more resources. Your final choice, from among the resources in a box at the end of each line, depends upon such factors as your own preference, the ready-made materials and equipment available to you, and preparation requirements or production services available. Media specialists can assist you with answering these questions and, with making choices of resources, locating or producing materials, and using any necessary equipment.

Exercise 6.

What example or resource might you select to supplement any verbal presentations in lectures designed to help students achieve the following performance objectives? More than a single resource may be used for each objective.

a. Compare Beowolf with three other legendary folk heroes with respect to five common characteristics.

b. Identify the special features of cardiac muscle that differentiate it from skeletal muscle.

c. Given a number less than 1000, represent it in the Egyptian, Roman, and Babylonian systems.

d. Explain the threads that link past artistic traditions to those of 20th Century art forms.

The following examples or resources might be selected to support or replace verbal presentations relevant to student achievement of the performance objectives.

For **a**, you might prepare a table of characteristics and heroes on the chalkboard or as an overhead transparency, then play recorded excerpts from selections that describe the various folk heroes and fill in the table as each characteristic is heard. In this way, students hear the descriptions and can participate mentally with you in identifying characteristics.

For **b**, since muscles are used in movement, it would be effective to have a brief motion picture sequence that shows, either through special photography or by means of animation, how the two kinds of muscles function differently.

For **c**, the representations can most easily be shown by writing on the chalkboard or by using an overhead transparency.

Item **d** may require a more complex presentation than a single, visual display.

The instructor could select or have help in preparing numerous slides or in using a videodisc that illustrates art forms from the past and the present in keeping with the intent of the objective. The slides might be shown with accompanying explanations, or the narration could be recorded and the slide/tape program presented as a segment of a lecture. The alternatives for resources are continuing to expand.

IV. SELECTING PRESENTATION FORMAT

The general format of the lecture involves making an introduction, presenting the content, and summarizing. The procedures you use in lecturing will reflect your **intention** to:

- ☐ Extend the factual knowledge of students about a topic or subject.
- ☐ Prepare students to understand ideas, concepts, principles, and rules relative to the subject.
- ☐ Prepare the students to use the information, ideas, concepts, principles, and rules in problem-solving and other practical or creative situations.
- ☐ Help the students develop a positive attitude toward the subject.

Presentation formats can be grouped within two paired categories, **formal** or **informal** and **deductive** or **inductive** methods.

Formal and Informal Methods

Some instructors are most comfortable when making their entire presentation to a class without having any interruptions during their delivery. This is the **formal** method. While much of it can be verbal, the instructor may write on the chalkboard, show visual materials, give demonstrations, and take other steps to present the content clearly. In the **informal** method, the instructor stops frequently to allow students to ask questions and to pose questions for student responses. In this method, in addition to questions and answers, students may be encouraged to make comments that can lead to productive discussion among themselves and with the instructor.

What advantages and disadvantages do you see with each of these methods?

Exercise 7.

This exercise is in three parts:

A. Under each heading list both advantages and disadvantages of the method.

Formal Lecture Method

Advantages	Disadvantages

Informal Lecture Method

Advantages	Disadvantages

B. Which *intentions* at the beginning of this section might best be accomplished by each lecture format?

Formal

Informal

C. State your preference for one method or the other (or combination) and your reasons.

A list of the advantages and disadvantages for each method follows.

Formal Lecture Method

Advantages	Disadvantages
Large amounts of content can be covered during the period.	Does not permit students to raise questions or make comments at opportune time.
Instructor can maintain the continuity and flow of ideas, presenting material as planned for the time period.	Reinforces the passive acceptance of the presentation.
Convenient for maintaining a planned schedule for treating the content.	Limits amount of information on how and whether students are achieving lecture objectives.

Informal Lecture Method

Advantages	Disadvantages
Encourages students to be more active during the period.	Not all students will ask questions voluntarily.
Allows instructor to ask questions that check levels of student understanding and the effectiveness of instructor communication.	Continuity of lecture may be disrupted since instructor can be drawn away from content being presented.
Permits students to raise points and get guidance while the topic is being presented.	Planned time schedule may be upset.
Creates opportunity for the spontaneous exploration and follow-up of new ideas.	Questions by some students may be of little interest or value to other students.
Provides some clues for improving future lectures on the topic.	The spontaneous activities for a few may be distracting or frustrating to others.

By comparing your lists in Exercise 7 Part A, with those suggested, you can better judge the suitability of each method for yourself. Besides selecting a method according to your own teaching style, the choice of one method over the other is greatly dependent upon the objectives being served.

In answer to Exercise 7 Part B, formal lectures may be most satisfactory when presenting factual information and preparing students to develop an understanding of concepts and principles. These are the first two statements of intentions at the beginning of this section. The next two statements there can most likely be handled effectively by the informal method. For Part C, the method selected should depend upon the specific situation. The style and skills of an instructor and the level of preparation in the topic may greatly influence the decision to use one or the other method. What many successful instructors do, is alternate formal and informal approaches during a lecture period to accomplish specific purposes. By mastering the two modes, formal and informal, you can better judge their appropriate uses in your own lectures.

Deductive and Inductive Methods

The *deductive* method is often considered an expository technique whereby an instructor tells students both generalizations and the evidence in support of the generalizations. It starts with a statement, a definition, concept, principle, or rule. This is followed by examples, illustrations, or applications. The examples can be presented by the instructor or drawn from students by questioning and discussion. Students are thus led to see the relationship between the generalization and specific situations that relate to it. Here is an example of the deductive method:

An instructor in a Health Science course states that, *carbohydrates comprise the sugars and starches in our diet*, a principle of nutrition. Students then are asked to give examples of carbohydrates in these two groupings. They suggest bread, rice, barley, and other grains as starch-based carbohydrates and various fruits and vegetables as sugar-based carbohydrates.

The *inductive* method reverses the process. Facts, examples, or situations are stated or observed; from them the generalization is derived. The instructor might present it or students may be encouraged and guided to discover it. If a Health Science instructor shows a class slides picturing various individuals and indicates the type of daily activity and dietary caloric intake of each person shown, the relation between energy input and output could be derived by students as the relationship to gain, loss, or stability of body weight. This relationship becomes the generalization from the examples presented.

The inductive method is characterized by discovery or inquiry techniques by which students may receive facts or make observations. By developing relationships and asking questions, students can be led to find and specify appropriate generalizations. What are the advantages or disadvantages of these two methods?

Exercise 8.

Place a number before each statement according to whether it is:

1. An *advantage* of the *deductive* method
2. An *advantage* of the *inductive* method
3. A *disadvantage* of the *deductive* method
4. A *disadvantage* of the *inductive* method

______ a. Can present the instruction more rapidly.

______ b. Students may be more mentally active while formulating the generalization.

______ c. Often few students participate, the majority wait for the answer.

______ d. Teaches a process by which students can derive their own conclusions in important matters beyond the classroom.

______ e. May permit verbalization of principles without understanding the fundamentals.

______ f. Usually perceived by students as being more orderly and logical.

______ g. More possibility for overlooking contribution from student's experience.

For Exercise 8, **a** and **f** are advantages of the deductive methods; **b** and **d** are advantages of the inductive method; **e** and **g** are disadvantages of the deductive method; and **c** is a disadvantage of the inductive method.

The teaching methods we have been examining can be employed in various arrangements. An instructor may find it beneficial to alternate between formal and informal techniques or from deductive to inductive methods during different sections of a lecture. The two groupings can be intermixed. A formal presentation may be employed with the deductive method, while informality can implement the use of an inductive procedure. The decision on which approach to use should be based upon the objectives or outcomes to be reached.

Turn to **gray sheet**, page 58, and make use of the information in this section for some planning of your own in Exercise E.

V. CREATING CONDITIONS FOR SUCCESSFUL LEARNING

In addition to organizing the lecture content, choosing the resources, and selecting the methods of delivery, successful learning can be assisted by:

- ☐ **Recognizing student preparation**
- ☐ **Providing for student participation**
- ☐ **Controlling physical conditions**

Recognizing Student Preparation

Most instructors have some general information about the students enrolled in their courses and their readiness to take a course. The more you know about your students, the better you can adapt your lectures to their interests, experience, and levels of preparation for your course.

Exercise 9.

List 5 types of information concerning your students, their background, and interest, that would be especially helpful to you as you prepare your lectures.

1.

2.

3.

4.

5.

Compare your answers with the five statements listed in Exercise 10 on the next page.

Exercise 10.

Write under each item how you might gather data from the students:

1. Previous courses taken in the subject field

2. Academic preparation for this course in requisite areas

3. Skills in necessary basic areas (reading, writing, math, etc.)

4. Possible future uses to be made of the course content

5. Experiences students expect or desire in the course

For Items 1, 2, 4, and 5, a questionnaire might be prepared for students to complete during the first class period. Analysis of the replies should give you an idea of the preparation levels and expectations of your students. This information might also be used for counselling and advising.

For Item 3, special diagnostic tests recommended by English and Mathematics departments could be used. Your Professional Development Office can assist you with getting help in selecting, procuring, using, and interpreting the results of such diagnostic tests. Introductory courses or tutorial help in English and Math may be desirable for some inadequately prepared students.

While extensive course modification may not be possible after you gather and analyze data about a current class, the information can help you to:

- ☐ **Decide on the depth of treatment or emphasis necessary for individual topics.**
- ☐ **Select examples and illustrations that relate to student experiences and interests.**
- ☐ **Group students for class or outside-class activities.**
- ☐ **Decide on projects or assignments.**

The fact that you attempt to learn more about your students can itself serve to motivate and further interest them in your course.

Another aspect of student preparation is their readiness for each lecture. They may need out-of-class readings, review of previous lecture material, or prior preparation through lab or field work. How can you best ensure that students will be prepared when they come to a lecture so each can gain what is essential from your presentation?

Exercise 11.

State procedures you might use to encourage students to prepare themselves before attending a lecture.

Compare your list with the items below.

- ☐ Make clear in advance that each lecture is based directly on required readings and other preparatory activities.
- ☐ Provide a list of the vocabulary, main concepts, and other key points that should be studied or reviewed prior to the lecture.
- ☐ Provide a list of questions for guidance when studying the required readings.
- ☐ Give a quiz at the start of the period covering preparatory materials and activities.

You may have listed other items. Obviously there are a number of different actions that could be taken to encourage students to prepare for a lecture.

Providing for Student Participation

The lecture method most frequently employs one-way communication, and may result in students being passive receivers of information. The amount and kind of participation and mental activity encouraged and required of students directly affect their interest in the lecture and what they learn. One way to stimulate participation and mental activity prior to a lecture is to inform students what they will be required to learn, and how the lecture will be related to their readings and practical activities. Another way of providing for student participation is through some type of active involvement as the lecture proceeds.

Exercise 12.

List some ways you can provide for student participation in a lecture to:

a. Inform them what they are required to learn.

b. Encourage their mental participation as the lecture proceeds.

To inform students of what they are required to learn, here are two recommendations.

1. Provide a hand-out sheet to each student which enumerates the performance objectives to be treated in the lecture, OR
2. List the objectives on the chalkboard or on a projected transparency so students may refer to them as the lecture proceeds.

In addition to informing students of what they are to learn, you can help ensure the mental involvement of students during the lecture in various ways. Check your list against the items in Exercise 13.

Exercise 13.

Considering your own lecture objectives, the nature of the content, and desired learning outcomes, which items would you select for encouraging mental participation? Add any additional items you had listed in Exercise 12.

- ☐ Teach note-taking skills.
- ☐ Refer to lecture outlines.
- ☐ Review homework in class.
- ☐ Refer to examples in texts.
- ☐ Set questions for small group discussion.
- ☐ Use media for exploration.
- ☐ Encourage student comments.
- ☐ Relate to students positively.
- ☐ Organize for different learning styles.
- ☐ Show enthusiasm for your subject.
- ☐
- ☐
- ☐ Teach listening skills.
- ☐ Provide worksheets for completion.
- ☐ Respond to student questions.
- ☐ Draw upon student experience.
- ☐ Raise critical questions.
- ☐ Facilitate student interaction.
- ☐ Set realistic reading assignments.
- ☐ Listen and keep eye contact.
- ☐ Provide for feedback.
- ☐ Involve students in problem solving.
- ☐
- ☐

Controlling Classroom Conditions

The successful presentation of a lecture depends on the physical conditions of the room and on the mode of presentation. They include seating arrangement, illumination and light control, ventilation and temperature control, controlling outside distractions and disturbances, and presentation skills.

Seating Arrangement

Arrange the chairs in the classroom so that each student easily can see the instructor, the chalkboard, and materials that are displayed. When students cannot comfortably see and read information being presented, they become frustrated and lose interest.

Illumination and Light Control

A suitable light level should be maintained in the classroom for viewing instructional activities and for note-taking. High light level at the front of the room tends to focus student attention.

Sufficient light must be reflected from the chalkboard to insure the necessary contrast for good viewing. Beware of glare or unusual bright spots caused by the sun or other outside light sources which reflect from display surfaces. Control unwanted light with window blinds or shades. When projection equipment is used, be sure the room light level is controlled so that no light falls on the screen to impair the picture image.

Ventilation and Temperature Control

A comfortable temperature should be maintained in the room. The room thermostat may have been preset at a suitable level, but if the room becomes too warm or too cold, resetting the thermostat may become necessary. Open the windows to refresh the air and help to control temperature in warm weather—inadequate oxygen levels can be a significant cause of student inattention. Encourage students to be aware of the problems caused by fuel economies or power shortages and to dress appropriately.

Outside Distractions and Disturbances

An instructor may have little control over outside distractions, but simply closing a blind, a window, or door often can help significantly and provide a more suitable environment to promote student attention and learning.

Presentation Skills

Presentation skills can be improved through practice and by checking facilities, equipment operation, sound, and visibility prior to the use of any media. Ensure that the students are able to see and hear clearly from all parts of the classroom.

- ☐ **Chalkboard summaries are most effective when they are clear and well organized.**
- ☐ **Charts and illustrations have more impact when they are large and simple.**
- ☐ **Overhead transparencies allow you to build concepts from simple to complex with overlays. They also enable you to keep eye contact with students under regular lighting conditions.**
- ☐ **Television, videodiscs, films, slides, and computer projection can be used to enlarge, explore and sequence visual displays.**
- ☐ **Microphones and tape recorders amplify sound. Check sound levels before the class begins.**

Turn to **gray sheet**, page 58, and complete Exercise F.

VI. PLANNING TO EVALUATE LECTURE EFFECTIVENESS

The evaluation of lectures should be recognized as an integral part of total course planning. Ways to measure student achievement should be planned at the same time as the course objectives and methods of instruction are being formulated.

Evaluation can serve two purposes. The first is to provide an indication of how well the students have mastered the content of lectures. The second is to provide the professor with information that can guide planning for future course improvements.

Suggestions for Using Classroom Tests

- ☐ Announce tests well in advance of administering them so students can prepare themselves. This process can help motivate students to consolidate their learning.
- ☐ Indicate clearly the objectives and type of test so students know how to prepare. Student preparation techniques for recall tests differ considerably from those used for higher level intellectual skills tests.
- ☐ Use tests periodically through a course, rather than only at mid-term and at the end of the course. Weekly or end-of-topic tests can give you a better indication of student learning, and, just as important, students will be aware of their own progress and the directions for needed further study.
- ☐ Provide students with test results promptly, within a few days. When students receive feedback on a test promptly, the value of the test is increased and the student benefits from timely correction of misinformation and incorrect ideas.
- ☐ Review test questions with students or otherwise provide an opportunity to discuss the test on an individual basis. For some students, this review may be as valuable a learning experience as preparation for the test.
- ☐ Minimize the threat of tests by observing the above suggestions so that students see tests as an integral part of their learning experience and an opportunity to demonstrate their accomplishments.

Measuring Student Learning

The tests you write should reflect the levels of learning you expect from students. For some levels of knowledge, which involve the memorizing of facts and concepts, there are various types of objective tests which are appropriate. Those most often used are: multiple choice, true/false, and matching tests.

When students are expected to demonstrate their ability to organize concepts, express their own ideas, or engage in analytical studies, their progress can be evaluated appropriately through written assignments, short answer, and essay tests.

Recognition of the various types of learning indicates that paper and pencil tests are not always sufficient and that other types of performance and problem-solving tests are necessary. By planning tests as a part of the total instructional process you will most likely select the evaluation process that best serves your purpose and enables the students to more effectively consolidate their learning.

Gathering Information to Improve Lectures

There are various aspects of evaluation that can provide data to help you improve your lectures and related activities.

If your tests are reliable and well constructed, you will have an indication of how well students have learned the content. In those areas where the majority of students do not have sufficiently high marks, it may be appropriate to:

- ☐ **Change the manner of presentation.**
- ☐ **Reorganize the content.**
- ☐ **Include additional relevant examples and illustrations so that the lecture content may be more readily understood by students.**
- ☐ **Check that the students have sufficient practice opportunities to apply knowledge they have learned.**

During the lecture students may express attitudes by facial expression, levels of attention, and participation in class activities or discussions. At the end of the lecture, students may exhibit further interest through their questions or involvement in class-related activities. These are among many behaviors that are indicators of positive or negative student attitudes that can provide useful **indirect** guides to you for revising specific portions of a lecture or course.

More direct indicators of student attitudes toward your lecturing can be obtained by asking students to complete an attitude or opinion survey. The following form for faculty evaluation is comprehensive and was developed to survey student opinions regarding the quality of teaching they are receiving.

STUDENT EVALUATION OF TEACHING *

Instructor____________________ Dept.__________ Course #_____ Year____ Quarter___
Teaching observed (give approximate number of each) Lectures_______ Labs_______
Conference-Discussion-Seminar_______ Other (specify)________________________

A. Each of these statements describes a basic component of teaching. Give the instructor an overall rating for each component, reserving the highest scores for unusually effective performance.

	Low — High Score
1. Has command of the subject, presents material in an analytic way, contrasts points of view, discusses current developments, and relates topics to other areas of knowledge.	1 2 3 4 5 6 7
2. Makes him/herself clear, states objectives, summarizes major points, presents material in an organized manner, and provides emphasis.	1 2 3 4 5 6 7
3. Is sensitive to the response of the class, encourages student participation, and welcomes questions and discussions.	1 2 3 4 5 6 7
4. Is available to and friendly toward students, is interested in students as individuals, is him/herself respected as a person, and is valued for advice not directly related to the course.	1 2 3 4 5 6 7
5. Enjoys teaching, is enthusiastic about his/her subject, makes the course exciting, and has self-confidence.	1 2 3 4 5 6 7

B. These items are not covered in the statements above and thus extend the evaluation.

	Low — High	Doesn't apply
6. Has increased my appreciation of the subject.	1 2 3 4 5	______
7. Keeps well informed about the progress of the class.	1 2 3 4 5	______
8. Anticipates problems and makes difficult topics easy to understand.	1 2 3 4 5	______
9. Is an excellent speaker.	1 2 3 4 5	______
10. Quickly grasps what a student is asking or telling him/her.	1 2 3 4 5	______
11. Presents the aesthetic and emotional values of the subject.	1 2 3 4 5	______
12. Relates class topics to student lives and experience.	1 2 3 4 5	______
13. Gives interesting and stimulating assignments.	1 2 3 4 5	______
14. Gives examinations that require creative, original thinking.	1 2 3 4 5	______
15. Givcs cxaminations that have instructional value.	1 2 3 4 5	______

C. Additional items may be presented by the instructor and/or department.

D. You are invited to comment further on the course and/or effectiveness of instruction.

* Adapted from a form used at U.C. Davis.

Alternative Questionnaire Formats

The five questionnaire formats outlined below may be used to get feedback on such factors as:

- ☐ The topic—interest, value, importance
- ☐ The instructor—competence, organization, enthusiasm
- ☐ The lecture—presentation rate, use of resources
- ☐ The assignments—complexity, relationship to lectures and course goals and objectives

1. Adjective Checklist

Underline the words that come close to telling how you feel about the topic.

unnecessary	useless	right on
needed	too easy	dumb
stimulating	easy	worthless
too difficult	exciting	boring
useful	far out	challenging

2. Rating Scale

Check the extent to which you agree or disagree with the statements below:

	Strongly Agree	Agree	Not Sure	Disagree	Strongly Disagree
1. The classroom presentation today was well organized.					
2. The pace of the lecture was confusing.					
3. The visuals distracted me from learning.					
4. The handouts were relevant to the presentation.					
5. The objectives were clear.					
6. I did not feel free to ask questions.					
7. I enjoyed this learning experience.					

3. Semantic Differential

How do you rate this course? Check the appropriate place in each scale.

1. How organized (logical, coherent, and complete) is the subject material?

UNORGANIZED — — — — — — — ORGANIZED

2. To what extent are homework and lab activities related to the classroom lectures?

RELATED — — — — — — — UNRELATED

3. How often are the students encouraged to ask questions?

SELDOM — — — — — — — OFTEN

4. How willing is the instructor to help you or other students?

WILLING — — — — — — — UNWILLING

4. Ranking

Rank the activities used in the last unit. 1 for the most useful to 4 for the least valuable.

	Ranking
the guest speaker	______
the film	______
the question/answer periods	______
the instructor's verbal presentation	______

5. Open Response Questions

1. What is your reaction to having guest speakers in class?

2. What uses did you find for the handouts in the last lecture?

3. What comments do you have on the organization of my presentation?

4. What suggestions do you have about the language I use in lecturing?

5. What types of questions did you find challenging?

Teaching Performance Rating Scale

The following guidelines may be useful for developing your own form for reviewing the quality and instructional effectiveness of your lecture.

Preparation

1. **Objectives and requirements stated**
2. **Knowledge of content (depth, accuracy)**
3. **Organization of content (introduction, body, summary)**
4. **Range of examples, illustrations, and applications**

Presentation

1. **Pace**
2. **Student involvement (discussion, questions, other types of participation)**
3. **Use of examples and instructional resources**
4. **Correlation with other activities (lab, field, homework)**

Personal Traits

1. **Enthusiasm**
2. **Style (speech, gestures, appearance)**
3. **Sense of humor**
4. **Rapport with students**

Complete Exercise G on **gray sheet**, page 59.

Two further techniques you might use for evaluating the effectiveness of your lectures are:

- ☐ Invite one or more colleagues or a member of your Professional Development Office staff to sit in on a lecture and then meet with you to offer constructive evaluation.
- ☐ Videotape your lecture for constructive criticism and/or your own personal review.

In each case, develop a list of criteria or key points to evaluate.

VII. SUMMARY OUTLINE

1. SELECTING THE CONTENT

Course Goals
Topic Outline
Performance Objectives

II. ORGANIZING THE CONTENT

Factual Foundations
Conceptual Understandings
Principles and Rules
Problem Solving and Creative Applications

III. CHOOSING EXAMPLES AND RESOURCES

Media Selection Diagram

IV. SELECTING PRESENTATION FORMAT

Formal and Informal Methods
Deductive and Inductive Methods

V. CREATING CONDITIONS FOR SUCCESSFUL LEARNING

Recognizing Student Preparation
Providing for Student Participation
Controlling Classroom Conditions
Seating arrangement, illumination and light control, ventilation, temperature control, outside distractions, and presentation skills

VI. PLANNING TO EVALUATE LECTURE EFFECTIVENESS

Measure Student Learning
Suggestions for Using Classroom Tests
Gathering Information to Improve Lectures
Types of Student Evaluation Forms

REFERENCES AND RESOURCES

Dill, David D. and associates. **What Teachers Need to Know.** San Francisco: Jossey-Bass Inc., 1990.

Eble, Kenneth E. **The Aims of College Teaching.** San Francisco: Jossey-Bass Inc., 1983.

Ericksen, Stanford C. **The Essence of Good Teaching.** San Francisco: Jossey-Bass Inc., 1988.

Gagne, Robert M. **The Conditions of Learning.** (4th ed.) New York: Holt, Rinehart and Winston, 1985.

Goodlad, John I., Roger Soder, and Kenneth A. Sirotnik. **The Moral Dimensions of Teaching.** San Francisco: Jossey-Bass Inc., 1990.

Kemp, Jerrold E. and Don C. Smellie. **Planning, Producing and Using Instructional Media.** (6th ed.) New York: Harper and Row, 1989.

Mager, Robert F. **Making Instruction Work.** Belmont, CA: Lake Publishing Company, 1988.

McKeachie, Wilbert J. **Teaching Tips: A Guidebook for the Beginning College Teacher.** (8th ed.) Lexington, MA: D.C. Heath and Company, 1986.

Weimer, Maryellen. **Improving College Teaching.** San Francisco: Jossey-Bass Inc., 1990.

VIII. APPLICATION EXERCISE

Exercise A.

Choose a course that you teach. Select content for a lecture using the process described. Complete each of the following. You will be asked to continue with this example after reading subsequent sections of the text.

1. Course title:

2. State a course goal.

3. List 3 topics to be treated relevant to the goal.

4. For one of the topics, list 3 supporting subtopics.

5. For each selected subtopic, develop a performance objective. Include at least two of them on intellectual levels higher than recall of information. Use the back of the sheet if necessary.

Exercise B.

Refer to the objectives you wrote for the topic on the previous page. List 3 of them in the spaces provided below. Then for each one list facts on the left side of the page and the concepts the facts lead to on the right.

List at least three items in the facts column for each objective. Also note the form used in the concept development as described in Exercise 2.

Objective #1____

____

Facts	**Concept (Form 1, 2, or 3)**

Objective #2____

____

Facts	**Concept (Form 1, 2, or 3)**

Objective #3____

____

Facts	**Concept (Form 1, 2, or 3)**

Exercise C.

State a principle, that would be taught or derived, for one of the objectives you wrote under Exercise B.

Principle

List the concepts relating to this principle. Beside each one indicate whether

(a) students should already have competency with it, or,

(b) students may not understand the concept.

Concepts	Check one for each concept	
	a	b

Exercise D.

For the principle you stated in Exercise C, develop two problem-solving activities you might use during the lecture or as follow-up outside assignments.

1.

2.

Exercise E.

Look back over your answers to previous A, B, and C exercises on the gray sheets. Select the methods you might use in order to treat a selected topic. Describe the procedure you would then follow in preparing for the lecture and the resources you would use.

(a) Method

(b) Preparation

(c) Resources

Exercise F.

Complete the planning for your lecture topic. Indicate the specific teaching activities and the participation activities for students before, during, and as follow-up.

	Teaching activity	**Student activities**
Before Lecture		
During Lecture		
Follow-up to Lecture		

Exercise G.

Section F of this module suggests a number of techniques you may consider using to gather ideas for improving your lectures. Which ones interest you — in what priority order?

______ a. Analyzing the results of student tests

______ b. Observing student reactions in and out of class

______ c. Using attitudinal surveys with the students

______ d. Asking a colleague or Professional Development Office representative to observe my teaching and offer comments

______ e. Videotaping my lecture and then personally analyzing it or reviewing it with a Professional Development Office representative

CONDUCTING DISCUSSIONS

Module Developers:	Ron J. McBeath Janice M. Lane
Editorial Associates:	Oswald B. Carleton Jerrold E. Kemp Damon G. Nalty Robert J. Simas
Editorial Consultant:	Richard B. Lewis

CONDUCTING DISCUSSIONS

Information presented through the lecture process is easily lost because the learner is not actively involved in using the new information. Procedures which aid in the active use of information should be part of every course. One such procedure is discussion. As a teaching method, discussion involves a group of students in a face to face exchange of facts, ideas, and opinions. Learning takes place on intellectual levels higher than solely the recall of information, as students think about the subject under discussion.

This module will help you conduct and evaluate discussions by exploring the characteristics of three general discussion patterns and the range of purposes they serve. It is organized under the following headings:

I. The Discussion Process

II. Patterns of Discussion

III. Purposes of Discussions

IV. Preparing for Discussions

V. Conducting Techniques

VI. Evaluating Discussions

VII. Summary Outline

VIII. Application Exercise

I. THE DISCUSSION PROCESS

Because the exchange of information in a discussion requires participation, a discussion is conducive to classroom interaction and the development of relationships. Instructors also find discussions useful in identifying student misconceptions, learning problems, and attitudes toward a subject. By interacting with individual students in a group discussion, the instructor has an opportunity to establish a direct interpersonal relationship, a possibility not readily available in the lecture process.

What purposes do you have for using the discussion process? Focus on one specific purpose for a particular class of say thirty students that could be divided into two or up to five groups.

Now try Exercise 1 below:

Exercise 1.

State one major purpose you have for conducting discussions.

____

____

____

Activity:

Indicate which statement below most closely relates to the purpose you listed.

______ A. To achieve my purpose, I must provide a well structured and controlled discussion with the whole class.

______ B. My purpose can best be achieved through allowing the students to determine the flow of the discussion in small groups, with only indirect influence on my part.

______ C. Achieving my purpose is dependent upon a highly collaborative interaction between myself and my students in a group of 12-18.

For this exercise, answers A, B, or C may apply. The choice you made should be based upon your instructional purpose and the characteristics of the student group, as well as your own preference or past experience with the discussion process.

If you found difficulty in selecting a statement describing how to achieve your purpose, your purpose for having discussions may be too general to fit into any single category. The more specifically you are able to identify your purposes or objectives, the more likely you are to reach them. The preparations you make, and techniques you use, for conducting discussions depend significantly on specified purposes.

Some of your instructional purposes may be better reached through a different instructional approach, say, lectures or self-paced learning. Discussions should be regarded as only one aspect of the instructional program. For some instructional objectives, however, discussions may be more effective than any other process.

Discussions establish the opportunity for face-to-face interaction between students and instructor, and among students. Whereas lecturing involves presentations from the instructor to the student, discussion requires an exchange of ideas and information. In lecture classes, students feel that their main tasks are to listen attentively, take notes, and respond on tests with the appropriate answers. Discussions present opportunities for students to express their own reactions and interpretations and to be exposed to a variety of attitudes.

Each technique can be used effectively to serve different functions.

Exercise 2.

Place the letter L beside those functions which you think best apply to lectures and the letter D beside those which you think apply to discussions.

________ Dispensing information

________ Relating and promoting thought about information already acquired

________ Raising the level of student involvement

________ Covering a large amount of material efficiently

________ Developing two-way communication

________ Formulating and expressing ideas and opinions

Your labels from Exercise 2 should be L, D, D, L, D, D.

Discussion requires active participation by both instructor and students. The instructor is placed in a different position from that of making presentations with prepared lecture notes. In a discussion, he is more open to challenges and his leadership role may be that of a guide and counsellor. His image as the dispenser of information may be changed to that of a well-informed resource person or group participant. Students have increased responsibility to contribute meaningful observations to the group. As participants are called upon to react openly to information, their knowledge, attitudes, and beliefs are open to evaluation by others.

While there may appear to be an element of uncertainty for both students and instructor within group discussion, there is also a good opportunity for giving positive reinforcement, building trust, and creating a positive relationship. The instructor can easily and naturally encourage students to respond to each other through extrinsic means such as verbally acknowledging contributions and through non-verbal gestures like affirmative nods of the head. The instructor can gain student respect and trust by openly contributing personal ideas and beliefs as a participating member of the group.

As their confidence and skill with discussion procedures increase, students require less extrinsic reinforcement from the instructor and generate their own internal or intrinsic reinforcement through making progress and developing a sense of achievement.

Exercise 3.

After reading the group descriptions, relate the purposes to the groups.

(Time frame: first three weeks of the semester.)

GROUP A — This group is composed of lower division students who must take the class to fill their general education requirement in science. The students have limited experience and show no particular interest in science as a field.

GROUP B — Upper division students make up this group. The students have chosen this class as part of their selected major. They have taken several courses in this field and have used the discussion process in the prerequisite courses.

GROUP	DISCUSSION PURPOSES
______	define terms, clarify content
______	test hypotheses, involve in problem solving
______	evaluate alternatives, share responsibility in decision making
______	motivate participation, build rapport

The answers are A, B, B, A.

The group A students require more attention in terms of encouragement and clarification of content. Most of the students in this group are aware of their lack of background and interest. The purposes of discussions with this group initially should be to motivate participation, define terms, and develop their confidence with the content and the discussion process.

Group B students are sufficiently advanced in their studies and content preparation so that they will be ready to move into higher levels of thinking by participating in discussions. Their preparation in both content and discussion techniques gives them the basic requirements for testing hypotheses, sharing responsibilities in decision making, evaluating alternative solutions and being involved in problem solving.

II. PATTERNS OF DISCUSSION

The three basic patterns of discussion are: instructor-directed, group-centered, and collaborative.

In the **instructor-directed** pattern, the discussion is leader-centered. It is a controlled discussion and the professor is normally the person in control. Brief questions and answers are common rather than a free exchange of ideas. Also, because the leader directs, questions are generally addressed to the instructor.

In contrast, the **group-centered** pattern has these characteristics: It is a free-flowing exchange of ideas without the directive influence of a leader. It is cooperative in that the participants provide the direction and control the pace. It is open-ended in that the discussion can go in any number of directions, depending on the student reactions and interactions.

The third pattern is **collaborative**. The professor is a participant with the students and is regarded as a contributor but assumes neither a dominant nor a passive role. The collaborative pattern is often task-oriented and focused on problem solving. All participants share responsibility for decision making.

Exercise 4.

Select from the list of characteristics the three which apply most appropriately to each discussion pattern. Write them down under suitable headings.

CHARACTERISTIC	PATTERNS		
	Instructor-Directed	Group-Centered	Collaborative
1. controlled 2. cooperative 3. shared responsibility 4. free-flowing 5. task-oriented 6. leader-centered 7. open-ended 8. question and answer 9. problem solving			

The discussion characteristics should be classified as below:

Instructor-Directed	Group-Centered	Collaborative
controlled	free-flowing	task-oriented
leader-centered	cooperative	shared responsibility
question and answer	open-ended	problem solving

As you have seen from the different patterns of group interaction, all discussions do not take place in the same way. They will vary according to the pattern chosen, the purposes intended, the extent of subject knowledge the participants bring to the session, and the amount of experience students have had with the discussion method. The following model summarizes these points to help you to see how these different factors interact and influence the roles of participants.

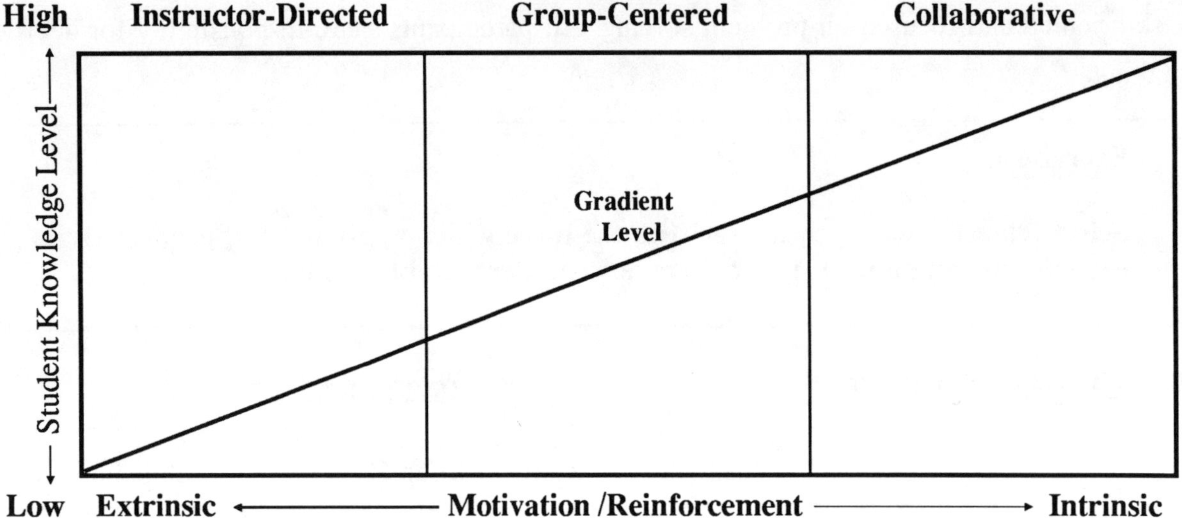

As indicated in the model, each pattern of discussion requires some *motivation* or *reinforcement*. The type and amount of reinforcement varies. In instructor-directed discussions the emphasis is placed on the instructor giving *extrinsic reinforcement* through encouraging participation, and recognizing contributions in an open and positive manner. As students progress through the discussion process and participate in collaborative discussions, the opportunity and need for extrinsic reinforcement are reduced.

Students are *intrinsically reinforced* by becoming involved, making contributions to the discussion, and developing confidence in their own skills. Because of the sense of satisfaction they develop, the students are more open to challenges and to challenging each other.

III. PURPOSES OF DISCUSSIONS

The purposes which discussions serve are examined next, in terms of the three patterns described in the model.

Instructor-Directed

A direct relationship exists between each pattern and the amount of knowledge on the subject which students bring to the discussion, and the type of guidance and reinforcement required. The *instructor-directed* pattern is well suited to an orientation discussion because students most often start the semester with limited background in the subject. They expect clarification of terminology and information. Questions and answers should be brief.

The instructor-directed pattern is also an appropriate way to introduce discussion procedures to students, because the instructor both guides the process of learning and motivates participation. Through this procedure the instructor is helping to reduce any ambiguity students may have on the topic and is building a foundation for the other patterns of discussion.

Some purposes which can best be served by *instructor-directed* discussion are to:

motivate participation
provide for interaction
recognize contributions
define terms
clarify content and objectives
identify assumptions

Group-Centered

The group-centered pattern is probably most effective when students have had prior experience with the leader-directed group discussion. Otherwise, the discussion could easily turn into a free-for-all with no direction and little learning taking place. Students must know what is expected of them and this is gained through experience with the discussion method.

Do not be misled by the term *group-centered.* A clear purpose is still a critical factor in the group process; i.e., the group is working toward a recognized goal, although the goal can be changed by consensus. As stated earlier, the group-centered pattern is a free-flowing, cooperative exchange where group members have responsibility for the conduct of the discussion. In order to progress, students require an adequate background of knowledge in the subject area and familiarity with terminology and basic concepts. Based on their knowledge and experience, they are expected to explore hypotheses and examine assumptions. There is less opportunity and less need for extrinsic reinforcement. The students are rewarded by the exchange of ideas and satisfaction which comes from making a contribution to the discussion.

The purposes of the group-centered discussion are compared below with the instructor-directed pattern:

Instructor-Directed	**Group-Centered**
motivate participation	**build on experience**
provide for interaction	**strengthen relationships**
recognize contributions	**raise questions**
define terms	**explore hypotheses**
clarify content	**formulate ideas**
identify assumptions	**examine assumptions**

Collaborative

The collaborative pattern is the most difficult, and is one that a group can probably handle better after they have had experience with the previous patterns of discussion. Because all members share decision-making responsibility, they must have a strong grasp of their subject matter. In this type of collaborative effort, participants are obliged to accept and integrate ideas from each other, critically evaluate alternative solutions, and formulate criteria for making judgments. The instructor, after cooperatively establishing the procedures, functions principally as a resource person in this type of discussion.

A great deal of challenging and probing with little extrinsic reinforcement may take place during the interchange of ideas. Contributions will be acknowledged, but members may in turn be asked to support their statements with concrete examples and facts. With a high level of cooperation, group members will gain respect for each other's knowledge of the subject and the skills they demonstrate in evaluative thinking. This type of collaborative discussion brings intrinsic reinforcement to each participant.

The purposes of the collaborative group are here compared with the previous two sets.

Instructor-Directed	Group-Centered	Collaborative
motivate participation	build on experience	**involve in problem solving**
provide for interaction	strengthen relationships	**share responsibilities**
recognize contributions	raise questions	**compare alternatives**
define terms	explore hypotheses	**test hypotheses**
clarify content	formulate ideas	**base action on criteria**
identify assumptions	examine assumptions	**modify assumptions**

Exercise 5.

Indicate which discussion pattern, Instructor-Directed, Group-Centered, or Collaborative, would be most appropriate for the following purposes:

1. A U.S. History instructor wants her students to use their knowledge of the electoral process in order to develop a joint proposal for a new and efficient presidential electoral procedure.

____

2. The instructor knows from marking their first test that his English students have had trouble distinguishing the differences between metaphor and simile. He wants to help his students understand the difference more clearly and avoid further ambiguity.

____

3. A science instructor wants the students to come up with as many different ideas as possible for generating new sources of energy.

____

Question 1 deals with proposing and comparing different alternatives to find the best solution to a problem. The *collaborative* group pattern would probably lend itself best to this purpose.

Question 2 involves clarification of content and could probably be handled well by the *instructor-directed* group discussion.

Exploring new ideas is the purpose in Question 3, and would lend itself to the *group-centered* pattern. There are a number of important reasons for using discussion. All relate to moving students from being receivers of information to being active participants in the learning process.

IV. PREPARING FOR DISCUSSIONS

Two practical matters which require attention in the initial stages of preparing for a discussion are: the selection of a problem or topic, and the consideration of group size and possible seating arrangements. Decisions related to these matters will depend upon the purpose of the discussion and the choice of a discussion pattern.

Selecting a Problem

Keep in mind the levels of student knowledge and their experience with the discussion process while considering and selecting a problem for discussion. The process of specifying a problem should involve student participation. This step is important. If the problem is arbitrarily set by the instructor, many students may not be motivated or prepared to participate. One way to involve students in planning is to offer several options to the group from which they select. Selecting a good discussion problem and setting its parameters may be the most important requirements in preparing for an effective group discussion.

Problems selected should be:

- ☐ Directly relevant to and significant in the development of the course.
- ☐ Suited to the background experience, preparation, and interests of the participants.
- ☐ Appropriate for the use and development of discussion skills in the time available.
- ☐ Intellectually stimulating within the competence of the students.

Exercise 6.

Which of the two discussion questions stated below would be more suitable for use early in a freshman course on American History? The one hour discussion group is made up of 18 students of average ability and mainly from white, middle class homes.

______ a. Could the Civil War have been prevented if the leaders had made wiser decisions?

______ b. What examples can you give to describe the difference between a revolution and a civil war?

Item **b** is the better choice. The question is more suited to the early phase of the course and the students' background, since it is helping to clarify and define terms as well as challenging students to use examples from their previous knowledge. In order to discuss item **a** in a productive manner students would need more background knowledge of the variables and would require a high level of discussion skill to be able to handle such a general topic in the time available.

As you select your problems and write them for student consideration or discussion activity, always state them in sufficiently broad terms for student contributions, but not so vague that specific responses would be discouraged.

Group Size and Arrangement

A group of 10 to 15 participants seated in a circle is generally considered as being effective for discussion purposes. Interaction is important and can be significantly limited if the group is too large. Under large group conditions it is common to find a few of the more assertive participants dominating the discussion. One alternative is to divide a class into smaller groups.

Seating arrangements most likely to be effective are those that permit the participants to maintain eye contact. This can be achieved easily by arranging chairs or tables in a circle or by having the participants seated around a large table. If it is not possible to change from a lecture seating arrangement, the role of the instructor is often strongly directive and the amount of give and take among the participants is limited.

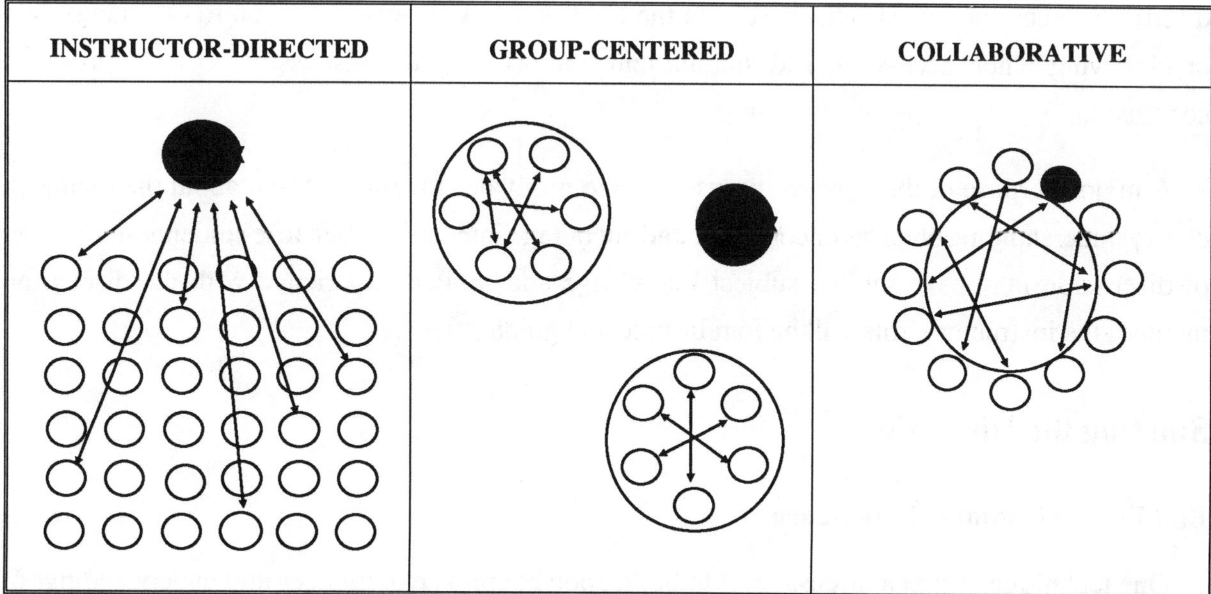

Now turn to the **gray sheets**, pages 95-97, to develop a discussion plan according to the appropriate pattern. Complete Items 1 and 2 on *Purposes and Topics*.

V. CONDUCTING TECHNIQUES

There are three important questions that need to be asked when planning a discussion:

- ☐ **What is the purpose of the discussion?**
- ☐ **What is the pattern of interaction?**
- ☐ **What are the procedures or techniques that could be most effective?**

Once you have formulated your purposes and selected the most suitable discussion pattern, there are a number of techniques available for starting up, keeping going, maintaining flexibility and generalizing. These techniques are outlined next to assist you with conducting discussions in each of the instructor-directed, group-centered, or collaborative patterns.

The patterns should be regarded as broad headings which overlap and from which variations can be developed to help you meet your course objectives. Some of the techniques presented under one pattern are applicable in the other patterns.

INSTRUCTOR-DIRECTED DISCUSSION

In an instructor-directed discussion, the instructor as leader is responsible for initiating the discussion, encouraging participation from the class, keeping the discussion on track, interpreting or clarifying when necessary, and summarizing or bringing the discussion to an appropriate conclusion.

A major purpose of this type of discussion is to motivate students to think about their subject, clarify understanding of terms or concepts, and encourage interaction. Because students at this level of discussion may have limited subject knowledge and limited experience with the discussion method, the instructor's role will be to reinforce and guide students.

Starting the Discussion

Building on Common Experience

One technique to start a discussion is to build upon common experiences and understandings of the group. Common experience may come from a previous learning activity such as a *reading assignment*, a *lecture*, or *studying a video*. You may wish to start out the discussion by listing terms and concepts which the class might find difficult and by asking for additions to the list. Encourage group members to explain what a certain term or concept means to them. Or you may have the group discuss a provocative statement by the author of a reading assignment. Frame a question that will encourage students to state the meaning or importance of the assignment.

Common experience for the students may also come from their school environment, geographical location, subject interest, or the occurrence of a political event. For instance, most students attending a university share common knowledge about environmental and ecological problems. This may be used as a point of departure for a discussion on the importance of conserving natural resources.

Questioning

The questions used to start a discussion can range from seeking additional information to provoking further interest in the discussion subject. Develop clear and succinct questions to meet specific objectives. Avoid vague, complex or wordy questions. Poorly worded questions may be confusing and threatening.

The questions that follow may discourage student participation:

The Binding Question usually includes the answer and leaves no alternative open.

Poverty causes revolutions, don't you agree?

The Closed Question permits only a *yes* or a *no* response and limits further interaction.

Were Washington Irving and James Fenimore Cooper contemporaries?

The Vague Question is too complex and needs to be more clearly defined.

How can democratic nations eliminate poverty?

The Why Question does not always get actual reasons for behavior or events. People often become defensive in trying to explain why. Change a ***why*** question to a ***what*** question for better results in a discussion.

Why are sanctions appropriate against military aggression?

In contrast to the inhibiting questions, an open question is more likely to encourage participation by the students. When a question starts with ***what***, the students feel that you want them to contribute and that you regard their information input as valuable.

Exercise 7.

1. Select the phrasing which is more likely to open up discussion.

_______ a. Did the Federalists support Washington after he became President?

_______ b. To what extent did the Federalists support Washington after he became President?

2. Which of the following questions would allow a student to respond more freely?

_______ a. Don't you think that's the reason why the Indians reacted the way they did?

_______ b. What do you think caused the Indians to react the way they did?

3. Label the following questions as either open or closed.

_______ a. Do you like discussion groups?

_______ b. What do you like or dislike about discussion groups?

_______ c. What do you dislike about this problem?

_______ d. You don't like this problem, do you?

4. Select the better worded question.

_______ a. Of what importance to the outcome of the American Revolution was the naval action off Cape Henry?

_______ b. Assuming that naval action cannot be separated from land campaigns in the analysis of the American Revolution, and assuming further that the war could not have concluded prior to 1871, and if we accept Washington's decision to apply force to the Southern sector as the proper decision, what was the significance of the naval action off Cape Henry in bringing about the final outcome of the American Revolution?

In questions 1 and 2, **b** is the better answer in both cases because open-ended responses are called for. In question 3, **a** and **d** are closed; **d** is also binding, **b** and **c** are open questions. For question 4, **a** is better worded than **b**, which is too complex. Students responding to **b** would probably spend too much time in discussing what the question should be rather than discussing the problem.

Timing

Don't hurry with your questions. The instructor who cannot wait inadvertently destroys a planned discussion. A question is asked. A few seconds of silence follow. The instructor feels uncomfortable and asks another question slightly different from the first, or even worse, immediately answers the question. Both of these actions will discourage students from responding for two reasons. *They have had insufficient time to think about a response*, and *even interested participants will be put off if the thinking and answering are done for them.* Allow ample time for a response, fifteen seconds may be required to give students a chance to do some reflective thinking. The pause will also create an expectation that their responses are desired as well as required.

Keeping It Going

To keep a discussion going, the instructor should involve the students, reinforce their successful participation, clarify any apparent confusion, handle digressions, and summarize periodically.

Involve students by asking for illustrative examples and by encouraging them to react to each other's comments and questions.

Student: *What does the term "detente" mean?*

Instructor: *Can anyone else explain the meaning of this term for Trudy?*

Reinforce students during the discussion by recognizing contributions and encouraging participation. It helps considerably to know and use the names of the students. Avoid the indiscriminate use of praise, qualify your statements as in the following examples:

Thank you, Bill. Well stated. Does anyone else have something to add?

Very good Jane, you qualified your point clearly.

Bob, your comment advanced the discussion to a new phase. Would anyone like to respond to Bob's idea?

Clarify apparent confusion with a comment or by using a question to focus attention on the ideas or content of the discussion. For example:

Let's clear up this point before we continue.

If I hear you correctly, are you telling me that . . . ?

Handle Digressions Promptly

Here are three techniques for keeping the discussion on track and enabling a productive interchange.

- ☐ Take firm measures to prevent misleading statements from becoming distractions by asking questions or calling for clarification.
- ☐ Bring digressions to a limited closure by offering a temporary resolution or a working definition. Gain approval from the group to set the matter aside, and proceed.
- ☐ Put questions off with a promise that they will be answered in the course of the discussion. If this promise is made, be sure to honor it otherwise your credibility as an effective leader may be lost.

Summarize Periodically

To identify the most significant ideas, remind the group of its progress, its unfulfilled commitments, and the time remaining. In the summary statement, select points that have been made and list them in a brief, simplified form. For example: *Thus far you have identified five.... As I write them, please verify my accuracy and be sure I have included all points made.*

Be careful not to jump to conclusions or make premature decisions. Students may sometimes try to find a solution to a problem with insufficient information or reasoning. Don't feel compelled to summarize if no conclusion has been reached. It is quite possible that there may be no solution. If students, through the discussion method, are helped to see that some intellectual questions lack quick, simple answers, they may be encouraged to keep thinking, reading, and probing the subject.

Maintaining Flexibility

Flexibility when conducting a discussion enables you to draw upon your students' experience. Good discussions depend upon more than the logical pursuit of a single idea. If you're too intent and rigid in your attempt to reach a specified outcome, you may preclude a significant student contribution. Allow students to explore areas which seem important to them and show them that you believe in the validity of their ideas. Flexibility allows students to bring forth their ideas and questions so that they can be acted upon. This in turn, may heighten their enthusiasm for discussion.

Generalizing

We have considered techniques for starting a discussion, keeping it going, and allowing for flexibility. The final technique is generalizing. How can you best apply, interpret, integrate, or summarize what has taken place during the discussion? If your discussion purpose has been one of fact finding, you might want to review the main facts discovered and consider with the group the next step to interpret or use the facts. This action may lead into the purpose of your next discussion session.

Your decision on how to generalize at the end of a discussion will directly relate to the purpose of the discussion. If seeking a course of action was the agreed upon purpose, then your generalizing statement should focus on the course of action and perhaps review the kind of reasoning which led to this group decision. Whatever method you use, remember that generalizing is a necessary part of the discussion process to bring it to an appropriate conclusion and confirm for the group what has been accomplished.

GROUP-CENTERED DISCUSSION

Starting the Discussion

A group-centered discussion is free flowing, cooperative, and open-ended. The instructor seldom intervenes and allows the group to carry the discussion. However, the instructor must do careful advance planning to set the scene and create an opportunity for a satisfactory and productive discussion.

One prerequisite for a group-centered discussion is to prepare the students in terms of both subject matter and discussion techniques. The students will need to have reached a reasonable mastery of the topic in order to explore hypotheses, raise questions, shape ideas, and consolidate information. Group-centered discussion might best be planned for midway through a course when students have the necessary subject background and skills learned in instructor-directed discussions. This type of discussion is especially productive for students when they have had a common background from assigned readings or other experiences relevant to the topic.

If the discussion is to be built around a reading assignment, give students a list of questions, work sheets, or exercises on which to focus their attention and organize their thoughts. The preparation should require more than memorization of facts and should help students to apply ideas and analyze information. This kind of guided preparation stimulates thinking and provides a structure for the students when they consider forthcoming discussions.

Once this background work has been done, these further steps should be completed before the discussion begins.

1. Make sure all students understand the problem or issue to be discussed.
2. Hand out any materials that would be helpful, such as diagrams, definitions or criteria lists.
3. Establish an appropriate seating arrangement in small enough groups so that all members can participate.
4. Establish discussion guidelines with the group in advance, such as the need for:

goals	acceptance of ideas	cooperation
relevance	staying on the subject	flexibility
clarity	participation by all	
brevity	sensitivity to others	listening

5. Select one participant to serve as group manager. The manager is a non-contributing member of the group, and does not make substantive contributions. The manager will facilitate the progress of the group by ensuring that the discussion guidelines accepted by the group will be respected. The manager will observe the progress of the discussion and will intervene only to bring to the attention of the group, deviations from their guiding rules, and to assist them to progress toward accomplishing their purpose.
6. Select recorder(s) to take notes of the major points under discussion.
7. Establish a reasonable time frame for the discussion.
8. Determine how to end the discussion and evaluate the outcome.

Keeping It Going

Keeping a discussion going depends upon having a purpose and having some elements which can become focal points within the topic. Sub-questions or sub-topics should be provided by the instructor, usually as preparation exercises. It is critical that students understand their roles as discussion participants. Lay the groundwork and establish criteria for a discussion of this type in a prior class session. Make it clear that in order for the discussion to develop and keep going, all students have the responsibility to come to the session prepared and expecting to participate. Their contributions are going to provide the content, the direction, and the dynamics of the discussion. Keeping a group-centered discussion going depends on the group members and on the competence of the manager.

Maintaining Flexibility

Because there is no instructor directly controlling the group-centered discussion, maintaining flexibility is the responsibility of the group. This is one of the criteria which the group may wish to establish in advance. Maintaining flexibility might mean not allowing one or two members of the group to dominate and take the discussion over. Keeping it moving toward its purpose, while still allowing for purposeful exploration, is the responsibility of each group member. The manager can aid the group in this task.

Maintaining flexibility may also mean re-evaluating the intended purpose of the discussion. If all group members agree that midway through the discussion a different topic or approach to a problem would be more beneficial to their learning, the group may change the direction of a discussion to suit their needs. Because a group-centered discussion lends itself to exploration and expansion of ideas, flexibility is a natural and essential characteristic of the process.

Generalizing

Generalizing can be considered the culminating phase of the discussion. Each group member may contribute to this process, although guidance from the instructor is desirable at this point. The whole purpose of this phase of the discussion is to bring it to an acceptable conclusion whether by summarizing, reviewing, interpreting, or analyzing. Most students, if they have been active in a discussion, may find it hard to recall the major points covered by the discussion. Therefore, bringing it all together in a concise summary is desirable.

Since a group-centered discussion lends itself to exploration and expansion of ideas, a specific conclusion may not be reached. Reviewing and summarizing the contributions may be all that is needed to draw the discussion to a close. There are several ways in which this can be accomplished:

1. The recorder(s) may be asked to read back the notes.
2. Major items of information may be recalled by the group and put on a chalkboard or overhead transparency.
3. Parts of an audiotape or videotape of the discussion may be played back.
4. The instructor or a member of the group may volunteer to summarize items of concern, asking for contributions from the group.

Generalizing should provide an opportunity for the students to consider what was accomplished, and decide whether the ideas formulated in this discussion merit further exploration and testing that might lead to a particular action or a solution to the problem. The generalizing phase thus provides an opportunity for evaluating the outcomes of the discussion.

COLLABORATIVE DISCUSSION

The collaborative discussion also has distinct patterns, purposes, and procedures and is often task oriented. The instructor acts as a contributing group member but takes neither a dominant nor a passive role. However, students need to know that the instructor is supportive, a good listener and as an expert, is interested in their ideas.

In order to function effectively in this role, it is essential for the instructor to have built up credibility with the students. This can be established by the way in which the first two levels of discussion with the class are handled, or credibility may be established through a reputation given by former students.

Starting the Discussion

Prior to starting a collaborative discussion, the instructor needs to have done advance planning with his students to prepare them for the process. Because collaborative discussion lends itself to testing hypotheses and solving problems, students should have reached a sufficiently high level of subject mastery to engage in this kind of thinking. To prepare the students adequately for a collaborative discussion, the instructor may have presented several lectures on the topic, assigned relevant reading and asked students to complete some independent research or study. These exercises should involve them in critical thinking and analysis.

Guidelines for Starting a Collaborative Discussion

- ☐ Make sure all group members know the specific topic to be discussed or the problem to be resolved. Sub-topics and sub-problems should also be reviewed.
- ☐ Hand out appropriate materials, such as diagrams, definitions, or criteria lists.
- ☐ Break into groups small enough to enable all group members to participate in the discussion.
- ☐ Select a manager for each group. The manager can also be a participating member.
- ☐ Select a recorder for each group to document the appropriate findings.
- ☐ Set a time frame for the discussion.
- ☐ Make certain that all group members understand their function and the function of a collaborative discussion. This kind of preparation should be undertaken in a previous class session.
- ☐ Determine the manner of evaluating the outcomes of the discussion.

Keeping It Going

Keeping a collaborative discussion going is the responsibility of the group as a whole. The success of this aspect of the discussion depends on a number of factors:

- ☐ How well are the students prepared?
- ☐ Do they have an adequate background to discuss the problem?
- ☐ Are students clear as to the objectives of the problem?
- ☐ How much experience have group members had with the discussion method?
- ☐ How carefully has the instructor planned the problem to be resolved?
- ☐ Are sub-problems identified with sufficient specificity?
- ☐ Is a solution to the problem feasible within the time frame established?

If group members have come adequately prepared, if they have sufficient experience with the discussion method, and if they have clearly in mind what they are to accomplish, the major prerequisites for keeping the discussion going will have been met. If the group digresses from its intended goal or stays on one topic too long, the manager should intercede and remind the group of its unfulfilled purpose and the time remaining for them to accomplish their goal. A technique that can be used effectively and productively in a collaborative discussion is probing, or intensive questioning. Probing should be used by group members to examine alternatives, analyze ideas, critique suggestions, and then come up with an appropriate solution to the problem.

Maintaining Flexibility

In a collaborative discussion where group members may be engaged in problem-solving or determining an appropriate action to be taken, maintaining flexibility is extremely important. Some group members may be intent on pursuing one avenue of interest or trying to persuade other group members to adopt their solution without allowing the whole group adequate time to set criteria and examine as many viable solutions as they can establish. Keeping options open allows exploration and testing of new ideas. It helps the group remain flexible and able to explore fruitful lines of thought which may emerge in the course of the discussion. These related topics may not be fully explored during the discussion period, but they can certainly be noted as important items which emerged from the discussion, and the group can then determine how they wish to handle them in the future.

Discussions should never be rigid. Even though they have an intended purpose, discussions are meant to help students react to information and use their critical faculties in applying and testing knowledge. The process of inquiry is of equal importance to the acquisition of information in a discussion. By maintaining flexibility within the discussion group, students will have the fullest opportunity to test and evaluate information.

Generalizing

In a collaborative discussion, students may be engaged in examining alternatives, finding the best solution to a problem, and deciding on possible action to be taken. Because the purpose of a collaborative group often includes coming to a group decision or consensus, generalizing will be part of this process. For the group to accomplish this purpose, summary, review, analysis, interpretation and application will be useful techniques for the group to employ.

Generalizing, although normally considered the culminating phase, may be valuable at intermediate times in the collaborative discussion. For example, group members may find it necessary to recap or review progress midway through the discussion. This could be accomplished by taking an inventory of the purposes of the discussion, reviewing notes, or summarizing progress. Generalizing at this point may give students a chance to consider and reflect before applying new information.

If the group as a whole has not been able to draw the discussion to an appropriate conclusion, the instructor may step in and aid the group by reviewing the objectives. With some guidance the group should use logic and creativity to relate all pertinent information and develop an action plan.

Exercise 8

Place the following conducting techniques or procedures under the type of discussion you think each one best fits. Some may be appropriate for all three patterns.

- ☐ set goals
- ☐ define roles
- ☐ be directive
- ☐ select a non-contributing manager
- ☐ select a contributing manager
- ☐ reinforce extrinsically
- ☐ bring discussion to an appropriate conclusion
- ☐ evaluate outcome
- ☐ handle digressions promptly
- ☐ probe

Instructor-Directed	Group-Centered	Collaborative

In answer to Exercise 8, your completed list might look like this:

Instructor-Directed	Group-Centered	Collaborative
set goals	set goals	set goals
be directive	define roles	define roles
handle digressions promptly	select non-contributing manager	select contributing manager
reinforce extrinsically	reinforce extrinsically	probe
bring to appropriate conclusion	bring to appropriate conclusion	bring to appropriate conclusion
evaluate outcome	evaluate outcome	evaluate outcome

Return to the **gray sheets**, pages 95-97. Complete sections 3, 4, 5, 6 and 7 on each page.

VI. EVALUATING DISCUSSIONS

Evaluation is an integral part of the discussion process. There are five important questions that need to be answered about evaluation: *why, when, who, what, and how?*

Why Evaluate?

Evaluation gives direction to a discussion plan. It helps to set goals or purposes and determine whether they are being achieved or are worth achieving. An evaluation is beneficial to the instructor and the students. It assists the instructor in determining what future learning experiences are desirable and it gives the participants a sense of accomplishment and indicates where improvements can be made.

When to Evaluate?

Evaluation procedures should be used before, during, and after a discussion session. Prior to the discussion the leader and/or the group should plan their purposes and assess the most appropriate patterns and procedures for reaching the selected goals. During the discussion process, leaders and group members should be alert to the progress being made. Midway through the discussion, a short review session can indicate whether the group is on its intended course. At the end of the session, the leader and the group members should take time to determine which experiences were effective or pertinent and which could have been improved.

Who Should Evaluate?

Everyone who is involved in the discussion should have the opportunity as well as the responsibility to participate in evaluation. Because each group member, resource person, or leader may have a different perspective, evaluation would not be valid unless all participated.

What to Evaluate?

Both the outcomes of the discussion and the discussion process itself should be evaluated. The criteria set up should reflect the purposes, procedures, and patterns. The more specifically objectives are set, the more accurately the outcomes and the success of the procedures selected can be measured. Identify the levels of knowledge or intellectual skills, the types of attitudes or behavior to be developed and use this information as the basis for evaluation.

How to Evaluate?

The standard procedures for measuring knowledge, intellectual skills and student attitudes used in lectures and self-paced learning apply equally well to discussions. Modules in this series on constructing objective tests, essay tests, and on measuring student attitudes can help evaluation procedures.

USING PMR FORMS FOR PARTICIPANT EVALUATIONS

There are a number of methods which can be used to evaluate the significance of the discussion process *from the point of view* of the participants. One of the most widely used is a post meeting reaction (PMR) form which gives the group members an opportunity to express their opinions of the discussion at the end of the session. Since PMR's are completed anonymously, a participant can report personal evaluations without any fear of reproach.

The PMR forms are most effective when they are:

- ☐ **Brief and easily answered**
- ☐ **Developed with appropriate closed and open questions, tailored to fit the purposes and needs of the group**
- ☐ **Distributed and completed immediately following the discussion**
- ☐ **Tallied and reported back to the participants as soon as possible**
- ☐ **Implemented as guidelines for reviewing the process and future planning**
- ☐ **Used to make appropriate changes during the course**

The questions used in a PMR might relate to substantive items, interpersonal matters, matters of technique and procedure, or a combination of the above.

The following PMR forms have been designed to measure the effectiveness of the three basic patterns presented in this module: Instructor-Directed, Group-Centered, and Collaborative.

PMR FORM FOR INSTRUCTOR-DIRECTED DISCUSSIONS

Was the topic introduced and defined effectively?

4	3	2	1
Very effectively	Reasonably well	Ineffectively	Poorly

Did the instructor keep the discussion on track?

4	3	2	1
Very effectively	Reasonably well	Partially	Not at all

Were you given opportunities to ask questions and present information?

4	3	2	1
At all times	Frequently	Seldom	Not at all

Was your participation both invited and encouraged?

4	3	2	1
Very effectively	Reasonably well	Seldom	Not at all

In what specific ways could the discussion have been improved?

What specific concepts do you think should be considered in the next discussion?

PMR FORM FOR GROUP-CENTERED DISCUSSIONS

Were all the members prepared for a productive discussion?

4	3	2	1
The whole group	Most members	A few	None

Did you feel that the members of your group worked cooperatively?

4	3	2	1
The whole group	Most members	A few	None

Was the group successful at generating ideas on the topic?

4	3	2	1
Highly	Reasonably	Partially	Not at all

Did the discussion serve to meet the group's goals ?

4	3	2	1
Very effectively	Appropriately	Partially	Not at all

In what ways do you feel that your experience on the topic contributed to and benefited from the discussion?

In what ways do you feel you benefited from the discussion?

What comments or suggestions do you have for improving the next discussion ?

PMR FORM FOR COLLABORATIVE DISCUSSIONS

Were the goals of the discussion clear to the group?

4	3	2	1
Completely	Reasonably	Partially	Not at all

Did members of the group contribute to the progress of the discussion?

4	3	2	1
All members	Most members	A few members	None

What progress do you feel the group made toward its goals?

4	3	2	1
Goals achieved	Effective progress	Little progress	No progress

Did the discussion provide you with a sense of achievement and satisfaction?

4	3	2	1
High level	Moderate	Limited	None at all

In what ways did the discussion help you to examine and develop your own thoughts on the topic?

What barriers interfered in reaching the planned goals for the discussion and how do you think they could be better handled in future sessions?

Complete Item 8 on the **gray sheets,** pages 95-97.

USING OBSERVER EVALUATORS

Another method of evaluation is to use an observer-evaluator. This person, as a non-participant, can often see clearly what others who are involved in a discussion may overlook. The function of the observer-evaluator is to take notes describing and interpreting important aspects of the discussion for later evaluation by the group. Elements of the discussion which the observer-evaluator should focus on depend on the purposes and the pattern of the group and the criteria established for participation. Such criteria might include the content and flow of interaction; the achievement of group and individual objectives; the information offered by participants; the logic of their remarks; and the atmosphere and organization of the discussion.

The observer-evaluator may even want to draw a diagram of interaction to help assess the relationship among members of the group. The diagram can reveal who is talking to whom, how often each member participates and any dominating persons.When a member speaks, an arrow is drawn from his or her position toward the person to whom the remark is addressed. Subsequent remarks in the same direction are indicated by short cross marks on the arrow. If a person speaks to the entire group, a larger arrow points toward the center of the group. An example diagram is shown below.

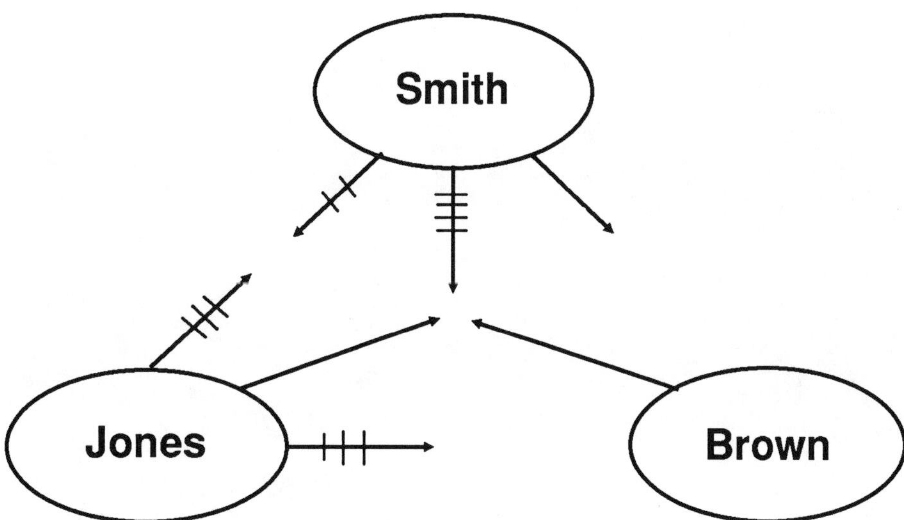

Other techniques for observer evaluation include using audiotape or videotape of the discussion. By listening to or viewing the tapes, all group members can act as observer-evaluators and assess the interactions and progress of the group.

Allow the participants to describe their own performance, this permits them to appraise their contribution from the broader perspective of the group. Encourage constructive statements and questions so that the group members will be better able to understand the discussion process and their progress in relation to the group.

Some persons may be overly critical of themselves, reinforcing their fears or seeing relatively unimportant errors in performance; others may be oblivious to their own mistakes and need further insight and development in the skills of self appraisal. Discussions reveal temperament, attitudes and skills in personal relations, as well as grasp of the subject.

Frequently, we think of evaluation as the end of the learning experience, whereas, it is also the beginning of future planning. The ability to evaluate your own contribution as a discussion leader or participant, to modify purposes and procedures of the group, and to follow up on your modifications is of critical importance. The evaluation techniques described here can help you to improve yourself and your method of assisting others through the discussion process.

VII. SUMMARY OUTLINE

I. THE DISCUSSION PROCESS

Relating purposes to instructional needs

II. PATTERNS OF DISCUSSION

Instructor-Directed
Group-Centered
Collaborative

III. PURPOSES OF DISCUSSIONS

Sets of specific purposes within each pattern differ

IV. PREPARING FOR DISCUSSIONS

Selecting a problem
Group size and arrangement

V. CONDUCTING TECHNIQUES

Instructor-Directed
- Starting the discussion — build on experience, questioning
- Keeping it going — involve, reinforce, clarify, digressions
- Maintaining flexibility — avoid domination, rigidity
- Generalizing — summarize, feedback

Group-Centered
- Starting the discussion — topics, materials, managers, recorder
- Keeping it going — questions, sub-topics, ground rules
- Maintaining flexibility — exploration
- Generalizing — summarize, analyze, feedback

Collaborative
- Starting the discussion — set goals, roles, materials, group size
- Keeping it going — preparation, problem focus, probing
- Maintaining flexibility — keep options open, observe time limits
- Generalizing — summarize, interpret, take action, evaluate

VI. EVALUATING DISCUSSIONS

Why, when, who, what, how to evaluate
Using PMR forms for participant evaluation
Using observer evaluators

REFERENCES AND RESOURCES

Brilhart, J. **Effective Group Discussion**. Dubuque, IA: William Brown and Co., 1989.

Eble, K. (Ed.) **Improving Teaching Styles: New Directions for Teaching and Learning.** San Francisco: Jossey-Bass Inc., 1980.

Fawcett Hill, William. **Learning Through Discussion.** Beverly Hills, CA: Sage Publications, 1982.

Fuhrmann, B. G. and F. A. Grasha. **A Practical Handbook for College Teachers.** Boston: Little, Brown and Company, 1983.

Kahn, Susan. (Ed.) **To Improve the Academy.** Stillwater, OK: New Forums Press Inc., 1989.

McKeachie, W. J. **Teaching Tips: A Guidebook for the Beginning College Teacher.** (8th ed.) Lexington, MA: D.C. Heath and Company, 1986.

Potter, D. and Y. P. Anderson. **Discussion in Small Groups. A Guide to Effective Practice.** (3rd ed.) Belmont, CA: Wadsworth Publishing Company, 1976.

VIII. APPLICATION EXERCISE

INSTRUCTOR-DIRECTED DISCUSSION.

1. State the purposes of the discussion.

2. List the topics/sub-topics of the discussion.

3. Describe the prediscussion assignments/activities/handouts.

4. Write open response questions for the topics.

5. State two techniques you would use to keep the discussion going.

6. What would you do to maintain flexibility?

7. What steps would you do to have the students use the information generated?

8. Develop a PMR form (use a full page).

GROUP-CENTERED DISCUSSION

1. State the purpose(s).

2. List the topics/sub-topics.

3. Describe the prediscussion assignments/activities/handouts.

4. List guidelines on goals, participation, listening, managing, responsibility.

5. What role will the group manager have?

6. List two items to help maintain flexibility.

7. What would you do to have the students integrate and apply the information generated?

8. Develop a PMR form.

COLLABORATIVE DISCUSSION

1. **State the purpose(s).**

2. **List the topics/sub-topics.**

3. **Describe prediscussion assignments/exercises on topics and critical thinking skills.**

4. **What are the organizational guidelines for directions, functions, and responsibilities?**

5. **What steps would you take to keep the discussion advancing?**

6. **What would you do to encourage exploration of new ideas?**

7. **What would you do to have the students use and evaluate the ideas generated?**

8. **Develop a PMR form.**

IMPROVING INSTRUCTOR-STUDENT RELATIONSHIPS

Module Developers:	Ron J. McBeath Jeanne M. Lassen
Editorial Associates:	Oswald B. Carleton Jerrold E. Kemp Robert F. Rubeck
Editorial Consultant:	Richard B. Lewis

IMPROVING INSTRUCTOR-STUDENT RELATIONSHIPS

How important are contacts among faculty and students? What types of relationships contribute to learning? What types detract from learning? These and similar questions may be important to you.

From your view, do you think that a positive relationship will help you in terms of being able to capture students' attention, arouse interest, and communicate effectively? Is it your intention to build self confidence and a sense of achievement in students? Do you expect to challenge students to accept responsibility for their own decisions? Such expectations may appear to be too complex to work toward as realities in our classrooms. But are they?

To help you develop answers to these and other questions, this module is organized under the following headings:

I. **The Use and Misuse of Labels for Students**

II. **Classroom Atmosphere**

III. **Communication between Faculty and Students**

IV. **Skills for Facilitating Verbal Communication**

V. **Instructor Functions and Classroom Interaction**

VI. **Learning Styles and Classroom Interaction**

VII. **Accessibility for Interaction beyond the Classroom**

VIII. **Summary Outline**

IX. **Application Exercise**

Relationships among instructors and students can be improved. There are many factors to be considered. Some will help you; others can hinder your attempts to build a positive relationship to improve teaching and learning.

I. THE USE AND MISUSE OF LABELS FOR STUDENTS

An instructor who concentrates attention on course content, or instructional methods, may give only casual attention to student attitudes and the causes for those attitudes. Such a concentration may have significant impact on instructor-student relationships and learning. For example, rather than give thought to what individual students bring to a class, the instructor may have a tendency to place each student in a stereotyped category identified by a single label. Labels used in this way may hinder efforts to achieve rapport and develop communication links which can contribute to learning.

Exercise 1.

The following terms are often used to categorize and label various student attitudes; *curious, hostile, indifferent, attentive.* Write each one of these terms under either the positive or negative heading. Then write a term which describes the opposite condition as with the example, eager-bored.

Positive	Negative
eager	bored
________	________
________	________
________	________
________	________

Compare your sets of opposite terms with the ones following. Your words may not be the same, but should be similar.

Positive	Negative
eager	bored
curious	apathetic
relaxed	hostile
enthusiastic	indifferent
attentive	inattentive

These terms when used as arbitrary labels for a *single* aspect of behavior have very limited value for improving relationships. When they are organized into checklists or rating scales, they can be used to find out more about students and broaden the base of information for improving instruction.

You could, for instance, construct a matrix like this and use it to plot changes observed over a period of time.

Student Attitude Change Matrix

	1	2	3	4	5	
bored	______	______	______	______	______	**eager**
apathetic	______	______	______	______	______	**curious**
hostile	______	______	______	______	______	**relaxed**
indifferent	______	______	______	______	______	**enthusiastic**
inattentive	______	______	______	______	______	**attentive**

The adjectives you choose should relate to your instructional objectives and reflect the range of behaviors you are interested in developing. From such a base, steps can be taken to develop ways to improve instructor-student relationships in teaching and learning.

Turn to Section A on **gray sheet**, page 138, and complete Items 1, 2, and 3.

II. CLASSROOM ATMOSPHERE

Whether or not you are consciously attempting to establish an appropriate classroom atmosphere, it is important to recognize that you DO contribute to the atmosphere. The question is, how can you create it to work for you rather than against you? By your actions you produce both thoughts and feelings in your students which can be positive or negative. When feelings are positive, the students will be more inclined to participate and become involved with the learning tasks, whereas negative feelings can have the reverse effect.

The atmosphere you create should communicate to the students that you are moving *toward* them and *with* them rather than *away* from them or *against* them, and that your intentions are not adversarial, but cooperative.

In the following three exercises there are descriptions of classroom situations which, if occurring, could provide clues about the tone or atmosphere of the class as a group. Look for the descriptive clues indicating the type of atmosphere.

Exercise 2.

Mr. Fleet rushes into the classroom, does not acknowledge the presence of the students and begins immediately lecturing, saying, "We have a great deal of material to cover today and we must move along quickly if we are to finish this topic on time." He lectures rapidly and continuously, then as the bell rings, he packs up his notes and leaves promptly.

1. Underline key words in this scene which describe the atmosphere.

2. Is the atmosphere likely to be positive or negative? ____________________

1. Key descriptors you may have underlined are: *rushes*, *does not acknowledge students*, *lectures rapidly*, *leaves promptly*. Mr. Fleet's actions communicate that the presence of students is irrelevant to his task. By rushing in and leaving immediately after class, he indicates that he has little interest in interacting with students. He has effectively cut himself off from them. They will probably accept this and eventually make no attempts to communicate with him in or outside of class.

2. The general atmosphere created by Mr. Fleet has negative characteristics.

Exercise 3.

Ms. Long has taken several minutes to hand out the mid-term essay exam which must be completed in the hour-long class period. Before starting the exam, she takes about seven minutes to talk about the grading procedures on the test, the percentage of the overall grade for the class for which this test will count, she continues to discuss the term paper requirement, the reading assignment for the next class meeting, and several other bits of class business which she wants to cover.

1. Underline the key words in this scene which describe the atmosphere.

2. Would you characterize the mood as positive or negative? ____________________

1. Key descriptors in the second part are: *taken several minutes*, *before starting the exam*, *continues to discuss*. Ms. Long has given the students a contradictory message by handing out the test but proceeding to ignore its importance by discussing a whole series of class administrative concerns and tasks. Probably somewhat anxious over the test, the students may experience a rise in anxiety at being delayed from starting work on the test.

2. Ms. Long, probably without intending to, has created a negative atmosphere.

Exercise 4.

Mr. Goodman is leading a class discussion on a topic in which several students have expressed particular interest. He pressures no one to participate in the discussion but moderates the group so that everyone who wants to contribute has an opportunity to do so. He listens and responds to each comment or question with his full attention.

1. Underline the key words in this scene which describe the atmosphere.

2. How would you characterize the mood which Mr. Goodman created?___________

1. Key descriptors in the third scenario are: *student interest, pressures no one, moderates, opportunity, listens, responds, full attention.* Mr. Goodman uses material which is interesting from the students' point of view. He gives validity and worth to the contributions of the students in the discussion. He provides opportunity for students to speak if they choose, but does not pressure anyone who feels uncomfortable speaking to the group. By these means he has probably caused an atmosphere which is relaxed and productive.

2. Mr. Goodman has created an atmosphere that is positive.

Creating a Positive Atmosphere

There are various conditions and events which can cause positive or negative influences on instructor-student relationships. Positive conditions are those which will enable students to develop attitudes of confidence as capable learners, and a favorable attitude toward the subject.

Negative conditions are those which can cause students to doubt their own worth or capability, to lose self-respect, and to inhibit their motivation for learning. The types of conditions which lead to the five sets of attitudes listed below are reviewed on the following pages.

POSITIVE ATTITUDES		NEGATIVE ATTITUDES
Confidence	vs.	**Anxiety**
Challenge	vs.	**Frustration**
Self-Respect	vs.	**Humiliation**
Inquisitiveness	vs.	**Boredom**
Physical Comfort	vs.	**Physical Discomfort**

Confidence vs. Anxiety

Anxiety occurs in many students who are concerned with failure or with their inability to live up to unrealistic expectations they have for themselves or believe you have for them. Anxiety occurs when instructors threaten failure and reinforce it by continued adverse criticism of student work or participation. Instructors often communicate that they **expect** failure by reinforcing an already existing low level of confidence: "You probably won't understand this assignment, but try anyway." Such statements are sometimes made unconsciously, and may reflect an overall negative attitude on the part of the instructor.

Many students have high anxiety levels regarding their ability to do well in the course. These anxiety levels have often been created and reinforced, in other courses, over a period of years.

It is preferable to create a positive atmosphere which shows that it is worthwhile for the student to make a reasonable effort. A positive, supportive approach by the instructor helps the student to see that learning can provide a sense of achievement and a feeling of accomplishment.

Set realistic levels of expectation for the students by the way you make assignments, give presentations, conduct discussions, and set tests and grade examinations. You can do much toward motivating students' learning and building self confidence through **acknowledging** their comments and ideas, **encouraging** them in their pursuit of learning, and in **recognizing** their achievements. Students need to be recognized for work well done. It is particularly important when such recognition comes from an instructor who understands and appreciates their efforts.

Exercise 5.

Which of these instructor behaviors would increase the probability of student anxiety?

Item(s)________________

Which will reinforce confidence?

Item(s)________________

a. Express doubts about the ability of students to succeed on a test.

b. Acknowledge student contributions to discussions.

c. Praise student efforts on term projects.

d. Encourage students to keep up the good work.

e. Ignore a student's comment and proceed to invite another student to comment.

Items **a** and **e** contribute to anxiety. Items **b**, **c**, and **d** reinforce confidence.

Challenge vs. Frustration

If students are unclear or confused about course procedures, material to be covered, or work that is expected of them, they may become frustrated. Frustration occurs when students are blocked from achieving the goals which are set, or when they feel the goals are inappropriate or obscure. Students may also experience frustration from readings or other work which seem unclear or unnecessarily difficult. You are often in the position where you must clarify or reinterpret such information either in class or out of class. You should reassess the level of knowledge and experience of your students each semester to ascertain whether readings or assignments are too elementary or too advanced. Either extreme can frustrate students instead of challenging them.

When students experience challenge in a class, they usually feel motivated to do the work which is required. When they have adequate information about how to proceed, and about what is expected, they are stimulated to move forward instead of being immobilized by ambiguity. They recognize that creative effort, study, and work are required to reach the specified objectives.

Be as clear as you can in discussing course objectives, assignments, grading procedures and policies, and any other matters which involve an expected product or response from the students. If you are deluged with questions after explaining these points, perhaps you need to re-examine both the level of information and your intentions as well as the competencies, interests, and expectations of your students.

If students understand the course objectives and procedures, and are interested in the subject matter, they will be challenged.

Exercise 6.

Which of these instructor behaviors is likely to increase student frustration?

Item(s)________________

Which will challenge the students?

Item(s)________________

a. Gives contradictory directions for an assignment.

b. Asks questions to stimulate interest.

c. Assigns specialized readings too sophisticated for the course level.

d. Assigns repetitious readings in different sources.

e. Relates test items directly to course objectives.

Items **a**, **c**, and **d** can increase student frustration. Items **b** and **e** would challenge students.

Self-Respect vs. Humiliation

Humiliating moments in classrooms are part of the experience of almost every person. Humiliation is a feeling which strips away self-confidence and self-respect. When associated with classroom or other educational experiences, humiliation can reduce motivation for learning. Feelings of humiliation and embarrassment can cause students to give up and stop trying.

Often we embarrass others without any intention of so doing. The key is in the student interpretation of the intent. If students feel that they are being ridiculed or embarrassed, instructors run a high risk of losing their cooperation.

Feelings of self respect, dignity, and worth are necessary for personal achievement and success. Regardless of competency, all students need and have a right to receive respect as individuals. Instructors can avoid engendering a loss of self respect in students by not making comparisons of their performance with that of other students or people in other classes and by not belittling their responses, ideas, or efforts.

Keep in mind that it is difficult for some students to ask for help or explanations. Try to be encouraging and accepting, and don't humiliate or embarrass anyone who asks for your help. Student self respect can be enhanced by communications which carry the message that you perceive them as responsible adults, who deserve your respect. Your recognition of the individuality of each student, goes a long way toward creating mutual respect .

Exercise 7.

Which of these instructor behaviors is likely to cause student humiliation?

Item(s)_______________

Which will reinforce student self respect?

Item(s)_______________

a. Criticizes individual students in the presence of class.

b. Accepts ideas and opinions of students.

c. Listens carefully to students' comments.

d. Compares a group unfavorably with another class.

e. Encourages students to confer on problems they may be having in the course.

Items **a** and **d** would cause humiliation. Items **b**, **c**, and **e** would reinforce student self-respect.

Inquisitiveness vs. Boredom

Motivating inquisitiveness depends upon your interest and enthusiasm as much as the interest and experience students bring to the class. If you are bored with what you teach or how you teach, undoubtedly your students also will be bored.

Instructors can both sense and observe when their students are bored in class. Cues and signs such as doodling, vacant stares, reading, and nodding off should not be overlooked. Boredom can produce much anxiety and frustration for both instructors and students. In lecture classes, the causes may include voice quality, pace of speech, use of language, ambiguity of statements, lack of examples, and failure to activate student participation.

Another cause of boredom is required reading that is not clear, not interestingly written, too advanced, or too elementary. Class assignments sometimes require effort beyond the value of the experience, or lack relevance.

Examine these and other factors. Arrange for your students to give their reactions and suggestions about the course. What interests them most? What interests them the least? What kinds of classroom presentations and interaction hold their attention? What are their expectations of the course, of you, of themselves? Often, the opportunity for students to make some choices of topics and types of assignments can increase inquisitiveness. Try to elicit their special interest areas, ideas, suggestions, and alternatives. The mere fact that you ask them for suggestions may spark ideas not previously considered.

Exercise 8.

Which of these instructor behaviors probably cause students to be bored?

Item(s)_______________

Which will reinforce and stimulate inquisitiveness?

Item(s)_______________

a. Speaks in a quiet monotone.

b. Assigns work too elementary for class level.

c. Displays energy and interest in the subject.

d. Relates course content to student interests.

e. Involves students actively during presentations and classroom discussions.

Items **a** and **b** cause boredom. Items **c**, **d**, and **e** reinforce inquisitiveness.

Physical Comfort vs. Physical Discomfort

The problem of physical comfort is one over which you may have little control. The classroom may be too hot or too cold. The seats may be too small, too hard, or designed only for right-handed persons.

Be aware of the physical environment of your classroom, and make whatever adjustments are within your control to make it comfortable. Almost all students have suffered in a hot, stuffy classroom, but this situation may be changed. Check the windows and ventilation. If it is feasible and agreeable to you and your students, arrange for an alternative meeting place.

Long class sessions can cause undue discomfort. In classes longer than 1-1/2 hours, a break is essential. If students are uncomfortable, their attention will be lessened, their enthusiasm dimmed, and their responses inhibited.

Adjust room darkening facilities if the sun is shining on the chalkboard and creating a glare, or if light is falling onto a screen that is being used for slides or motion picture films. Also, check that projectors are in the best position to provide a full size picture that everyone can see.

Exercise 9.

Which of these instructor behaviors are likely to produce student discomfort?

Item(s)________________

Which will increase the probability of student comfort?

Item(s)________________

a. Lectures for 3 hours without a break.

b. Leaves window open with building construction occurring close by.

c. Closes window on a hot day.

d. Darkens room during a film showing in a daytime class.

e. Seeks rooms with appropriate seating and conditions for style(s) of instruction.

Items **a**, **b** and **c** would cause students to be uncomfortable. Items **d** and **e** would contribute to physical comfort. Your actions will influence and reinforce student attitudes in both positive and negative ways. The outcomes of all classroom situations are not completely under your control, yet with attention and constructive action, you can often improve poor working conditions.

Review various instructor actions, their impact on student attitudes, and significance for instructor-student relationships in the following exercise.

Exercise 10.

Complete the chart by filling the open boxes to indicate how
A. The action of the instructor
B. Influences student attitudes and behavior positively or negatively
C. Has impact on the instructor-student relationship

Action of Instructor **will influence** Attitude or Behavior in Students **and contribute to** Instructor-Student Relationship

A	B	C
1. Provides vague objectives. Teaches one thing and tests on another.	Feel frustrated. —lack of trust in instructor —confusion —anxiety —resentment	Students may choose not to interact—may withdraw or become hostile. (moving away or against)
2. Gives acknowledgement to all student comments in class.		Relationship may be positive and respectful. (moving toward and with)
3. Gives unannounced *pop quizzes* with no indication of their importance.	Feel a lack of trust and resentment, become guarded or suspicious.	
4. Gives unenthusiastic lectures and shows little interest in the course.		Relationship may be uncooperative and apathetic. (moving away or against)

Action of Instructor **will influence** Attitude or Behavior in Students **and contribute to** Instructor-Student Relationship

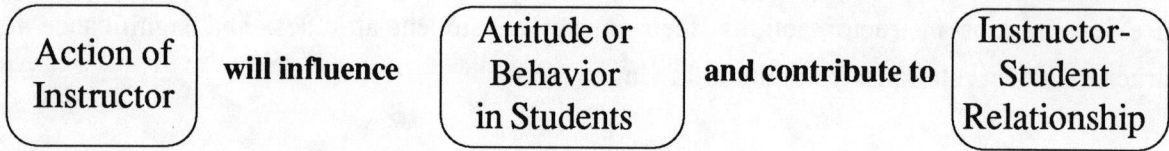

A	B	C
5. Clearly states the objectives of the course, grading methods and practices, and follows those guidelines.	Aware of responsibilities and able to make realistic decisions.	
6. Ridicules students for wrong answers.		
7. Exhibits enthusiasm and interest in presenting lectures or in conducting discussions.		
8. Encourages students and recognizes their contributions and achievements.		

Compare the boldface statements with your responses to Exercise 10 on previous pages.

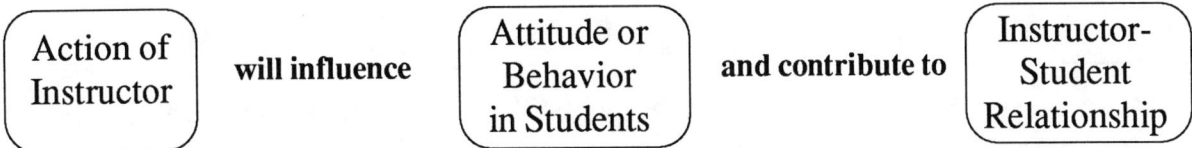

Action of Instructor **will influence** Attitude or Behavior in Students **and contribute to** Instructor-Student Relationship

A	B	C
1. Provides vague objectives. Teaches one thing and tests on another.	Feel frustrated. —lack of trust in instructor —confusion —anxiety —resentment	Students may choose not to interact—may withdraw or become hostile. (moving away or against)
2. Gives acknowledgement to all student comments in class.	**Feel a sense of self-confidence, and motivated to participate.**	Relationship may be positive and respectful. (moving toward and with)
3. Gives unannounced *pop quizzes* with no indication of their importance.	Feel a lack of trust and resentment, become guarded or suspicious.	**When students believe the actions of instructors are unfair, an adversarial relationship is likely to develop.** **(moving away or against)**
4. Gives unenthusiastic lectures and shows little interest in the course.	**Feel boredom and indifference.**	Relationship may be uncooperative and apathetic. (moving away or against)

Action of Instructor **will influence** Attitude or Behavior in Students **and contribute to** Instructor-Student Relationship

A	B	C
5. Clearly states the objectives of the course, grading methods and practices, and follows those guidelines.	Aware of responsibilities and able to make realistic decisions.	**Student interaction with an instructor who is seen as fair and clear, usually results in a cooperative and open relationship. Students know what is expected/where they stand. (moving toward and with)**
6. Ridicules students for wrong answers.	**Feel shame or guilt in relationship to their peers and their self concept, feel anger at the instructor and the situation.**	**Students may withdraw from participating in class and develop a defensive or hostile relationship. (moving away or against)**
7. Exhibits enthusiasm and interest in presenting lectures or in conducting discussions.	**Generate corresponding enthusiasm and interest in the course.**	**If students are involved and interested in the class they participate, put in effort, and reap greater benefit to themselves. (moving toward and with)**
8. Encourages students and recognizes their contributions and achievements.	**Feel self respect and confidence—motivated to success.**	**Students whose contributions are recognized by the instructor will see themselves as capable and continuing learners. Their relationship is likely to be participative. (moving toward and with)**

Turn to Section B on the **gray sheet**, page 138, and complete Items 1 and 2.

III. COMMUNICATION BETWEEN FACULTY AND STUDENTS

The process of communication enables you and your students to work toward the goal of building understanding and meaning through sharing information, feelings and beliefs. Clear communication depends upon having common ground with the students with regard to both experience and expectations. You can build common ground by communicating the objectives of the course, how it fits into their program, and what is required to succeed.

Communication is a two-way process which can be carried out by a variety of methods to develop mutual understanding, respect and positive interpersonal relationships. Each participant in the communication process shares responsibility for the outcome of the interaction.

Within the process there are many possibilities for misunderstanding and misinterpretation. The term *noise* is often used to describe conditions which interfere with communication. *Noise* can be a physical condition, such as bad light or distracting sound. *Noise* can also result from the mindset, language, and cultural differences of the sender and receiver. To overcome the effect of noise, the instructor should develop ways to get feedback through open communications. This will clarify misunderstandings and help students develop a sense of achievement.

The following sections deal with these five aspects of the communication process:

- ☐ **The Content of Communication**
- ☐ **Written Communication**
- ☐ **Non-verbal Communication**
- ☐ **Spoken Communication**
- ☐ **Mediated Communication**

The Content of Communication

In all communication, people express both thoughts and feelings. We express linguistic meanings (ideas and information), and emotional meanings (attitudes and values). In order to know their significance to communication, we should recognize the difference between linguistic and emotional meanings.

In higher education the emotional elements of communication are often neglected in favor of linguistic meanings. Students are not asked to feel; they are asked to think. Yet in all circumstances people think and feel simultaneously about events, processes, and people. To overlook the emotional aspects of interactions is to lose much of the meaning of communication.

If a student says, *I read the book you recommended*, the linguistic meaning is clear; but you have no idea of the emotional impact of the reading until you ask questions such as: *Did you like the book? What relevance did it have for you? How did it affect you? What will you do differently because you read the book?*

In and out of the classroom, students' responses are influenced by their interpretation of your projected thoughts and feelings about the course, yourself, and the class. You are evoking responses that are both positive and negative. Positive interactions will help spark student interest and can help motivate them to further study. Negative interactions have the reverse effect in the long term.

Humorous anecdotes and personal experiences often help students to grasp meanings and see applications. Students can be encouraged to offer examples from their own experience. By the relevance of the examples they offer and the class interaction, you can recognize the extent to which the class understands and what they feel about the ideas you wish to make clear. It is important to remember that the content is a means to an end, and that it is the student who makes meaning out of the communication and thereby learns.

Written Communication

Written communication is a part of every class experience. Instructors write course objectives, topic outlines, exercises, assignments, and tests. If instructions are not clear, students will be frustrated in their attempts to follow assigned procedures or tasks. As a result, their perceptions of instructors and assignments may be negative.

The students normally communicate with instructors in writing through term papers, tests, and assignments. So that they know what is to be evaluated, provide guidelines or criteria for them so that acceptable standards may be maintained. When assessing work, be consistent, avoid cynicism, and offer constructive suggestions.

Non-Verbal Communication

Non-verbal communication occurs through gestures such as raising a hand during a lecture, affirmative or negative nodding of the head, drumming fingers on desk or table, smiling or frowning. The meanings of these actions might be mutually clear, but other non-verbal messages may not be so easily interpreted. Nevertheless through studied observation of many students you become increasingly skillful in interpreting non-verbal behavior. Such skill can be of great value to you in improving your relations with students and in improving your instructional program.

Exercise 11.

Study the four types of student reactions presented in the matrix below and complete the interpretation exercise on the lower part of the page.

Student Reactions to the Situation	Behaviors Usually Observed or Recognized	Behaviors NOT Usually Observed or Recognized
Acceptance	Student is poised on the edge of the chair, writing very fast as you lecture, looking up to nod affirmatively.	Student takes notes consistently throughout a lecture and returns eye contact.
Resistance	Student glares at you, folds arms across chest, and makes a half turn away from you in his chair.	Student looks out the window, passes notes back and forth with the person next to him, stifles yawns.

Circle the appropriate term in the boxes below.

	Behaviors Usually Observed or Recognized	Behaviors NOT Usually Observed or Recognized
Acceptance	Enthusiasm Anger Attentiveness Apathy	Enthusiasm Anger Attentiveness Apathy
Resistance	Enthusiasm Anger Attentiveness Apathy	Enthusiasm Anger Attentiveness Apathy

Do your interpretations agree with those noted on the next page?

Student Reactions	Behaviors Usually Observed or Recognized	Behaviors NOT Usually Observed or Recognized
Acceptance	Enthusiasm	Attentiveness
Resistance	Anger	Apathy

Analysis of the behavior patterns this way is one approach to studying non-verbal behavior by direct observation. Caution is advisable, since it is possible to misinterpret student behaviors. Many times you may be misled by the behavior of students who are reacting to conditions not associated with the class situation.

Another way to study student-instructor behavior is to have a videotape recording made of one or more class sessions; this technique helps in making judgments of non-verbal behavior you might have overlooked during the class.

Spoken Communication

Verbal interaction is the prevailing method of communication in most classrooms. It may also be the easiest type to misunderstand. Four components that relate to the intellectual and emotional content of verbal interaction and influence the clarity and impact of verbal communication are:

Assumption(s) (speaker and listener)	The belief held by the participants about the situation and the people in the interaction process.
Intent (speaker)	The purpose for stating the message.
Message (speaker)	The actual verbal communication.
Reception (listener)	The interpretation and internal response to the verbal communication from others.

Do not assume that you and your students have similar assumptions regarding the information and its value. Try to recognize your assumptions and learn about those of your students. Check your assumptions with your students, ask for reactions or feedback so that you may establish some common ground or frame of reference.

Once you have determined the **purpose or intent** of your message, develop it to fit both your intentions and the experience of your students. If your **intent** is not clear, students will react according to their **reception** and **interpretation.**

Organize the facts and concepts in your message and use examples to add clarity and relevance. Be as positive as you can when you stimulate students' feelings. When your verbal communications are clear to the students both linguistically and emotionally, you are likely to get positive and understandable responses.

Exercise 12.

Read this example of an instructor's message where the intent is not clear and which could be received and interpreted in a positive or negative way by students. Complete the exercise by circling the appropriate italicized word below.

Instructor's Message	Instructor's Assumption	Instructor's Intent
Stated during a class discussion of a reading assignment that students complained was too difficult: "Come on, it's easy, you can do it. You can do better than that."	The students are capable but not trying hard enough.	To motivate the students to do better and to liven up the discussion.

A student who perceives the intent to be encouraging and well meaning would probably have a ***positive/negative*** reception of the message.

A second student who perceives the intent to be a *put down* of the abilities of the class would probably have a ***positive/negative*** reception of the message.

The first student will probably have a positive reaction to the message and will not take offense. The student assumes with the instructor, that the class is capable but not very involved at the moment.

The second student may have a negative reaction to the message and may be offended, particularly if he or she has doubts about his or her own capabilities. From the instructor's perspective the learning is easy, but from the student's point of view, it may seem difficult.

Mediated Communication

Media is a term used to denote a variety of instructional resources which may be chosen to supplement words and provide concrete illustrations of concepts, processes, or principles. Realistic images and sounds can provide aural and visual clarification.

Typical resources available to supplement lectures include:

- ☐ **films, videotapes, videodiscs, and computer programs**
- ☐ **still pictures, slides, and overhead transparencies for projection**
- ☐ **audiotapes and disc recordings**
- ☐ **real objects and models**
- ☐ **displays, diagrams, and charts**

The decision to select one or more resources should be based on the objectives of your communication, the needs of your students, the nature of the instructional situation, and the characteristics of the medium. The decision will also be related to the availability of media resources at your institution.

When used effectively, media modify the role of the instructor. They provide an opportunity for the instructor to be less a dispenser of information and to become more involved in facilitating student discussion. The instructor is less involved in transmitting information and is thus able to participate more with the students.

The instructor plays a key role in setting the stage and focusing students' attention, and in assisting them to interpret and apply the information they receive. You can do this through giving an introduction and raising questions prior to the presentation, making the presentation under good viewing and listening conditions, and afterwards by providing suitable follow-up discussion or related activities.

The students can also make use of various forms of media in making presentations to the class. Facilities for producing slides, overhead transparencies, charts, audiotapes and videotapes are becoming quite common. Check with the media services personnel to find out more about the services, resources, and guidelines available to you and your students.

Media well used, bridge the gap between symbols and reality.

Turn to Section C on the **gray sheet**, page 139, and complete Items 1, 2, and 3.

IV. SKILLS FOR FACILITATING VERBAL COMMUNICATION

Three basic skills to facilitate communication are: **Listening**, **Questioning**, and **Reacting to Student Communication.**

Listening

Many breakdowns in communication can be attributed to unmotivated, inattentive listening by students and instructors. Patterns of human interaction are such that if students feel an instructor is not listening they will probably give up trying to be heard. If your students feel that you acknowledge and recognize them, they will be motivated to communicate.

Here are four points to guide you in developing your own listening skills.

1. **Keep eye contact with the student. This communicates willingness to attend to what is being said.**
2. **Try not to be preoccupied with your own thoughts or responses. Don't rush ahead merely waiting to talk again.**
3. **Attempt to get behind the words. What does the student think and feel about him/herself? The situation? Listen to voice tone, and the words chosen, observe gestures and other body action, all of which contribute to the communication.**
4. **Indicate that you are following the conversation and that you understand what is being said.**

Questioning

Use questions to seek information, provoke discussion, and facilitate further inquiry. There are many kinds of questions and many reasons for asking them. Some types of questions can help you to reach your objectives, others may not.

Questions that Inhibit

Some questions can open communications among people, other questions hinder or inhibit. Some of the types of questions which can stifle further interaction are listed on the next page.

The Binding Question:

This question includes the answer. It is a way to make a statement rather than ask a question.

No one is going to flunk a test unless he's having a lot of trouble, isn't that so?

The Soliciting-Agreement Question:

This question suggests that the person who is asked must agree with the speaker.

You really don't think your term paper is up to par, do you?

The Forced-Choice Question:

This question limits the possible responses, none of which might be the answer one might really want to give.

Do you want to do this assignment over or do you want me to record an "F" for it?

The Double-Bind Question:

This question implies a no-win situation:

Have you quit cutting class?

The "Why" Question:

Questions which ask why, do not always elicit answers that reveal actual reasons for behavior or events. People can become defensive in trying to explain why:

Why are you late?

Why didn't you turn in your paper?

Why don't you put more time into studying?

Closed Questions:

This type of question can limit a student's response by setting up parameters and narrowing choices. Extremely closed questions can limit the answer to "yes" or "no."

You don't want to take the test today, do you?

You don't like this class, do you?

Questions that Enrich and Facilitate Responses

As opposed to closed questions, which structure the response, open questions provide opportunities for answers that express what students really want to say.

Closed: *You didn't like the book I recommended, did you?*

or

Open: *Did you like the book I recommended?*

What was your reaction to the book?

The open question asks for a free response of the opinion, thoughts, and feelings of the student. It creates an opportunity for a student to be heard in words of his/her own choice. When you start the question with the word ***what*** the listener is more inclined to assume that you are seeking information and more likely to provide an informative answer.

Exercise 13.

Following are examples of closed, soliciting agreement, binding, double-bind, forced choice or *why* questions. Formulate an open question that could be substituted for each.

Closed or inhibiting	1. *Why did you cut classes all those weeks?*
Facilitating	
Closed or inhibiting	2. *You feel nervous about taking the test because you're unprepared, right?*
Facilitating	
Closed or inhibiting	3. *You don't really believe that theory, do you?*
Facilitating	

Facilitating responses:

1. What were you doing when you weren't coming to class?
2. How do you feel about taking the test?
3. What is your belief about the theory?

Reacting to Student Communication

To develop positive feelings of interrelationship with students, several types of instructor reactions can serve constructive purposes. Here are some examples:

You seem to be saying. . . If I hear you correctly, is this what you mean. . .

Such statements encourage students to expand or clarify their communication and provide means to emphasize key ideas or ensure accuracy. They also let students know they have been heard, and acknowledge what has been said.

Here are further examples that indicate that you have received what was said, and felt. Note that these statements should reflect feelings expressed by students, but not be judgmental.

You seem to be very excited about the project . . . You seem to be a bit hesitant.

Spoken Communication Skills Summary

Listening	**Maintain eye contact.**
	Listen with full attention.
	Ascertain feelings and emotions.
	Interpret non-verbal behavior.
	Indicate that you follow what is being said.
Questioning	**Use open questions to facilitate responses.**
	Avoid closed inhibiting questions.
	Avoid *why* questions.
	Employ *what* questions.
Reacting	**Encourage expansion and clarification of ideas.**
	Emphasize key ideas and ensure accuracy.
	Reflect the feelings expressed by the students.
	Use comments that are not judgmental.

Turn to Section D on the **gray sheet**, page 139, and complete Items 1, 2, and 3.

V. INSTRUCTOR FUNCTIONS AND CLASSROOM INTERACTION

Five different functions of an instructor are outlined below. They reflect personal characteristics, course expectations, the tasks you undertake, and the classroom environment. The way you perform these functions will contribute to your teaching style and the student interactions. They are:

The Expert, Formal Authority, Counselor, Facilitator, and Model

The Expert

In your chosen subject, you are accepted as an expert. As such, your purpose is to impart information that is relevant to the course objectives. Depending upon the instructional mode, students may participate with you, as in a discussion class or a seminar, or mainly listen to you, as in a lecture class. In both cases, students expect you as the authority to confirm or deny the validity of interpretations and conclusions in the course materials.

There are rigid experts and flexible experts, some who are defensive and some who welcome challenge. There are experts who draw out the ideas from others and those who turn them off. Students will respond to your style, the way you perform your functions as an instructor. Present your subject in a way that encourages questions or interpretations. Make the students feel they can ask questions or offer ideas to enhance or clarify a discussion. Communicate enthusiasm for your subject, to inspire enthusiasm among your students. In summary:

- ☐ Solicit and respond to student comments and questions.
- ☐ Be enthusiastic about your subject.
- ☐ Relate to students in a positive manner.
- ☐ Be approachable and willing to listen to others.

Exercise 14.

Please circle the word that best describes the instructor as an expert.

a. informed b. informal c. collaborative

Item **a**, *informed*, best fits the description of the instructor as expert.

The Formal Authority

You are the representative of your department, school, and the university. You must satisfy the many administrative and management demands such as attendance, grade sheets, and add/drop cards. You must also clarify and interpret these administrative requirements for your students. In addition to representing authority from beyond the classroom, you also serve as a formal authority when presenting your course objectives, assignments, procedures for tests, evaluation and grading deadlines, and standards. In this role of formal authority, students perceive you as the controller.

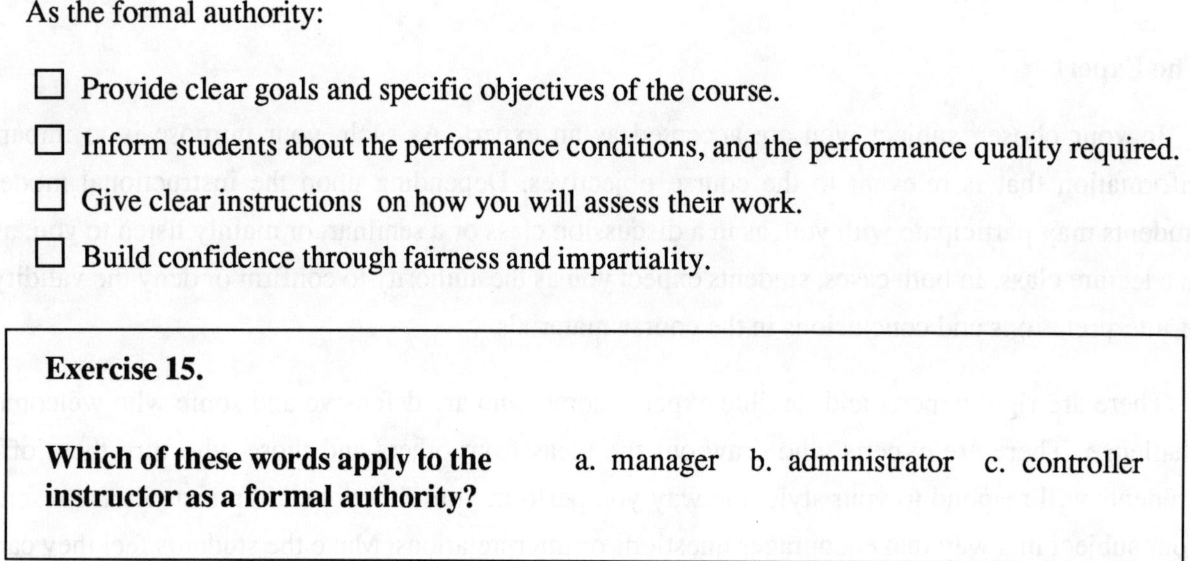

As the formal authority:

- ☐ Provide clear goals and specific objectives of the course.
- ☐ Inform students about the performance conditions, and the performance quality required.
- ☐ Give clear instructions on how you will assess their work.
- ☐ Build confidence through fairness and impartiality.

Exercise 15.

Which of these words apply to the instructor as a formal authority? a. manager b. administrator c. controller

All Items **a, b** and **c**—the manager, administrator, and controller—fit the description.

The Counselor

As counselor you often serve as a link between your profession, and students who aspire to careers in your field. You serve as a recruiter, identifying students who show promise, ability, and interest. To the students in your class, you represent the values and style of your discipline. As a counselor, your interaction with students will include answering questions, discussing aspects of the field, giving advice when sought, and listening.

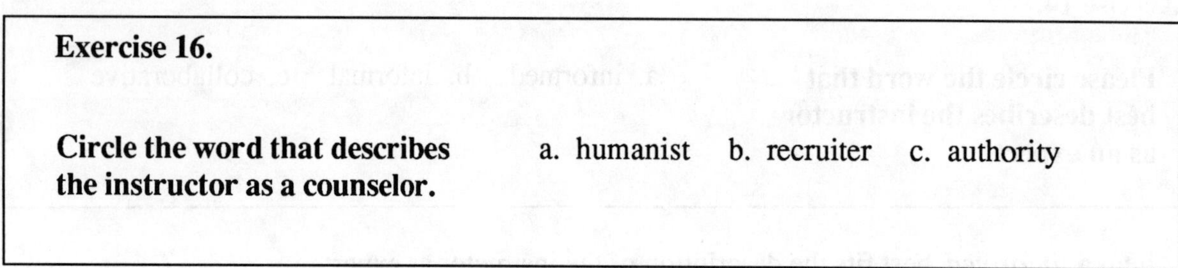

Exercise 16.

Circle the word that describes the instructor as a counselor. a. humanist b. recruiter c. authority

Item **b**, *the recruiter*, best fits the description of the instructor as counselor.

The Facilitator

As facilitator your function focuses more on your ability to elicit information from your students, to help them discover, and define, their own goals and skills. As a facilitator, you do not impose your own standards, instead you assist them to formulate their own goals and plans of study within the context of the particular situation. You interact with students as a guide, asking questions, listening, and suggesting rather than directing actions.

Most instructors experience this function when supervising individualized study or conducting independent study courses. This function requires a collaborative interaction between instructor and student. As a facilitator you come to know students as individuals and respond to their particular needs and learning styles. It is by this interaction that students will get to know you as an individual.

Exercise 17.

Circle the word(s) that describe the instructor as facilitator. a. non-directive b. collaborative c. formal

Items, **a**—non-directive, and **b**—collaborative, are suitable descriptions for the instructor as facilitator.

The Model

You also function as a model for students who seek to emulate some aspect of your intellectual ability, drive, skill, or enthusiasm. Your students see you as symbolic of your profession. You may or may not be aware of your role as a model, but in this important function, you are teaching by example rather than by direction.

Exercise 18.

Circle the word(s) which best describe the instructor as a model. a. symbolic b. directive c. consulting

Item **a**, *symbolic*, best describes the instructor as model.

As you have read the descriptions of the five instructor functions, you may have thought about how you performed each of them and the overall style you have developed. Some factors that may have influenced your performance are listed below. Can you think of others?

- ☐ The purposes of the course of instruction.
- ☐ The image you hold of yourself as an instructor.
- ☐ The expectations, interest, feelings and abilities of your students.
- ☐ The classroom atmosphere and conditions in which interaction has taken place.
- ☐ The conscious and unconscious choices you have made of which function to emphasize.
- ☐ The way you feel physically or mentally at moments of decision.

Exercise 19.

Below are examples of *student* comments or questions to instructors. Use the appropriate letter from the list to indicate the teaching function students are likely to perceive.

A. Expert

B. Formal authority

C. Counselor

D. Model

E. Facilitator

______ 1. *Are the term papers due on May 12 or May 15?*

______ 2. *I wish I knew as much as you do about the topic. I really want to learn as much as I can about it.*

______ 3. *Thank you for listening. I appreciate your encouragement.*

______ 4. *Do you think we would have gone on to fight a full-scale war in Vietnam if Kennedy had lived?*

______ 5. *Could you tell me more about the professional association you talked about so I could inquire about student membership?*

______ 6. *I'm glad you helped me sort through all those ideas I had for a thesis topic. Now I feel I can make a choice based on some good considerations.*

You probably recognize the possibility of alternative answers. How do yours compare with those selected below?

1. Formal authority	B	4. Expert	A
2. Model	D	5. Counselor	C
3. Counselor	C	6. Facilitator	E

These functions of an instructor affect teaching style and influence decisions on procedures, assignments, activities, and evaluation techniques. The total impression of these elements strongly influences student responses. If students accept your role as a provider of information (expert), generally they will respond as they believe appropriately, probably limiting their approaches to questions of fact. Thus, if you wish to encourage a variety of interactions, your program must include a variety of clearly defined functions and alternative styles.

Exercise 20.

Mr. Byrd teaches an upper division Social Psychology class. He has a strong belief that students should make as many choices as possible in determining their own educational goals. He sees his role as a guide to help students discover what is important and how to pursue their goals. He wants them to define for themselves what they will learn.

Mr. Byrd has prepared a bibliography of suggested readings around which much of the class discussion is focused. He encourages each student to choose a specific topic of study within the broad field of Social Psychology and to communicate to him what they have learned. They may write a traditional term paper, present a class lecture, lead a discussion, compile an annotated bibliography, or choose an alternative method of presentation. In this way, Mr. Byrd hopes to provide each student with an equal chance to succeed.

Choose the term which best characterizes Mr. Byrd's approach to this class.

Expert	(knowledgeable)
Formal Authority	(the administrator)
Counselor	(the recruiter)
Facilitator	(non-directive)
Model	(symbolic)

Probably you consider that Mr. Byrd as an instructor sees his principal role as a **facilitator** of student learning. Rather than directing the students to learn specified content, he believes their interests will motivate them to study those areas of most importance to them. Further, Mr. Byrd makes a continuing effort to identify and appreciate the different learning styles of his students.

Turn to section E on **gray sheet**, page 140, and complete Items 1, 2, and 3.

VI. LEARNING STYLES AND CLASSROOM INTERACTION

All students have different learning styles. These styles reflect their personal characteristics, attitudes toward learning, past experience in instructional situations, and learning skills they have acquired. These styles may conflict with an instructor's ideas of how students should learn. A successful instructor helps students to build on their strengths, overcome limitations and broaden their approaches to study. Six generalized learning styles are described as opposing pairs.

Competitors	**Collaborators**
Avoiders	**Participants**
Dependents	**Independents**

The Competitors

Competitors usually achieve success in learning because they are motivated to perform better than others. The classroom process is seen as a win-lose situation. They want to score points and receive rewards in the form of attention from the instructor, high grades, and recognition, even negative recognition such as envy by the other students, influences their behavior.

The Collaborators

Collaborators cooperate fully, by their own initiative, with the instructor and other students. By sharing their own thoughts and listening to those of others, they feel they reap the most benefit from their educational experiences. They are willing to take risks and explore alternatives.

The Avoiders

Avoiders do not appear to exhibit interest in either the content of the course or in participating with the instructor and other students. They seem either remote from the process or threatened by the content. This characteristic may be a general trait, but is often related to a specific course, and sometimes a particular professor.

The Participants

Participants like going to class and being with other students. When encouraged, they will interact with others to learn course content and participate in classroom procedures. They can be guided into taking some responsibility for their classroom experiences and thereby benefit intellectually as well as socially and emotionally.

The Dependents

Dependents exhibit little curiosity and learn only what is required. They view the instructor as a source of structure and authority. They expect clear guidelines and detailed directions for their assignments. They prefer responding to *hard facts* rather than to making future predictions based on subjective judgments.

The Independents

Independents think for themselves and are confident of their own abilities. During the course they learn what is of value to them. They prefer to work by themselves rather than with others. They like to select their own challenges and follow their own interests.

Exercise 21.

John is a 20 year old junior in Mr. Byrd's class. He feels anxious about the choices he has been asked to make about a term project. He has taken mostly lecture courses which used objective tests based on textbook readings. He has had little experience in doing research, and feels at a loss to choose a topic. He wishes Mr. Byrd would just assign a text and give multiple choice tests like everybody else. It is getting close to the time when Mr. Byrd wants to have decisions from the students about their topic choices. John still hasn't made a choice. He decides to see Mr. Byrd for help.

Which term characterizes John?

competitor

collaborator

avoider

participant

dependent

independent

John's style is dependent. He hasn't had many opportunities to choose what he will study and prefers to have his instructor decide what he is to learn. There are numerous alternatives an instructor could suggest to this student. What would you be inclined to do?

Exercise 22.

Choose a course of action you would take when reacting to John's concerns about selecting a topic. Circle the appropriate letter.

A. Tell him you know just the thing that would be sure to spark his interest—it's an exciting area you've wanted to research for a long time now. Load him up with a stack of your own books and turn him loose.

B. Tell him any topic within the broad field of the course would be fine, just come back and check it out with you before he starts working on it.

C. Ask him if he has come across areas in the readings for the course that have interested him which he would like to know more about and might like to pursue as a topic.

D. Ask him about his major field of study and his other interests in or outside of school to get an idea of the areas he values that might help in his choice of a topic.

E. Tell him you would prefer that he choose a topic without your influence entering into the decision.

Depending upon this student's image of himself and of you, he may have differing reactions to each of the responses. Here are some of them.

A. John would probably be greatly relieved that you gave him a topic. He would probably struggle through even if he thought it was the dullest, most irrelevant material he had ever read. It would be better than going back and telling you that he didn't think much of your *exciting area.* He might not get much personal satisfaction out of your suggestions, but he would certainly complete the assignment and pass the course. By being as directive as you were, you effectively communicated **your** interests to **him** but found out nothing about his concerns or interests.

B. John would go away feeling just as anxious as he did before seeing you. He faces the same decision. You gave him no new information and you probably gave him the impression that you wanted to discuss neither the topic to be chosen nor his feelings about the choice.

C. John might still feel threatened by making a choice, but at least he would have further reinforcement that you want him to pursue a topic of importance to him, therefore it is crucial that he make the decision. It is possible that in discussing the readings, he will reveal some area that has sparked his interest and you can encourage him to explore it further.

D. John would probably be pleased that you asked about his outside interests. He might be able to give you enough information about himself, his goals, and values so that both of you can identify areas in the course content that relate to his interests.

E. John would certainly know he had to make his decision alone and would still feel anxious. He would probably think you didn't mean what you said when you told the class you were there to help or guide them in the pursuit of learning.

Mr. Byrd is trying to make the learning experience for his students as meaningful and individualized as possible, but conflicts or clashes in teaching-learning styles can occur. Students like John can feel threatened when faced with choices or challenges not encountered previously. Mr. Byrd's approach is saying, "I want you to be free," but John is saying that he doesn't know **how**. Mr. Byrd, because of his own facilitative philosophy of teaching and learning, will attempt to help John move from a dependent position to a more independent one. By encouragement and support of John's attempts to be independent, Mr. Byrd will enable John to develop confidence in his own abilities.

Summary of Learning Styles

The six categories of learning styles outlined: competitors, collaborators, avoiders, participants, dependents, and independents, are generalized and simplified. However, they serve to point out that there are many styles of learning that require different kinds of instructor-student interaction. When an instructor and a group of students interact, each individual responds in a unique way. Interaction with a student who is highly dependent and needs structured guidance would differ from that of an independent student who is seeking challenges and new interests.

The five instructor functions will need varying degrees of emphasis depending on the different types of students in the class. Some students will need information from the expert, others need the guidance of the facilitator, or encouragement from the model. The avoiders may respond better from the counselor functions and be helped to recognize why they are taking the class, what they may gain from it, and what effort is needed for a satisfactory pass. In each instance the interactions will be dynamic and different, the needs and purposes of each person are always unique.

When you are able to draw upon a constantly broadening background of experiences that enables you to choose the appropriate method for achieving successful interactions, your functions as an instructor improve.

Turn to section F on the **gray sheets**, pages 140-141, and complete Items 1 and 2.

VII. ACCESSIBILITY FOR INTERACTION BEYOND THE CLASSROOM

One of the important concerns of students is having access to instructors. Many instructors often contend that they are spending a disproportionate amount of time with students, leaving insufficient time for other important activities such as class preparation, departmental and university committee work, or independent research and writing. Yet, it is often through out-of-class contact that instructors experience their greatest effectiveness and rapport with students.

Research studies of college and university faculty members indicate that those instructors who had the most frequent contact with students outside of class were chosen most often by other faculty and students as having contributed most to the personal and educational development of students. Those faculty with frequent contact expressed the beliefs that students learn best when instructors take a personal interest in them, and that contact outside class is a vital part of a student's total education.

Exercise 23.

Rate the following actions of an instructor that indicate high or low accessibility and availability.

High/Low **Action of Instructor**

______ 1. Acknowledges and greets students in passing them on campus.

______ 2. Spends most of time out of class off campus.

______ 3. Keeps catch-as-catch-can office hours.

______ 4. Is always in a hurry to be somewhere else.

______ 5. Makes students feel welcome as office visitors, not intruders.

High accessibility is indicated by numbers 1 and 5. Low accessibility by numbers 2, 3, and 4.

Those faculty who interacted more frequently out-of-class differed from other faculty in significant ways in their teaching practices. Their classroom participation practices were more interactive. These faculty also more often than other teachers invited students to help with class plans and policies, encouraged students to participate in discussion, and asked for student evaluations of their courses. These instructors were open to discussing in class, points of view other than their own, and were apt to encourage discussion when relating course material to other fields and issues.

Exercise 24.

Rate the following actions of an instructor which would indicate high or low accessibility.

High/Low **Action of Instructor**

______ 1. Makes time to talk with students before and after class.

______ 2. Is prepared with information to answer educational and career questions, or can direct students to relevant resources.

______ 3. Makes no changes or modifications of course plans based on student input or interest.

______ 4. Learns names of students in class.

______ 5. Spends most of class time in one-way communication, talking *at* instead of *with* students.

______ 6. During class encourages students to have meetings outside class. States office hours and keeps them.

High accessibility is indicated by numbers 1, 2, 4, and 6. Low accessibility by numbers 3 and 5.

Usually, teacher attitudes and methods in the classroom serve as good indicators to students about the accessibility of the instructor beyond the classroom. Conversely, those faculty whom students find inaccessible give clues that faculty-student contact belongs in the classroom on a formal basis.

Instructors who provide opportunities for interaction through being accessible, report they believe their style aids them in meeting student needs and permits them to influence positively student decisions about selecting fields of study, choosing careers, and formulating personal philosophies. When questioned, students concur in this belief about the relative value of faculty influences on their lives.

Turn to Section G on **gray sheet**, page 141, and complete Items 1 and 2.

VIII. SUMMARY OUTLINE

I. THE USE AND MISUSE OF LABELS

Positive, Negative, Matrix

II. CLASSROOM ATMOSPHERE

Creating a Positive Atmosphere

Confidence	vs.	Anxiety
Challenge	vs.	Frustration
Self respect	vs.	Humiliation
Inquisitiveness	vs.	Boredom
Physical comfort	vs.	Physical discomfort

III. COMMUNICATION BETWEEN FACULTY AND STUDENTS

The content of communication
Written communication
Non verbal communication
Spoken communication
Mediated communication

IV. SKILLS FOR FACILITATING VERBAL COMMUNICATION

Listening — eye contact, indicate following
Questioning — inhibiting and facilitating
Reacting — encourage, clarify, non judgmental

V. INSTRUCTOR FUNCTIONS AND CLASSROOM INTERACTION

Expert, Formal Authority, Counselor, Facilitator, Model

VI. LEARNING STYLES AND CLASSROOM INTERACTION

Competitors, Collaborators, Avoiders, Participants
Dependents and Independents

VII. ACCESSIBILITY FOR INTERACTION BEYOND THE CLASSROOM

High accessibility — Low accessibility
Instructor actions — Student reactions
Impact and Influence

REFERENCES AND RESOURCES

Barth, Roland S. **Improving Schools from Within.** San Francisco: Jossey-Bass Inc., 1990.

Bateman, Walter L. **Open to Question.** San Francisco: Jossey-Bass Inc., 1990.

Braskamp, Larry A., D.C. Brandenburg and J.C. Ory. **Evaluating Teaching Effectiveness.** Beverly Hills, CA: Sage Publications, 1984.

Cronbach, L.J. and R.E. Snow. **Aptitudes and Instructional Methods: A Handbook for Research on Interactions**. New York: Irvington, 1977.

Eble, K. (Ed.) **Improving Teaching Styles: New Directions for Teaching and Learning**. San Francisco: Jossey-Bass Inc., 1980.

Fuhrman, B.S. and A.F. Grasha. **A Practical Handbook for College Teachers**. Boston: Little, Brown and Company, 1983.

McKeachie, W.J. **Teaching Tips: A Guidebook for the Beginning College Teacher**. (8th ed.) Lexington, MA: D.C. Heath and Company, 1986.

Perry, W.G. **Forms of Intellectual and Ethical Development in the College Years**. New York: Holt, Rinehart and Winston, 1970.

Sax, Gilbert. **Principles of Educational and Psychological Measurement and Evaluation.** (3rd ed.) Belmont, CA: Wadsworth Publishing Company, 1989.

Wilson, Robert C. and Jerry G. Gaff. **College Professors and Their Impact on Students**. New York: John Wiley and Sons, 1975.

IX. APPLICATION EXERCISE

Answer each question on improving instructor-student relationships in terms of your own instructional situation.

A. Labels for Students

1. What *labels* do you frequently assign to individual students as you observe their behavior?

____

____

2. Which *labels* are negative and which are positive?

Negative:______________________________

Positive:______________________________

3. Develop a checklist or rating scale for measuring student attitudes.

B. Classroom Atmosphere

1. What kind of an atmosphere do you feel you create in your classroom?

a. During the first meeting of the course?

b. As the semester progresses?

2. List three steps you could take to create a more positive atmosphere.

a.______________________________

b.______________________________

c.______________________________

C. Communication Between You and Your Students

1. **What different types of communication do you engage in with your students?**

2. **Which ones do you feel are most successful?**

3. **Which ones do you feel need improvement?**

D. Facilitating Communication

1. **State the skills in which you feel most capable.**

2. **Which ones would you like to improve?**

3. **List four suggestions offered in the module that might help you to improve communications.**

   a.

   b.

   c.

   d.

E. Classroom Instructor Functions

1. State which of the five functions you feel most capable.

a. ______________________ b. ______________________ c. ______________________

d. ______________________ e. ______________________

2. Which ones would you like to improve?

a. ______________________ b. ______________________ c. ______________________

d. ______________________ e. ______________________

3. List four suggestions offered in the module that might help.

a.

b.

c.

d.

F. Student Learning Styles

1. Name three different students in a past or present class.

Identify their learning styles.

a. ______________________ ______________________

b. ______________________ ______________________

c. ______________________ ______________________

2. What specific recognition, encouragement, or help might you give each student?

a.

b.

c.

G. Your Accessibility to Students Beyond the Classroom

1. State three instructor actions you use to provide high accessibility.

a.

b.

c.

2. State three low accessibility actions you would like to improve.

a.

b.

c.

CONSTRUCTING MULTIPLE CHOICE TEST ITEMS

Module Developers:	Robert Simas Ron J. McBeath
Editorial Associates:	Oswald B. Carleton Jerrold E. Kemp Jeanne Lassen Carole R. Smith
Editorial Consultants:	David Cohen Richard B. Lewis

CONSTRUCTING MULTIPLE CHOICE TEST ITEMS

The multiple choice test has an important place in student evaluation. Effective test items probe various levels of student understanding, discriminate between achievers and non-achievers, and help to pinpoint and diagnose learning problems. They require time and skill to develop, but are quick to administer and score. They need to be used with other types of measurement to provide a balanced evaluation. This module is divided into seven sections.

I. Seven Rules for Item Construction

II. Four Additional Tips

III. Bloom's Taxonomy

IV. Six Levels of Test Items

V. Summary Outline

VI. Review Test on Writing Items

VII. Application Exercise

By examining examples of well-written test items, and by practice in revising items yourself, you will gain expertise in the construction of test items, and you will be better able to assess the value of the multiple choice test format for your particular testing needs. To make the exercises that follow as practical as possible, you will be asked to construct test items for your own subject field.

The following are some samples of **factual statements** which are used as the basis for multiple choice test items subsequently in this unit:

a. Seattle is the city with the largest population in the Pacific Northwest.

b. Kurt Vonnegut, Jr., wrote *Player Piano.*

c. John F. Kennedy was assassinated in 1963.

d. Every ecosystem must have a continual external source of energy.

Now, turn to the **gray sheet**, page 175, and complete **A** in the spaces provided, write three factual statements of your own that could be used as a basis for developing multiple choice test items for a course in your field.

I. SEVEN RULES FOR ITEM CONSTRUCTION

A multiple choice test item is composed of two parts: the *statement* or *stem* and the *answer choices*. In the ***stem,*** the problem is presented as either a question or as an incomplete statement. The ***choices*** include one correct response and several plausible distractors.

Rule 1. Present a single, definite statement to be completed or answered by one of the several given choices.

Compare these examples:

1. **Poor Item:** In the Northwest,
   a. timbering is the primary industry.
   b. the average yearly rainfall is 30 inches.
   c. annual income is higher than the U.S. average.
   d. Seattle is the most populous city.*
2. **Better Item:** In the Northwest area of the United States, the city of largest population is
   a. Eugene.
   b. Portland.
   c. Seattle.*
   d. Spokane.

In Item 1, the statement, *In the Northwest...*, does not focus student attention on the purpose of the item. Does the choice to be made concern the industry, climate, economics or demography of the Northwest? Of course, the instructor knows what the task posed by the statement or the stem is intended to involve. Since alternative **d** has been keyed as the correct answer, we infer that the instructor wanted to measure demographic knowledge.

Item 2 is a rephrasing of Item 1. Now the statement presents a single, definite directive. The students know what to look for. The task is clear: from the given homogeneous choices, select the one which is the name of the most populous city in the Pacific Northwest.

Exercise 1.

Items 1 and 2 exhibit a violation of the rule that the statement should present a single, definite directive. In neither item does the statement give sufficient information for the student to select the answer. Revise each of these item stems and/or choices.

1. **Poor Item:** Henry Fielding was

   a. an American architect.
   b. a British author.*
   c. a contemporary of James Milton.
   d. not sufficiently recognized for his talent until after his death.

Revised Item:

2. **Poor Item:** Humidity is indicated as a

   a. percentage.*
   b. fraction.
   c. decimal.
   d. numerical ratio.

Revised Item:

For Item 1, a possible remedy is to revise the statement in the form of a question that presents a specific problem to the student: "Of what nationality was the novelist Henry Fielding?" Choices might then be: (a) English (b) American (c) Irish (d) Australian. Notice that by clarifying the problem presented by the statement, the choices need revision. The revised choices are more homogeneous than the original set.

You may have taken a different approach and concentrated on Fielding's profession. Of course, the choices for the items **a** through **d** should relate directly to the statement you wrote. The important concern is to ensure that the statement gives the student a clear understanding of the criterion to be used in selecting the correct choice.

Item 2 could better indicate the answer wanted by changing the statement to read "Humidity level is indicated in television weather reports as a . . . "

This statement would focus student attention on the specific response that is needed.

If you used other means to improve the initial items, and if your improvements complete or modify the statements so that students correctly understand the task, then you have met the requirements of Rule 1 and you are well on the way to writing effective multiple choice items.

Now, it is your opportunity to work on your own items. Refer again to the **gray sheet**, page 175, and complete **B**. For each of the statements you wrote in **A**, construct a multiple choice test item that conforms to the first rule, that each statement clearly formulates a specific task.

Rule 2. Keep student reading efforts to a minimum and eliminate irrelevant material.

This rule means: avoid wordiness and complex sentences, and eliminate irrelevant material in both the statement and the response choices. Compare these examples:

1. **Poor Item:** Kurt Vonnegut, Jr., a controversial contemporary American fiction writer and social critic, wrote which of the following books?
   a. Shogun
   b. Player Piano*
   c. The Women's Room
   d. Dynasty

2. **Better Item:** Kurt Vonnegut, Jr. wrote which of the following books?
   a. Shogun
   b. Player Piano*
   c. The Women's Room
   d. Dynasty

The inclusion of extraneous material in Item 1 tests the student's reading ability more than knowledge. Item 2 gets directly to the core of the matter; the pairing of an author's name with the title of one of his books.

3. **Poor Item:** John F. Kennedy was assassinated

a. in the year 1961.
b. in the year 1963.*
c. in the year 1965.
d. in the year 1968.

4. **Better Item:** John F. Kennedy was assassinated in the year

a. 1961.
b. 1963.*
c. 1965.
d. 1968.

Item 3 clearly illustrates a violation of Rule 2. If the same words are needed with each choice, it is better to eliminate non-essential repetition by placing the words in the statement of the item as has been done in Item 4. By reducing the student's reading load in this manner, both the validity and reliability of the test as a whole can be improved. Revise the Poor Items in Exercise 2.

Exercise 2.

3. **Poor Item:** The Beaufort scale, developed in 1805 by Admiral Sir Frances Beaufort of the British navy, is used on weather maps to indicate

a. air pressure.
b. air temperature.
c. precipitation.
d. wind velocity.*

Revised Item:

4. **Poor Item:** When a cold front passes

a. the wind direction usually changes from southwest to northwest.*
b. the wind direction usually changes from northwest to southwest.
c. the wind direction usually changes from northeast to southwest.
d. the wind direction usually changes from northwest to southeast.

Revised Item:

Item 3 presents distracting, irrelevant material. It would be much better to phrase the statement in the following manner: The Beaufort scale is used on weather maps to indicate, (a) air pressure (b) air temperature (c) precipitation (d) wind velocity. Likewise, under Item 4, the response choices can be simplified. Include the repetitious phrase in the stem, so that the item reads: When a cold front passes, the wind direction usually changes from (a) southwest to northwest (b) northwest to southwest (c) northeast to southwest (d) northwest to southeast.

Refer to the **gray sheet**, page 175, and review the multiple choice items which you developed. Do the items conform to Rule 2 which requires that student reading effort should be kept to a minimum and irrelevant words eliminated?

Rule 3. Ensure that only one response is considered best or correct by experts in the field.

No doubt you have often read multiple choice test questions for which there is more than one correct choice from the responses provided. Such questions create frustrating experiences for students and provide instructors with little insight into problems students may be having. Rule 3 is demonstrated by the following examples.

1. **Poor Item:** An example of an egg-laying animal is the

    a. porpoise.
    b. platypus.*
    c. wallaby.
    d. eagle.

2. **Better Item:** An example of an egg-laying mammal is the

    a. porpoise.
    b. platypus.*
    c. wallaby.
    d. eagle.

Item 1 exemplifies a question with more than one correct choice. Both the platypus and the eagle are egg-laying animals. To improve the question, Item 2 has been re-written to specify the category of egg-laying mammal.

3. **Poor Item:** Thumb-sucking is likely to produce greatest psychological trauma

    a. during infancy.
    b. in the preschool period.
    c. before adolescence.*
    d. during adolescence.
    e. after adolescence.

4. **Better Item:** Thumb-sucking is likely to produce greatest psychological trauma from

    a. birth to 2 years.
    b. 3-5 years.
    c. 6-12 years.*
    d. 13-20 years.
    e. 21 years or older.

In Item 3 there may be confusion between response **c**, **a**, or **b** since the term *before adolescence* may be thought to include preschool and infancy. Specific age periods, as shown in Item 4, will reduce ambiguity. In Exercise 3, revise the response choices to make them mutually exclusive.

Exercise 3.

5. **Poor Item:** The ingredient used as a leavening agent is

    a. baking powder.
    b. baking soda.
    c. yeast.*
    d. arrowroot.

Revised Item:

6. **Poor Item:** An advantage of multiple choice test items over essay questions is that the former

    a. can be graded with a test-scoring machine.
    b. can be scored more rapidly and objectively.*
    c. are better for measuring ability to organize material.
    d. require less time to formulate.

Revised Item:

The violations of Rule 3 are fairly obvious. In Item 5, the statement is so vague that answers **a** and **c** would have to be considered correct. This flaw could be corrected by having the statement read . . . *The leavening agent used principally in baking bread is* . . . Likewise, 6 is confusing. Responses **a** and **b** can be interpreted to mean nearly the same thing. To overcome this difficulty, response **a** can be altered to read something like, *provide a narrow sampling of content.* This then becomes another incorrect response.

Now refer to your **gray sheet**, page 175, and examine the response choices for the items which you wrote. Are the choices mutually exclusive? Is there only one correct answer possible? If you need to, revise your items to meet the criterion of Rule 3.

Rule 4. **Avoid negative statements; if negatives must be used, CAPITALIZE, <u>underscore</u>, or otherwise *highlight* the negative term.**

The use of negatives or exceptions is often employed as a smoke screen under the mistaken supposition that the student who knows his subject will have no trouble in unraveling the answer. In reality, questions such as these emphasize reading skills more than cognitive skills. Under the pressure of testing, and being accustomed to seeing positive more often than negative statements in most resource materials, many people can easily miss a negative word or prefix.

Now review the four examples under Rule 4:

1. **Poor Item:** In considering ideal environmental conditions in a classroom, physical comfort will not be ensured without

   a. the temperature set at 60°, the relative humidity at 50%.
   b. the temperature set at 72°, the relative humidity at 72%.
   c. the temperature set at 68°, the relative humidity at 25%.
   d. the temperature set at 68°, the relative humidity at 50%.*

2. **Better Item:** The most ideal environmental conditions set to ensure physical comfort in a classroom are

   a. temperature 60°, relative humidity 50%.
   b. temperature 72°, relative humidity 72%.
   c. temperature 68°, relative humidity 25%.
   d. temperature 68°, relative humidity 50%.*

Item 1 under Rule 4 is unnecessarily complicated. The statement contains two confusing negatives, *not....without.* By simple conversion, the statement can be changed to become a straightforward question as in Item 2.

3. **Poor Item:** In all ecosystems, maintenance will not be possible without a continual external source of

   a. energy.*
   b. living adult organisms.
   c. plant spores.
   d. oxygen.

4. **Better Item:** Ecosystems <u>cannot</u> be maintained <u>unless</u> they have a continual external source of

   a. energy.*
   b. adult living organisms.
   c. plant spores.
   d. oxygen.

Item 3 illustrates the same problem of two negatives used in the question, with a different solution exemplified.

In Item 4, the negative words have been underscored. Revise the Poor Item in Exercise 4.

Exercise 4.

1. **Poor Item:** Which of the following is not a characteristic of good multiple choice test items?

   a. discriminates among student achievement levels.
   b. helps diagnose learning difficulties.
   c. frequent use of negative statements.*
   d. requires skill and time to develop.

Revised Item:

In the case of Item 1, essentially the same knowledge could be measured if you asked, positively, *Which of the following is a characteristic of multiple choice test items*? There could follow such choices as: (a) usually encourages originality, (b) frequent use of negative statements, (c) discriminates between student achievement levels, (d) quick and easy to write.

2. **Poor Item**: Which one of the following men was not a signer of the Declaration of Independence?

   a. John Adams
   b. Benjamin Franklin
   c. George Washington*
   d. Thomas Jefferson

Revised Item:

In Item 2, the phrase *was not* could be easily misread as *was*. Highlight the word **NOT**.

Check your own items on the **gray sheet**, page 175.

Rule 5. Use only plausible and attractive alternatives as incorrect response choices.

Plausible and attractive alternatives can be easily generated by administering a stem as an open-ended question to a sample group of students. Their responses could provide plausible alternatives.

1. **Poor Item:** The vessel carrying oxygenated blood from the heart to the body is

   a. trapezius muscle.
   b. forebrain.
   c. patella tendon.
   d. ascending aorta.*

2. **Better Item:** The vessel carrying oxygenated blood from heart to the body is

   a. vena cava.
   b. pulmonary artery.
   c. femoral artery.
   d. ascending aorta.*

In Item 1, three of the four alternatives can be eliminated from consideration because they obviously have nothing to do with the circulatory system. The choices have been rewritten in Item 2 so that they include the correct answer and plausible, but incorrect, responses.

In Item 3 below, an incorrect answer does not give the instructor, or the student, information about the nature of the possible misconception.

3. **Poor Item:** What is the intelligence quotient of a student who has a mental age of 10 and a chronological age of 8?

   a. 75
   b. 100
   c. 125*
   d. 150

4. **Better Item:** What is the intelligence quotient of a student who has a mental age of 10 and a chronological age of 8?

   a. 80
   b. 102
   c. 118
   d. 125*

Each of the choices above is an answer that could result from common formula errors made in computing the intelligence quotient. In this respect, these incorrect alternatives are plausible. By analyzing the nature of an incorrect response, both the student and the instructor can pinpoint the source of the error and gain insight into a possible learning difficulty. Complete Exercise 5.

Exercise 5.

1. **Poor Item:** Button Gwinnett is most famous as a/an

   a. early American novelist and essayist.
   b. co-signer of the Declaration of Independence.*
   c. pitcher for the San Francisco Giants.
   d. Revolutionary War hero.

Revised Item:

Response **c** on Item 1 is an obvious give-away that accomplishes little educationally. A more plausible alternative would be something such as *Post-Revolutionary War architect.*

2. **Poor Item:** To measure students' understanding of a textbook chapter, a 20-item multiple choice test would be better than a 5-item test because

a. students will receive higher scores.
b. a sharper pencil is required.
c. the amount of guessing will be reduced.
d. the test will have higher level of content validity.*

Revised Item:

In Item 2, choice **b** is probably one that would not even be considered, let alone selected by a student. A better choice for **b** might be *students can be compared to one another.*

You may have written similar choices to provide the student with plausible alternatives from which to choose. Your selection of specific incorrect responses should help you diagnose misconceptions or learning difficulties. How do the choices for your own items on the **gray sheet**, page 175, conform to the criterion of Rule 5? Take time to look them over. Revise them if necessary.

Rule 6. Avoid giving clues to the correct option.

Items may contain clues that either direct students to the right answer or reduce the number of choices from which they must select. Clues can take various forms as in these examples:

1. **Poor Item:** B.F. Skinner has found that negative reinforcement in learning

a. serves to obliterate a response.
b. never has an effect.
c. always decreases the behavior which it follows.
d. when removed increases the behavior.*

2. **Better Item:** B.F. Skinner has found that negative reinforcement in learning

a. serves to obliterate a response.
b. has no effect.
c. decreases the behavior which it follows.
d. when removed increases the behavior.*

Item 1 exhibits another example of unintentional clues to which a test-wise student becomes sensitive: the inclusion of an *always* or *never* in a statement makes it immediately suspect. Options **b** and **c** are eliminated with a fair degree of confidence because of their absolute tone. This leaves only two viable choices, the student has doubled the odds at guessing the correct answer. Item 2 is well phrased and tests the same information as the previous item.

3. **Poor Item:** The smallest particle of any chemical element that can exist by itself and retain the qualities that distinguish it as an element is an

    a. electron.
    b. neutron.
    c. atom.*
    d. molecule.

4. **Better Item:** (i) The smallest particle of any chemical element that can exist by itself and retain the qualities that distinguish it as an element is a/an

    a. electron.
    b. neutron.
    c. atom.*
    d. molecule.

    or (ii) The smallest particle of any chemical element that can exist by itself and retain the qualities that distinguish it as an element is

    a. an electron.
    b. a neutron.
    c. an atom.*
    d. a molecule.

Item 3 demonstrates a common and easily corrected error. Two of the four choices are effectively eliminated because they begin with consonants. Since the statement ends in the indefinite article *an*, which is used only before words beginning with vowels, *atom* or *electron* are the obvious choices. Avoid these clues by providing for both forms of the article **a/an** or use **the** in the statement.

A lesser preference is to exclude articles from the statement and include them with the choices. This approach is illustrated in Item 4 (ii). Besides the clues given by articles, another obvious clue can be the grammatical number of the verb. The use of a singular verb form would preclude any choice stated as a plural, and vice-versa. The criterion used to eliminate incorrect response choices should be knowledge of the subject area itself, not of English grammar.

5. **Poor Item:** The boiling point of water is

   a. 424° F.
   b. 282° F.
   c. 212° F at sea level, in an open container.*
   d. 100° F.

6. **Better Item:** The boiling point of water at sea level in an open container is

   a. 424° F.
   b. 282° F.
   c. 212° F.*
   d. 100° F.

A further example of clues is visual highlighting of a correct answer by excessive length, usually caused by the inclusion of qualifying statements, as in Item 5. The solution is to include the qualifications in the statement, not the option. When this is done, as in Item 6, all the choices have visual homogeneity.

7. **Poor Item:** The major purpose of a student teaching internship is to

   a. give the intern an opportunity to practice teaching under the supervision of an experienced teacher.*
   b. assist school principals in selecting new teachers.
   c. assist the teaching profession to screen out unqualified teachers.
   d. permit observation of prospective teachers.

8. **Better Item:** The major purpose of a student teaching internship is to

   a. practice teaching under the supervision of experienced teachers.*
   b. assist school principals in selecting new teachers.
   c. assist the teaching profession to screen out unqualified teachers.
   d. permit observation of prospective teachers.

A final example of a clue illustrates the phenomenon often referred to as the clang *association.* This occurs when one choice repeats words or phrases used in the statement. Thus, this one choice seems to *sound out* as the most probable, the only one that really fits with the statement.

In Item 7, choice **a** echoes the stem of the word *internship* by referring to the *intern.* In Item 8, this clue has been eliminated as well as the length clue. Complete Exercise 6.

Exercise 6.

1. **Poor Item:** An example of an extinct animal is an

   a. sloth.
   b. eskimo curlew.*
   c. pocket gopher.
   d. wombat.

Revised Item:

2. **Poor Item:** In what way did the styles in women's clothing in 1950 differ from those in 1900?

   a. They showed more beauty.
   b. They showed more variety.
   c. They were easier to clean.
   d. They were easier to live in, work in, move in, and were generally less restrictive.*

Revised Item:

3. **Poor Item:** When used in conjunction with the T-square, the left vertical edge of a triangle is used to draw

   a. vertical lines.*
   b. slant lines.
   c. horizontal lines.
   d. inclined lines.

Revised Item:

Item 1 is an example of a grammatical clue. It would be better if the statement read, *An example of an extinct animal is a/an...* The inclusion of the articles in the statement permits an unbiased consideration of each choice. Another format would be to include the article with each response.

In Item 2 the correct answer is signaled by its length. In the case of this particular item, option **d** could be changed to read, *They were more functional.* This change would make all four options homogeneous, equally plausible, and similarly phrased.

Upon reading Item 3, you probably were struck by the obvious "clanger." What else would you expect to draw with the *vertical edge of a triangle* except *vertical lines*? A much better test of student knowledge could be achieved by rewriting the statement to eliminate the word *vertical.* The new statement could read, *When used in conjunction with a T-square, the edge of the triangle which includes the right angle is used to draw...*

Check for any violations of Rule 6 in your own test items on the **gray sheet**, page 175.

Rule 7. Use as choices *all of the above* and *none of the above* sparingly, if at all.

The use of the phrase *all of the above* weakens the power of an item. The student merely has to compare two choices; if they are both acceptable, *all of the above* is the logical answer. On the other hand, if either one of the two choices is obviously unacceptable, not only is that choice eliminated, but so is the choice *all of the above.* In either case, the test-wise student can guess the correct answer without actually knowing the information.

Review the following examples:

1. **Poor Item:** What is the statistical term for the arithmetic average?

   a. mean*
   b. median
   c. mode
   d. all of the above

2. **Better Item:** What is the statistical term for the arithmetic average?

   a. mean*
   b. median
   c. mode
   d. central tendency

The folly of the choice, *all of the above*, in Item 1, is apparent. Choice **d** adds nothing to the test item. Perhaps it was used only because the test writer could not think of a fourth choice. A plausible alternative to *all of the above* could be, *central tendency*, a much better incorrect choice.

The use of *none of the above* can be better defended as a viable choice. Unlike the phrase *all of the above, none of the above* prevents a student from increasing the odds of guessing the correct answer. *None of the above* can be safely chosen only after each of the other items is read and eliminated as unacceptable. But, there are two major criticisms of this response. First, incorrect selection of *none of the above* provides no diagnostic information to help either the instructor or the student to pinpoint the nature of the student's misconception. Second, using it can reduce test reliability and discrimination by actually penalizing a person for knowing too much.

3. **Poor Item:** The purpose of the Bill of Rights was to

   a. free the slaves.
   b. give everyone the right to vote.
   c. ensure the freedom of individuals.*
   d. provide none of the above.

4. **Better Item:** The purpose of the Bill of Rights was to

   a. free the slaves.
   b. give everyone the right to vote.
   c. ensure the freedom of individuals.*
   d. establish the rights to free public education.

The first weakness is plainly evident; the second has been pointed up in Item 3. A competent student reading this item could reason that the purpose of the Bill of Rights was actually to limit the power of the central government. This is correct and, in this case, actually exceeds the level of understanding for which the instructor was testing. As a consequence, a student choosing response **d**, *none of the above,* would fail the item. The substitution of *none of the above* by a plausible distractor such as choice **d** in Item 4, strengthens the diagnostic power of the test item; and at the same time increases item reliability by clarifying the test writer's intent.

Now complete Exercise 7.

Exercise 7.

Make the corrections needed in these items.

1. **Poor Item:** Hitler first disobeyed the Versailles Treaty when he ordered troops to

   a. invade Poland.
   b. occupy Bavaria.
   c. occupy the Rhineland.*
   d. invade Austria.
   e. do none of the above.

Revised Item:

2. **Poor Item:** South Africa leads the world in the mining of

   a. bauxite.
   b. diamonds.*
   c. iron ore.
   d. all of the above.

Revised Item:

In Item 1, a solution to the undesirable use of *none of the above* is simply to delete this answer choice. There is nothing special about having five possible answers. The use of *none of the above* simply serves to confuse students, since some historical experts consider Hitler's orders to rearm Germany as his first transgression of the Versailles Treaty, without which the subsequent invasions and occupations could not have occurred.

Item 2 is weakened by the use of *all of the above* as a choice. It would be much better to substitute a plausible incorrect option such as manganese or copper to test student knowledge of the South African economy.

When you wrote your own items on the **gray sheet**, page 175, did you avoid the traps of *all of the above* and *none of the above* response options? If you have included these choices, check your items again to determine whether you can justify using them. You may want to make revisions.

II. FOUR ADDITIONAL TIPS

In addition to the seven rules here are four tips for the construction of multiple choice items.

Tip 1. Avoid irrelevant sources of difficulty.

Typical sources of difficulty are ambiguous statements and esoteric terminology.

Exercise 8.

The major purpose of the contemporary United Nations organization in relation to total political structures is to:

a. maintain peace among peoples of the world.*
b. establish international law.
c. provide military controls.
d. form new governments.

What are two sources of difficulty in the item above?

(1)______________________________

(2)______________________________

First, the word *contemporary* is unnecessary as it could be a distracting qualifier that has no basis. Second, the phrase, *in relation to total political structures*, is an unnecessary complication of the question. The revised statement would be: *The major purpose of the United Nations is to ...*

Tip 2. Arrange response choices in a logical order.

For the sake of efficiency and ease of reading, it is suggested that answer choices be sequenced alphabetically in the case of proper names or terms, numerically in the case of figures, and chronologically in the case of dates. Students can follow the sequence more easily and concentrate on the cognitive task of identifying the correct response without having to re-order the information.

Example Item

The government of the United States was declared in effect under the Constitution in

a. 1792.	a. 1776.
b. 1776.	b. 1785.
c. 1785.	c. 1789.*
d. 1789.*	d. 1792.

In this example item the choices are shown in random order and, in logical sequence. The logical order is preferred since it enables the student to read the series quickly for the correct answer.

Tip 3. Avoid patterns of responses. The correct answer should appear randomly in each response position and in approximately an equal number of times.

Many writers of multiple choice questions tend to bury correct answers in the middle position, choices **b** or **c** with the result that the extreme positions, **a** and **d** in a four option format are not used as often as might be expected. Such a response pattern, if detected by students, may lessen the validity of the test by establishing a response bias. To select appropriate response positions, a random sequence can be developed by several techniques: the roll of the die; the draw of a card; or a table of random numbers. Another simple procedure that can be used is to open a book at a random location and use the last digit of the right-hand page number to give you the position for your test item.

A Poor Pattern of Response Positions

Question	Correct Answer
1.	b
2.	c
3.	c
4.	b
5.	b
6.	c
7.	b
8.	d

A Better Pattern of Response Positions

Question	Correct Answer
1.	b
2.	d
3.	a
4.	c
5.	d
6.	a
7.	c
8.	b

Tip 4. Examine each test item to see that it relates directly to the specific instructional objective for which the student is being tested.

The test item should represent the intent of a performance objective that was established when the instructional unit was planned. Therefore, each test question should correlate directly with an objective.

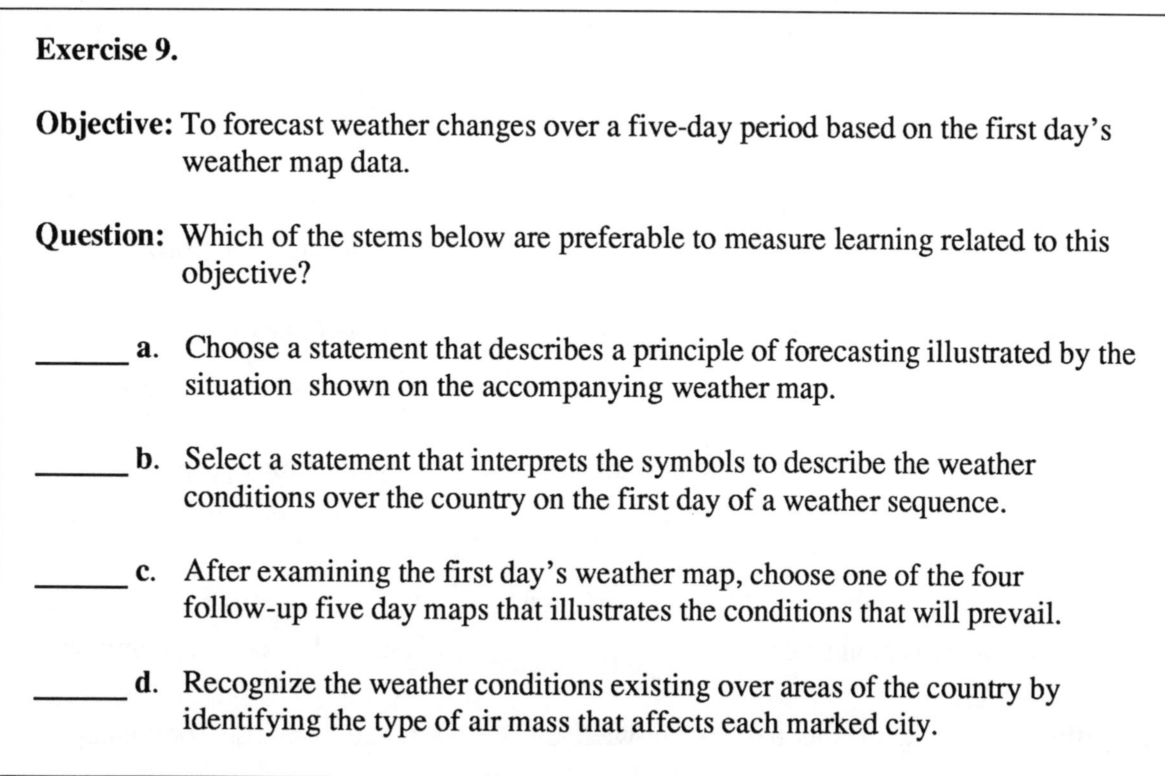

Exercise 9.

Objective: To forecast weather changes over a five-day period based on the first day's weather map data.

Question: Which of the stems below are preferable to measure learning related to this objective?

______ **a.** Choose a statement that describes a principle of forecasting illustrated by the situation shown on the accompanying weather map.

______ **b.** Select a statement that interprets the symbols to describe the weather conditions over the country on the first day of a weather sequence.

______ **c.** After examining the first day's weather map, choose one of the four follow-up five day maps that illustrates the conditions that will prevail.

______ **d.** Recognize the weather conditions existing over areas of the country by identifying the type of air mass that affects each marked city.

In this exercise, the performance objective requires *use* of weather forecasting principles. Therefore the test item should require such an application. Statement **c** does this and could be developed into an acceptable multiple choice test item. None of the other statements require the student to *apply* knowledge. They request the recall of information or facts and concepts about forecasting.

Again, refer to the test items you wrote on the **gray page**, page 175. Do they conform to the additional tips on constructing multiple choice tests?

III. BLOOM'S TAXONOMY

Performance objectives can be written on various levels within a classification schema, called a taxonomy. The most widely used one is that prepared by Benjamin Bloom and his colleagues for the cognitive domain of learning.

The six levels Bloom identified in the cognitive domain are described below. Action verbs typically used in the setting of objectives or writing test questions are included for each level.

BLOOM'S SIX COGNITIVE LEVELS

1. **Knowledge** — memorize and recall information	define, label, list, name, repeat order, arrange, memorize
2. **Comprehension** — interpret information in one's own words	describe, indicate, restate, explain review, summarize, classify
3. **Application** — apply knowledge to new situations	apply, illustrate, prepare, solve, use, sketch, operate, practice, calculate
4. **Analysis** — breakdown knowledge into parts and show relationship among parts	analyze, categorize, compare, test, distinguish, examine, compare
5. **Synthesis** — bring together parts of knowledge to form a whole; build relationships for new situations	arrange, compose, formulate, organize, plan, assemble, construct
6. **Evaluation** — make judgments on basis of criteria	appraise, evaluate, conclude, judge, predict, compare, score

IV. SIX LEVELS OF TEST ITEMS

When performance objectives are prepared that require student learning on these various intellectual levels, then test questions should measure the learning accordingly. Where appropriate, multiple choice questions need to be formulated for these levels.

Examples of Multiple Choice Items for Each Level of the Bloom Cognitive Domain Taxonomy

1. Knowledge Level

Objective: To identify early settlements in the colonies.

Test Item: The first permanent English colony in the New World was

a. Jamestown.*
b. Roanoake.
c. Plymouth.
d. Williamsburg.

2. Comprehension Level

Objective: To interpret the relation between an odd and even number.

Test Item: Let **A** represent an odd number and **B** represent an even number; then **A** minus **B** must represent

a. a prime number.
b. an even number.
c. an odd number.*
d. sometimes an odd and sometimes an even number.

3. Application Level

Objective: To calculate the mean of a set of scores.

Test Item: A student earned test scores of 42, 82, 69, 98, and 79. What is the mean score?

a. 69
b. 74*
c. 77
d. 83
e. 87

4. Analysis Level

Objective: Distinguish among factors that contribute to preparation of a quality photograph.

Test Item: Examine the sample photograph. What will correct the condition shown?

a. Use another negative.
b. Expose paper for a longer time.*
c. Develop paper for a longer time with the same exposure.
d. Use a stronger developer.

5. Synthesis Level

Objective: To propose a plan to solve an instructional problem.

Test Item: An instructor teaches a video production course. She wishes to add a new unit on using a word-processing program for script writing. Her students generally are blasé about studying. They prefer hands-on activities. In this case, they need motivation and detailed, specific instructions in order to be successful in using the new word-processing program. Which instructional technique would be the most beneficial to plan?

a. Assign a textbook chapter to read, followed by class discussion and the assignment to write a short paper on the subject.
b. Develop a self-instructional package consisting of an audio recording to guide students through the manual.*
c. Give students the program manual and have them read it through completely and then start working on the computer.
d. Give a lecture on the word-processing program, supported by overhead transparencies, followed by asking questions of the class.

6. Evaluation Level

Objective: To assess a physical condition in a patient after childbirth.

Test Item: You note while checking your patient 6 hours after delivery that the fundus is approximately 3 cm above the umbilicus and on the right side. You diagnose:

a. nothing is wrong.
b. a distended bladder.*
c. hypertrophy of the uterus.
d. postpartum hemorrhage.

Exercise 10.

Following are performance objectives on various levels of the Bloom cognitive domain taxonomy. First, indicate the level represented by each objective. Then write a multiple choice question that would serve as a test item for each objective.

Objective 1: To identify places in the campus library where various types of materials can be found.

Level: ______________________________

Test Item:

Objective 2: To search library locations for a specific reference need.

Level: ______________________________

Test Item:

Objective 3: To judge acceptability of written points of view in terms of a set of criteria.

Level: ___________________________

Test Item:

Here are suggested multiple choice test items that could test the three objectives. Your items certainly can be different, but the intent of relating to the stated objective should be similar.

Objective l: Test Item (Knowledge level)
Identify the floor in the main library on which the bound periodicals are located.

a. 1st
b. 2nd
c. 3rd*
d. 4th
e. 5th

Objective 2: Test Item (Application level)
To find a 1939 issue of the New York Times newspaper, where do you look in the library?

a. The 1st floor Reference section
b. The 2nd floor Microfilm section*
c. The 3rd floor Periodicals section
d. The 5th floor Documents section

Objective 3: Test Item (Evaluation level)
Read the three letters to the editor of the student newspaper concerning campus parking problems. Which one best meets the criteria of accuracy, objectivity, and practicality?

a. Article A
b. Article B
c. Article C*

Turn to the multiple choice items you wrote on the **gray sheet**, page 175. Do they relate to different levels of performance objectives? What levels are your items? Are they all in the recall and knowledge level or are some of them handling higher level intellectual skills such as comprehension, application, analysis, synthesis, or evaluation? Indicate the levels in the spaces provided.

There are ways to test learning and evaluate the achievement of objectives other than with multiple choice items. In particular, objectives on the levels of *synthesis* and *evaluation* might better be tested with other activities such as essay questions, and performance tests. Look beyond one method of testing for measuring the successful achievement of performance objectives in your course.

V. SUMMARY OUTLINE

I. SEVEN RULES FOR ITEM CONSTRUCTION

Present a single, definite statement to be completed or answered by one of the several given choices.

Keep student reading efforts to a minimum; eliminate irrelevant material.

Ensure that only one response is considered correct by experts in the field.

Avoid negative statements; if negatives must be used, CAPITALIZE, underline, or otherwise *highlight* the negative term.

Use only plausible and attractive alternatives as incorrect response choices.

Avoid giving clues to the correct option.

Use as choices *all of the above* or *none of the above,* sparingly, if at all.

II. FOUR ADDITIONAL TIPS

Avoid irrelevant sources of difficulty.

Arrange response choices in a logical order — alphabetically or numerically.

Avoid patterns of responses; the correct answer should appear in each of the response positions approximately an equal number of times and in a random order.

Examine each test item to ensure it relates directly to the specific learning objective for which the student is being tested.

III. BLOOM'S SIX LEVELS FOR TEST ITEMS

Knowledge	recall information	define, list, name
Comprehension	interpret information	describe, explain, review
Application	apply in new situations	use, solve, operate
Analysis	break down into parts	analyze, distinguish, test
Synthesis	integrate, form relationships	arrange, compose, organize
Evaluation	judge against criteria	appraise, evaluate, predict

VI. REVIEW TEST ON WRITING ITEMS

Directions: Read each of the following multiple choice test items. If the item violates one or more of the stated rules or tips, write down the number of the specific rule or tip violated. If the item does not violate any of the rules, put a check in the "OK" column. Answers are at the end of the test.

	Violations	OK
1. **An example of an extinct animal is an**	_______	_______

a. sloth.
b. eskimo curlew.*
c. pocket gopher.
d. wombat.

2. **John F. Kennedy was assassinated**	_______	_______

a. in the year 1961.
b. in the year 1968.
c. in the year 1963.*
d. in the year 1965.

3. **Thumb-sucking is likely to produce the greatest psychological trauma from**	_______	_______

a. birth to 2 years.
b. 3-5 years.
c. 6-12 years.*
d. 13-20 years.
e. 21 years or older.

4. **The ingredient used as a leavening agent is**	_______	_______

a. baking powder.
b. baking soda.
c. yeast.*
d. arrowroot.

5. **In the Northwest**	_______	_______

a. timbering is the primary industry.
b. the average yearly rainfall is 30 inches.
c. annual income is higher than the U.S. average.
d. Seattle is the most populous city.*

	Violations	OK
6. **The vessel which carries oxygenated blood from the heart to the body is called the**	________	________
a. trapezius muscle.		
b. forebrain.		
c. patella tendon.		
d. ascending aorta.*		
7. **South Africa leads the world in the mining of**	________	________
a. bauxite.		
b. diamonds.*		
c. iron ore.		
d. all of the above.		
8. **Kurt Vonnegut, Jr. wrote which of the following books?**	________	________
a. Shogun		
b. Player Piano*		
c. The Women's Room		
d. Dynasty		
9. **In all ecosystems, maintenance will not be possible without a continual external source of**	________	________
a. living adult organisms.		
b. plant spores.		
c. oxygen.		
d. energy.*		

Answers: **1.** Rule 6 **2.** Rule 2, Tip 2 **3.** OK **4.** Rule 3 **5.** Rule 1
6. Rule 5 **7.** Rule 7 **8.** OK **9.** Rule 4

REFERENCES AND RESOURCES

Cangelosi, James S. **Evaluating Student Achievement.** White Plains, NY: Longman, 1990.

Ebel, Robert L. and David A. Frisbie. **Essentials of Educational Measurement.** (4th ed.) Englewood Cliffs, NJ: Prentice-Hall Inc., 1986.

Gay, L. R. **Educational Evaluation and Measurement.** (2nd ed.) Columbus, OH: Charles E. Merrill Publishing Company, 1985.

Gronlund, N. E. **How to Construct Achievement Tests**. Englewood Cliffs, NJ: Prentice-Hall Inc., 1987.

Gronlund, N.E. and Robert L. Linn. **Measurement and Evaluation in Teaching**. (6th ed.) New York: Macmillan, 1990.

Hopkins, Kenneth D., Julian C. Stanley, and B.R. Hopkins. **Educational and Psychological Measurement and Evaluation.** (7th ed.) Englewood Cliffs, NJ: Prentice-Hall Inc., 1990.

Popham, W. James. **Modern Educational Measurement.** (2nd ed.) Englewood Cliffs, NJ: Prentice-Hall Inc., 1990.

Sax, Gilbert. **Principles of Educational and Psychological Measurement and Evaluation.** (3rd ed.) Belmont, CA:Wadsworth Publishing Company, 1989.

Shrock, Sharon A. and William C. C. Coscarelli. **Criterion-Referenced Test Development.** Reading, MA: Addison-Wesley Publishing Company, 1989.

VII. APPLICATION EXERCISE

A. Write three factual statements derived from one of your courses, or your subject field. These will form the basis for the multiple choice test items you will develop.

Statement 1: ____

____

Statement 2: ____

____

Statement 3: ____

____

B. Write three different levels of multiple choice test items based on the statements above.

Item 1: Level__________

Item 2: Level__________

Item 3: Level__________

CONSTRUCTING TRUE-FALSE TEST ITEMS

Module Developers:	Robert Simas Ron J. McBeath
Editorial Associates:	Oswald B. Carleton Jerrold E. Kemp Jeanne Lassen Carole R. Smith
Editorial Consultant:	Richard B. Lewis

CONSTRUCTING TRUE-FALSE TEST ITEMS

This module presents guidelines for constructing true-false test items under these headings:

I. **The Simple Form**
II. **The Complex Form**
III. **The Compound Form**
IV. **Rules For Constructing True-False Tests**
V. **Summary Outline**
VI. **Review Test**
VII. **Application Exercise**

I. THE SIMPLE FORM

Each true-false test item consists of two parts: a *statement* and a *set of choices*. The statement is usually in the form of a declarative sentence. The student reads the statement and selects one response out of the set provided. The most common choice of format consists of dichotomous word pairs such as *true/false, right/wrong, correct/incorrect, fact/opinion*, and *agree/disagree*. This is the simplest and most commonly used form of the *true/false* test item.

A. Epistemology is the study of the nature of knowledge.	(True)	False
B. The United States Constitution is the highest law of the land.	(Fact)	Opinion
C. The Fourteenth Amendment to the Constitution is the most important amendment.	Fact	(Opinion)
D. In metric measurement, 1000 meters equals 1 kilometer.	(True)	False
E. The biological process by which experience shapes heredity is evolution.	(True)	False

Statement A is a declarative sentence: *Epistemology is the study of the nature of knowledge.* Statements B through E are similarly phrased as declarative sentences. This is the most commonly used phrasing for true-false items.

There are various ways in which a statement may be phrased.

F. Is 25% of 60 less than 13? Yes (No)

G. Some forms of animal life do not need to breathe air BECAUSE they get oxygen from water. (Yes) No

H. The formula for computing rho (Spearman-rank order correlation coefficient)

is $p = 1 - \frac{(6\Sigma D^2)}{N(N^2 - 1)}$

In this formula:

$p =$ rho (True) False

ΣD^2 = Sum of differences in the ranks True (False)

N = Number of pairs of ranks (True) False

Statement F is a question.

Statement G permits exploring cause-effect relationships by using a word functioning like *because.*

Statement H presents a series of related statements after the introduction. In each item above, the response for this **simple form** of the true-false test consists of two mutually exclusive options.

Criticism of these mutually exclusive options, in the **simple form**, includes:

- ☐ It is not always appropriate for the subject matter.
- ☐ The student has a 50/50 chance of guessing the correct answer.
- ☐ There is a poor range of discrimination, the student either knows or does not, either passes or fails.
- ☐ There is little diagnostic information revealed.

II . THE COMPLEX FORM

Attempts to remedy some of these inherent weaknesses have resulted in the development of the complex form from the simple, two-alternative form. Examine examples **I** through **L**.

<table>
<tr><td colspan="2">I. The acquisition of morality is a developmental process.</td><td>True</td><td>False</td><td>Opinion</td></tr>
<tr><td colspan="2">J. There are three stages in the development of morality: rules, moral realism, justice.</td><td>True</td><td>False</td><td>Opinion</td></tr>
<tr><td colspan="2">K. Using the general principle that all matter possesses inertia, indicate whether the item is true, false or cannot be determined.
An object that weighs 1 lb. at the equator weighs more than a pound at the north or south pole.</td><td>True</td><td>False</td><td>Cannot be resolved</td></tr>
<tr><td>L.</td><td>True</td><td>False</td><td>Converse True</td><td>Converse False</td></tr>
<tr><td>All dogs are mammals</td><td>√</td><td></td><td></td><td>√</td></tr>
<tr><td>All marsupials are kangaroos</td><td></td><td>√</td><td>√</td><td></td></tr>
<tr><td>All parasites are animals</td><td></td><td>√</td><td></td><td>√</td></tr>
<tr><td>No snakes are reptiles</td><td></td><td>√</td><td></td><td>√</td></tr>
</table>

The **statements** are made in identical form to the items in the previous section, but the **choices** have been modified to allow for more than two options.

In Item **I**, this modification measures the student's ability to distinguish between opinion and non-opinion, and to judge the truth or falsity of the latter.

Item **J** is another example of the complex form.

Item **K** tests both the student's understanding and correct application of rules, the same is true in Item **L**. These items, **I** through **L,** are examples of way s **true-false** items can be constructed to enhance the measurement effectiveness of the simple, two alternative, form.

III . THE COMPOUND FORM

To further strengthen the diagnostic capabilities of the true-false test item, the compound form adds conditional, completion, or fill-in response options, as shown in Examples **M** through **P**.

M. The cortex is the center of all mental processes, such as learning, memory, and perception. True (False)

If the statement is false, describe what makes it so: ***Cerebrum is center***

N. REM is an abbreviation for *repetitive* eye movement. True (False) ***rapid***

0. In early Greek education, the term *paidagogos* referred to slaves. (True) False ______

P. Cellulose and starch are compounds consisting of units of *Amino Acid.* True (False) ***sugar***

In the examples, the true statement requires no additional comment. However, identification of a false statement is not sufficient; the student must know why the statement is false and be able to correct it as in items **M**, **N**, and **P**. The advantage of this format is immediately apparent. The student must identify false statements and state the exact nature of the falseness. The limitation of the form is also apparent; with specificity comes scoring problems. Items can no longer be machine scored; for each false statement, the written response must be read and separately scored.

In review, there are three forms in which true-false items may be constructed:

- ☐ **Simple (two options)**
- ☐ **Complex (more than two options)**
- ☐ **Compound (combined with conditional, completion, or fill-in options)**

The next consideration is the construction of true-false items.

Turn to the **gray sheet**, page 197. Write three statements to complete **A**.

IV. RULES FOR CONSTRUCTING TRUE-FALSE TESTS

There are three basic rules to follow in writing true-false test items. They relate to *clarity, unintentional clues,* and *item relevance*.

Rule I. CLARITY. Use statements upon which clear-cut judgments can be made.

This rule means that each statement should be written in such a way that it is precisely described by one or the other answer options. Through thoughtlessness and inattention, the rule is frequently violated, with the result that the validity and, in some cases, the reliability of the question is reduced.

Review the examples below and underline the violations of the rule of clarity.

1.	Poor Item:	Shakespeare wrote in several different modes.	T	F
2.	Better Item:	Shakespeare wrote plays, poetry and essays.	T	(F)
3.	Poor Item:	Compass directions and locations should be capitalized.	T	F
4.	Better Item:	Compass directions are capitalized when referring to specific geographical areas.	(T)	F

Avoid the use of vague, indefinite, or ambiguous terms.

How many different concepts of *several* in Item 1 would you expect to find in a group of thirty students? Item 2 specifies three forms of writing: plays, poetry and essays. The statement is clear and precise. The student must now dccide if it is categorically true or false.

Item 3 is confusing to the student who knows the compass directions are capitalized when referring to specific geographical areas such as Southeast Asia, but are not when referring to general locations, such as *Drive* ***north*** *on Highway 280 to reach San Francisco.* Clarifying the statement to specify geographical areas as in Item 4 eliminates confusion.

5. Poor Item: The President of the United States is elected. T F

6. Poor Item: The President of the United States is usually elected. T F

7. Better Item: The position of President of the United States is an elected 4 year term of office. (T) F

Avoid broad, general statements in the interests of clarity, validity and reliability.

Item 5 is a broad, general statement in which truth and falsity cannot readily be determined. There are different qualifications that could be made. What about the instances where the Vice-President has taken over the presidency because of the death or resignation of the President? Attempts may be made to qualify the original statement, but they are rarely successful.

Does Item 6 solve the problem? No. The use of the qualifier, **usually**, adds little to the clarity of the statement. As we have already seen, words such as **usually** are open to interpretation. Just how frequent is **usually**? Is this everyone's interpretation?

Item 7 is a rephrasing of the two previous items. The emphasis has been shifted to the length of the term of office of the President. The test item is now specific.

8. Poor Item: Every body in the universe attracts every other body, therefore the moon rather than the moon and the sun together causes tidal actions. T F Cannot be determined

9. Better Items: a. Every body in the universe attracts every other body. (T) F Cannot be determined

b. The moon rather than the moon and the sun together causes tidal actions. T (F) Cannot be determined

Avoid including two ideas in one statement.

Item 8 demonstrates a violation of the rule of clarity. The statement contains two parts: the first states one of the basic laws of physics, while the second states what may or may not be an accurate application of that law. Two separate ideas are compounded into a single true-false statement, hence confusion and misinterpretation may result. If the student chooses the incorrect alternative, there is no way for the instructor to know which part of the compound statement is giving the student difficulty. In this case, the instructor has written the item to be correctly answered as false because the implication is false, yet the basic law is true. It is better to separate Items **9a** and **9b**.

Review Items 10 and 11 for clarity.

10.	Poor Item:	If an individual who is engaged in the retail distribution of automobiles carries through to completion a business transaction wherein he purchases a motor vehicle for the sum of two thousand five hundred and twenty-five dollars and at a subsequent date disposes of the said vehicle for the sum of one thousand six hundred and eighty-three dollars, the net loss on the completed business transaction involving the vehicle is eight hundred and forty-two dollars.	Yes/No Insufficient information
11.	Better Item:	If an item is bought for $2525 and resold for $1683, then $842 represents the net loss.	(Yes)/No Insufficient information

Avoid long or complex sentences.

What do you think of the way in which Item 10 is phrased? This example points out another very common violation. The statement is obviously too long and complex. Long, complex sentences test reading ability more than knowledge, comprehension, or problem-solving abilities. A clearer statement is expressed in Item 11. It now is a straightforward test of the computation of net loss.

Review Items 12 to 18 for negative statements or unattributed opinions.

12.	Poor Item:	None of the information in the instruction manual was unnecessary.	T	F
13.	Better Item:	All of the information in the instruction manual was necessary.	(T)	F

Avoid negative statements.

Another barrier to item clarity is the use of negative statements and especially the use of double negatives as in Item 12. Negative words, such as **no** and **not**, tend to be overlooked by students. Two negatives in the same sentence contribute to ambiguity of the statement, as for example, the **none . . . unnecessary** of Item 12. The intent of the statement is much clearer when phrased positively as in Item 13.

14. Poor Item:	The President of the United States is not elected by popular vote.	T	F
15. Better Item:	The President of the United States is <u>NOT</u> elected by popular vote.	(T) Opinion	F

Item 14 is one of those rare instances in which a negatively phrased statement cannot be avoided. It is a good idea to highlight a necessary negative word by either CAPITALIZING it or <u>underscoring</u> it or both, as has been done in Item 15.

16. Poor Item:	Americans can best be assured of an adequate standard of living through a government guaranteed annual income plan.	T	F
17. Better Item:	The current Congress of the United States unanimously supports a guaranteed annual income plan.	T	(F)
18. Better Item:	Americans can best be assured of an adequate standard of living through a government guaranteed annual income plan.	T	F (Opinion)

Avoid using unattributed opinion.

Item 16 demonstrates that another barrier to clarity is the use of an opinion without a specified source. Note the proposed solution in Item 17. Using unattributed opinion instead of a statement of fact can be confusing and should not be done unless the purpose of the test is for the student to discriminate between fact and opinion as in Item 18.

Guidelines for the Rule of Clarity

Avoid ambiguous/indefinite terms.

Avoid broad, general statements.

Avoid including two ideas in one statement, unless cause-effect relationships are being measured.

Avoid long or complex sentences.

Avoid negative statements, especially two negatives in the same sentence.

Avoid using unattributed opinion, unless discrimination between fact and opinion is specifically being measured.

Write revisions of the clarity violations below:

19. Poor Item:	In some cases, the U. S. Constitution gives certain powers to the federal government, or to both the federal and state governments. Some powers are not denied to states but are specified for the federal government and are called concurrent.	T	F
Revised Item:	____________________ ____________________		
20. Poor Item:	The *separate but equal* doctrine was not rejected by the Supreme Court in the Plessy vs. Ferguson decision.	T	F
Revised Item:	____________________ ____________________		
21. Poor Item:	Mt. Lassen, which is the last active volcano in the contiguous states, is located in the Cascade Range in Washington.	T	F
Revised Item:	____________________		

Statement 19 is too long and unnecessarily complex. Instead of measuring whether the student has achieved knowledge or understanding, a long complex sentence tends to measure reading comprehension. It is for this reason that such sentences should be avoided in tests to measure achievement. A possible revision might read: *Concurrent powers are those which the U. S. Constitution gives to the federal government and does not deny the states.*

Item 20 is an unnecessary use of a negative form. A much less confusing statement could be simply formed by replacing the phrase *not rejected* with the word *accepted*, or *confirmed.*

Item 21 is poorly written because it is a *double-header*, it contains two separate ideas one of which is true and one false. A student may know that Mt. Lassen is the last active volcano in the contiguous states and that it is not located in the Cascade Range, but may be in doubt about how to answer the question. The best approach is to divide the item into two statements, such as: (1) *Mt. Lassen is the last active volcano in the contiguous states*, and (2) *Mt. Lassen is located in the Cascade Range in Washington.*

22.	Poor Item:	Van Gogh rarely painted portraits of women.	T	F
	Revised Item:	______________________________		
23.	Poor Item:	Photographic *depth of field* is dependent on subject to camera distance.	T	F
	Revised Item:	______________________________		
24.	Poor Item:	A centrally-controlled economy is unresponsive to the public's needs.	T	F
	Revised Item:	______________________________		

In Item 22 the error is the use of the word *rarely. Rarely* is ambiguous, subject to different interpretations by different students. There is no easy way to edit Item 22 so that it is a good true-false test item. Knowledge about Van Gogh might better be tested on a different item format, say multiple-choice or matching items.

In Item 23 the statement is only a partial truth. At first glance, the answer may seem to be true but *depth of field* is also dependent on *both* the *focal length of the lens* and *the size of the aperture.* The statement would be better phrased as, *Subject-to-camera distance is one of the determinants of photographic depth of field.*

The Item 24 statement is merely an opinion. It cannot be judged either true or false. A simple remedy would be to add "opinion" as an additional response alternative. On the other hand, if the simple true-false format is to be maintained, the statement itself needs to be modified. The opinion should be attributed to some source, such as Keynes or Galbraith.

All of these revisions are only suggestions. If you wrote different statements to improve the poor items, and if your improvements resulted in a clear, unambiguous statement, then you've met the requirements of Rule 1, Clarity.

Now turn to the **gray sheet**, page 197, and complete **B** in the application exercise. Write three true-false test items which meet the criteria of the **Rule of Clarity**. Each statement should be straightforward, unambiguous, and phrased in a way that a clear-cut judgment can be made as to the truth or falsity of the item.

Rule 2. CUES. Avoid unintentional cues.

Doubtless you have seen test questions in which unintentional cues create problems. Words such as *always* and *never* in the item statement may give a test-wise student a clue to the correct answer.

THESE TERMS	are likely to indicate	**THESE ANSWERS**
always, every, none, each, without exception, uniformly, never, all.	⟶	FALSE INCORRECT WRONG, NO
usually, generally, often, sometimes, frequently, maybe, occasionally.	⟶	TRUE CORRECT RIGHT, YES

Avoid the use of specific determiners.

When a student who is unsure of the subject matter sees one of the specific determiners, he can improve his chances to guess the correct answer. Check the examples below:

25.	Poor Item:	T F	All plants photosynthesize.
26.	Better Item:	(T) F	Living plants possessing chlorophyll are capable of photosynthesis.
27.	Poor Item:	T F	Colonial powers are often racist.
28.	Better Item:	(T) F	The United Nations censured South Africa for its racial intolerance.

In 25, to guess the answer *false*, would be a reasonable conclusion. In Item 26 the specific determiner *all* has been removed and the statement has been modified in order to remove the cue. Item 27 is another example of unintentional cuing. The word *often* is not only ambiguous, and open to interpretation, but also it indicates the likely answer, *True*. Item 28 is much more specific.

Avoid answer patterns.

Answer patterns such as all *true*, all *false*, or alternating sequences of *true/false*, or *true/true/false/false*, should be avoided. Test-wise students can often discover answer patterns, therefore answers should be randomly distributed. Since some students have a consistent tendency to mark *true* when in doubt about an answer,while others favor *false* when they guess, the number of each type of correct answer should be *approximately* equal. The word *approximately* is stressed here because, if the number of each type of correct response is exactly equal, this might provide a cue to the student who is unable to answer some of the test items. The best procedure is to vary the percentage of true answers to between forty and sixty percent.

Avoid length cues.

Finally, the length of a statement can play a part in giving unintentional cues to the correct answer. There is a natural tendency to make true statements longer than false ones because true statements often require more qualification. This unintentional cuing can be overcome by lengthening the false statements through the use of qualifying phrases similar to those found in true statements.

Three Guidelines for Avoiding Unintentional Cues

Avoid the use of specific determiners; *all, none, never, always, generally.*

Avoid answer patterns. Responses should be both randomly sequenced and approximately evenly proportioned.

Avoid length cues. All statements should be of similar length.

Read and then revise Items 29 and 30 according to Rule 2.

29. Poor Item: T F All sounds, regardless of loudness, travel at the same speed.

Revised Item: ______________________________

30. Poor Item: T F An objective test is generally easier to score than an essay test.

Revised Item: ______________________________

In Item 29, the word *all* could be misleading. Change the item to read something like: *The speed of sound is not influenced by loudness.* The emphasis is shifted to the criterion, *loudness*, and the cue-word *all* is eliminated. Item 30 uses the term *generally*, which might lead the student to favor the *true* answer. A better statement would be, *An objective test is easier to score than an essay test.*

Now review the true-false items you wrote on your **gray sheet**, page 197. Are they free from unintentional cues? Revise items as necessary.

Rule 3. RELEVANCE. Relate test items to specific objectives.

Students expect relevance in all test questions and instructors lose credibility when students see a lack of relevance and the possibility of *trick* questions.

31. Poor Item:	T	F		Otto Rank was Sigmund Freud's personal secretary.
32. Better Item:	(T)	F		Major theorists of the Neo-Freudian School are: Otto Rank, Karen Horney, Alfred Adler, and Harry Stack Sullivan.
33. Poor Item:	T	F		Mark Twain was the pen name of Samuel E. Clemens.
34. Better Item:	(T)	F		Mark Twain was the pen name of Samuel L. Clemens.

Relate items to specific objectives.

Item 31 is an example of trivia. Item 32 treats more worthwhile content. Knowing major theorists of the Neo-Freudian School is more useful than being able to recount a fact of minor importance.

Avoid trivial content and details.

Another aspect of relevance is seen in Item 33. Did you see the reason for the falseness of the statement? If you missed it on your first reading, you are not alone, many people would. It is natural for people to concentrate on content, attending to concepts and relationships especially in a test. In this specific case, the author's middle initial is relatively unimportant. This is typical of trick questions, which can tell something about the teacher but little about the student. If the student were to mark *false*, the correct answer, would it be because he knew that the middle initial should have been an *L* instead of an *E*, or because the student could not connect Twain and Clemens. A more straightforward item is seen in Item 34, which contains no trickery, just a factual statement.

Revise Items 35 and 36 to eliminate the trivial content and details:

35. Poor Item: T F The earliest colonial record of the sale of slaves was in 1619 B.C. at Jamestown.

Revised Item: ______________________________

36. Poor Item: T F Igor Stravinsky, the Russian composer, was born in 1882.

Revised Item: ______________________________

Item 35 might have taken you a second reading in order to spot the easily overlooked trick detail. The simplest solution is to change **B.C.** into **A.D.** Now the emphasis is on testing the student's knowledge, not his reading ability.

Item 36 could be considered a trivial question unless it relates specifically to your objectives. The exact year of an individual's birth may be factual but relatively unimportant in regard to course objectives. A much more meaningful test question might be, *Igor Stravinsky was a modern (20th century) Russian composer.* The relevance of the question depends on your objectives.

This final rule, that all items should be relevant to specific objectives, and neither trivial nor directed toward unessential details, is fundamental. The choice of relevant and significant facts, concepts, principles, and problems is of basic importance in the construction of a useful, effective test. Not only must items be well constructed, but they must relate to the specific learning objectives for which the student is to be tested.

Review your test items on the **gray sheet**, page 197, to see that they meet the **Criteria of Relevance.**

V. SUMMARY OUTLINE

TYPES OF TRUE-FALSE ITEMS

THE SIMPLE FORM	Dichotomous word pairs True-False, Yes-No
THE COMPLEX FORM	Dichotomous word pairs plus an option column
THE COMPOUND FORM	Adds space for conditional, completion or fill-in responses

RULES FOR WRITING GOOD TRUE-FALSE TEST ITEMS

1. **CLARITY —Use statements upon which clear judgments can be made:**

   a. Avoid ambiguous/indefinite terms.

   b. Avoid broad, general statements.

   c. Avoid including two items in one statement, unless cause-effect relationships are being measured.

   d. Avoid long or complex sentences.

   e. Avoid negative statements, especially two negatives in one sentence.

   f. Avoid using unattributed opinion, unless discrimination between fact and opinion is specifically being measured.

2. **CUES —Avoid unintentional cues:**

   a. Avoid the use of specific determiners; for example, *all, none, never, always, generally*.

   b. Avoid answer patterns. Responses should be both randomly sequenced and approximately evenly proportioned.

   c. Avoid length cues, all statements should be of similar length.

3. **RELEVANCE — Relate to objectives:**

   a. Relate items to specific learning objectives.

   b. Avoid trivial content and details.

VI. REVIEW TEST

Read each of the following true-false test items. If the item violates one of the rules stated on the previous page, write down the specific rule violated. If the item does not violate any of the rules, put a check in the OK column. Answers are at the end of the exercise.

				Violation/OK	
1.	True	False	Otto Rank was Sigmund Freud's personal secretary.	___	___
2.	True	False	The *separate but equal* doctrine was not rejected by the Supreme Court in the Plessy vs. Fergusen decision.	___	___
3.	True	False	Americans can best be assured of an adequate standard of living through a government guaranteed annual income plan.	___	___
4.			The formula for computing rho (Spearman rank-order correlation coefficient) is $p = 1 - \frac{(6 \Sigma D^2)}{N(N^2 - 1)}$ In this formula		
	True	False	$p =$ rho	___	___
	True	False	ΣD^2 = Sum of differences in the ranks	___	___
	True	False	N = Number of pairs of ranks	___	___
5.	True	False	The speed of sound is proportional to loudness.	___	___
6.	True	False	Mt. Lassen, which is the last active volcano in the contiguous states, is located in the Cascade Range in Washington.	___	___
7.	True	False	All plants photosynthesize.	___	___
8.	True	False	The United Nations censured South Africa for its racial intolerance.	___	___

Violation/OK

9. True False Epistemology is the study of the nature of knowledge. ___ ___

10. True False Every body in the universe attracts every other body; therefore the moon, rather than the moon and the sun together, causes tidal action. ___ ___

11. Indicate the *truth/falsity* of each item and its converse: ___ ___

	True	False	Converse True	Converse False
All dogs are mammals				
All marsupials are kangaroos				
All parasites are animals				
No snakes are reptiles				

12. True False The President of the United States is elected. ___ ___

13. True False An objective test is generally easier to score than an essay test. ___ ___

14. True False None of the information in the instruction manual was unnecessary. ___ ___

15. True False Living plants possessing chlorophyll are capable of photosynthesis. ___ ___

16. True False Mark Twain was the pen name of Samuel E. Clemens. ___ ___

17. True False Shakespeare wrote in several different modes. ___ ___

18. True False The acquisition of morality is a developmental process. ___ ___

Answers: 1. (3) 2. (1e) 3. (1f) 4. (OK) 5. (OK) 6. (1c) 7. (2a) 8. (OK) 9. (OK) 10. (1c) 11. (OK) 12. (1b) 13. (2a) 14. (1e) 15. (OK) 16. (3) 17. (1a) 18. (OK)

REFERENCES AND RESOURCES

Cangelosi, James S. **Evaluating Student Achievement.** White Plains, NY: Longman, 1990.

Ebel, Robert L. and David A. Frisbie. **Essentials of Educational Measurement.** (4th ed.) Englewood Cliffs, NJ: Prentice-Hall Inc., 1986.

Erickson, Richard C. and Tim L. Wentling. **Measuring Student Growth.** Boston: Allyn and Bacon Inc., 1976.

Gronlund , N. E. **How to Construct Achievement Tests**. Englewood Cliffs, NJ: Prentice-Hall Inc., 1987.

Gronlund, N. E. and Robert L. Linn. **Measurement and Evaluation in Teaching.** (6th ed.) New York: Macmillan, 1990.

Hopkins, Kenneth D., Julian C. Stanley, and B.R. Hopkins. **Educational and Psychological Measurement and Evaluation.** (7th ed.) Englewood Cliffs, NJ: Prentice-Hall Inc., 1990.

Popham, W. James. **Modern Educational Measurement.** (2nd ed.) Englewood Cliffs, NJ: Prentice-Hall Inc., 1990.

Sax, Gilbert. **Principles of Educational and Psychological Measurement.** (3rd ed.) Belmont, CA: Wadsworth Publishing Company, 1989.

VII. APPLICATION EXERCISE

A. Write three factual statements from your own course or subject field which could form the basis for true-false test items.

Statement 1:

Statement 2:

Statement 3:

B. In the following spaces, write a true-false item appropriate for each of the concepts you have stated above.

Item 1. Simple:

Item 2. Complex:

Item 3. Compound:

CONSTRUCTING MATCHING TEST ITEMS

Module Developers:	Carole R. Smith Ron J. McBeath
Editorial Associates:	Oswald B. Carleton Jerrold E. Kemp Jeanne Lassen Philip C. Seyer
Editorial Consultant:	Richard B. Lewis

CONSTRUCTING MATCHING TEST ITEMS

This module presents guidelines for the development of matching test items. To give you practice with the ideas presented, you will have opportunity to develop and refine matching items for use in teaching or testing. The module is organized under the following headings:

I. **Components of Matching Test Items**

II. **Types of Relationships Used in Matching Test Items**

III. **Writing Clear Directions**

IV. **Writing Premises and Response Choices**

V. **Summary Outline**

VI. **Review Test**

VII. **Application Exercise**

I. COMPONENTS OF MATCHING TEST ITEMS

Three components of well written matching test items are: *an introductory statement*, *a set of premises*, and *a list of response choices*.

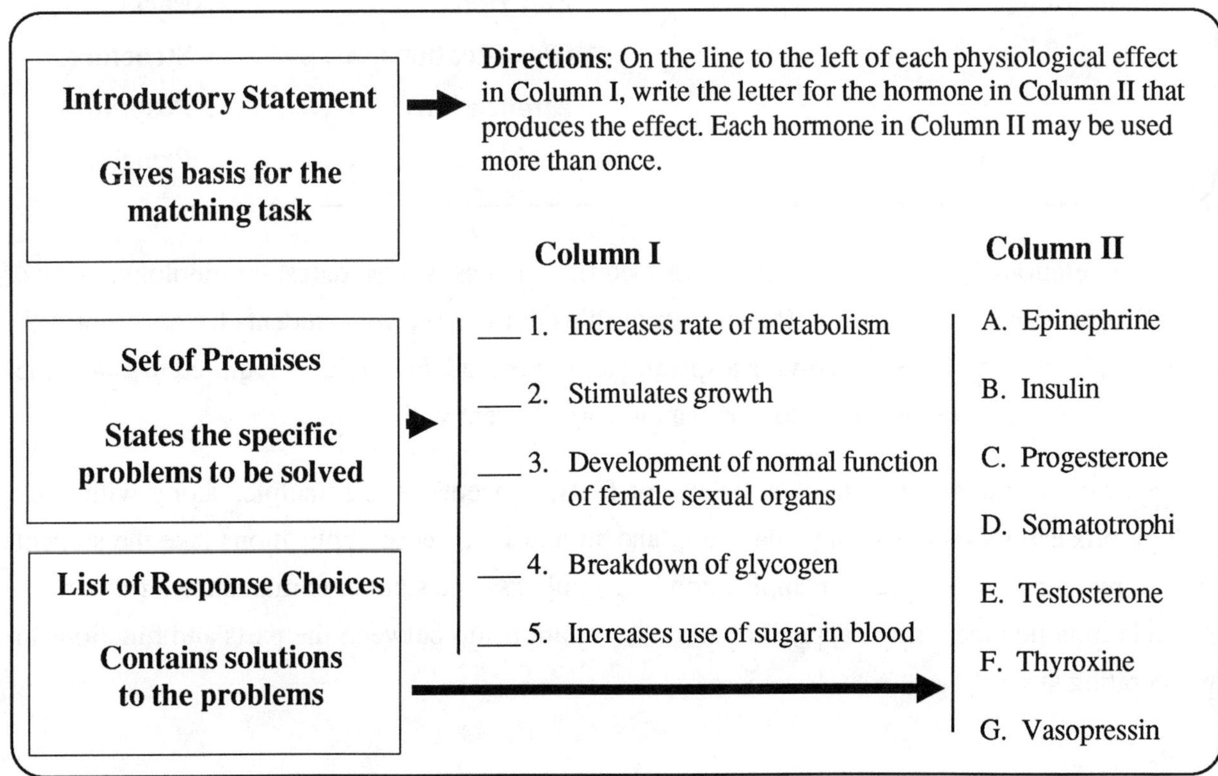

Introductory Statement
Gives basis for the matching task
Directions: On the line to the left of each physiological effect in Column I, write the letter for the hormone in Column II that produces the effect. Each hormone in Column II may be used more than once.
Set of Premises
States the specific problems to be solved
List of Response Choices
Contains solutions to the problems
Column I
___ 1. Increases rate of metabolism
___ 2. Stimulates growth
___ 3. Development of normal function of female sexual organs
___ 4. Breakdown of glycogen
___ 5. Increases use of sugar in blood
Column II
A. Epinephrine
B. Insulin
C. Progesterone
D. Somatotrophi
E. Testosterone
F. Thyroxine
G. Vasopressin

The *introductory statement*, which gives the basis for the matching task, is a set of directions to the student. The *response choices* tend to be briefer than the *premises*. The main purpose for using matching test items is to measure student ability to identify the relationship between a premise and a response.

II. TYPES OF RELATIONSHIPS USED IN MATCHING TEST ITEMS

Different types of relationships commonly used in matching test items are outlined below. The list is divided into two levels: relationships requiring *recall* of knowledge and relationships calling for the *application* of knowledge.

Relationships requiring *recall* of knowledge	**Definitions**	**Terms**
	Historical Events	**Dates**
	Achievements	**People**
	Statements	**Postulates**
	Descriptions	**Principles**
Relationships requiring *application* of knowledge	**Examples**	**Terms**
	Functions	**Parts**
	Classifications	**Structures**
	Applications	**Postulates**
	Problems	**Principles**

Recall relationships involve *remembering* specifics such as places, dates, terminology, events, as well as principles and theories. Recall relationships draw upon what students have memorized. For example, in a recall item involving a specific term, the student would be required to match the term with the correct definition or to match an historical event with a date.

Application relationships involve the *use* of facts, concepts, and principles along with such thought processes as interpreting, analyzing, and structuring. These applications take the student beyond recalling knowledge. An application item could ask the student to match the term with an example in which the term is applied or show the relationship between the parts and functions in an operating system.

Exercise 1.

Read this example, then answer Questions 1 and 2 below.

Directions: On the line to the left of each definition in Column I, write the letter of the defense mechanism described in Column II. Use each defense mechanism only once.

	Column I	Column II
______	1. Hunting for reasons to support one's beliefs.	A. Denial of reality
______	2. Accepting the values and norms of others as one's own even when contrary to previously held values.	B. Identification C. Introjection
______	3. Attributing to others one's own unacceptable impulses, thoughts, and desires.	D. Projection E. Rationalization
______	4. Ignoring disagreeable situations, topics, or sights.	

Question 1: What specific relationship is illustrated in the example above?

______ a. Achievements ....People

______ b. Foreign Words ....English Equivalents

______ c. Functions...Parts

______ d. Definitions ....Terms

Question 2: Does the example require recall or application of knowledge?

______ a. Recall of knowledge

______ b. Application of knowledge

The student is asked to match terms with definitions previously memorized in Question 1, so the answer is **d**. The answer to Question 2 requires only factual recall, so the answer is **a**.

Exercise 2.

Read the example, then respond to Question 1 and Question 2 below to indicate the relationship being illustrated and the level of knowledge.

Directions: On the line to the left of each conversational description in Column I, write the letter of the defense mechanism described in Column II. Use each defense mechanism only once.

Column I	Column II
______ 1. "My son can do no wrong."	A. Denial of reality
______ 2. "I missed because the sun was in my eyes."	B. Identification
______ 3. "Everyone is basically dishonest."	C. Introjection
______ 4. "I am Napoleon."	D. Projection
	E. Rationalization

Question 1: What specific relationship is illustrated by the example above?

______ a. Definitions.................................Terms

______ b. Problems...................................Principles

______ c. Examples..................................Terms

______ d. Functions...................................Parts

Question 2: Does the example require recall or application of knowledge?

______ a. Recall of knowledge

______ b. Application of knowledge

The answer to Question 1 is **c**. It requires the student to read examples and choose the term which applies to the situation. Since the test example requires students to apply knowledge about defense mechanisms to different examples, the answer to Question 2 is **b**.

Exercise 3.

Read through the two examples and complete the exercise below.

Directions: For each description in Column I, select the letter of the physical law that accounts for it. Each physical law may be used more than once. Mark your answers on the accompanying answer sheet.

Column I	Column II
______ 1. Equal force was applied to objects A and B. A had twice the mass of B. A traveled 10 feet; B, 20 ft.	A. The law of action-reaction
______ 2. Two astronauts in deep space push against each other and move in opposite directions.	B. The law of inertia
______ 3. Once in motion, a car is easy to push.	C. The law of motion
______ 4. If a force of 2 G's is applied to a cart, its speed will be 3 MPH: if 4 G's, 6 MPH.	

Directions: For each area in Column I, select the letter of the zone in Column II which identifies it. Each zone may be used more than once. Mark your answers on the accompanying answer sheet.

Column I	Column II
______ 1. Region of shallow water where light can penetrate	A. Aphotic zone
______ 2. Area of deep fresh water where no light can penetrate	B. Estuary
______ 3. Deep sea area where no light can penetrate	C. Littoral zone
______ 4. Zone where fresh water meets the sea	D. Neritic biome
	E. Profundal zone

Which example tests for application of knowledge?

______ a. First example ______ b. Second example

The correct answer is **a**, in the first example. The student reads a list of physical laws and applies them to novel situations. In the second example, the student matches terms and previously learned definitions.

Turn to the **gray sheet**, page 224, and using the guidelines below develop relationships for matching test items of your own. Complete **A.**

Guidelines for Matching Relationships

Relationships requiring *recall* of knowledge	**Definitions . . . . Terms**
	Historical Events . . . . . . Dates
	Achievements . . . . People
	Statements . . . . Postulates
	Descriptions . . . . Principles
Relationships requiring *application* of knowledge	**Examples . . . . Terms**
	Functions . . . . Parts
	Classifications . . . . Structures
	Applications . . . . Postulates
	Problems . . . . Principles

Relationships testing for recall involve, but are not limited to, specifics such as names, places, dates, events, and terms. Check to see whether your recall relationship fits one of the types listed. Do a similar comparison for your application relationship. If you need to revise the relationships that you wrote on the **gray sheet**, page 224, to fit the classifications of recall and application, do so now before continuing.

Now return to the **gray sheet**, page 224, to complete **B**. Write matching test items involving the recall relationship you have selected. In **C** on page 225, write items which test application of knowledge, again based on your selection in **A**. Include the necessary component parts: (1) an introductory statement of directions, (2) a set of premises, and (3) a list of response choices.

III. WRITING CLEAR DIRECTIONS

Exercise 4.

To help you write clear directions, read the two examples, then complete the exercise.

Directions: The following is a list of incomplete statements. Select the word or words from the list on the right that best describes or completes the statement.

	Column I	Column II
_____	1. The belt of calm air nearest the equator is called . . .	A. Doldrums
_____	2. Climate characterized by clear skies, dry air, and little rainfall is found in the area of . . .	B. Horse latitudes
_____	3. The wind belt immediately north or south of the doldrums is called the . . .	C. Polar easterlies
		D. Prevailing easterlies
_____	4. Most of the United States lies in the belt of winds known as . . .	E. Prevailing westerlies

Directions: In Column I are descriptions of geographic characteristics of wind belts. For each statement find the appropriate wind belt in Column II. Record your answer in the appropriate space on the answer sheet. Answers may be used more than once.

	Column I	Column II
______	1. Region of high pressure, calm, and light winds	A. Doldrums
______	2. The belt of calm air nearest the equator	B. Horse latitudes
______	3. A wind belt in the northern hemisphere typified by a continual drying wind	C. Polar easterlies
		D. Prevailing easterlies
______	4. Most of the United States is found in this belt	E. Prevailing westerlies

Which directions are written more clearly? _____ First _____ Second example.

This example is a better item because:_______________________________

The second example is considered the clearer of the two examples because the directions introducing the matching task are written in more specific terms.

Exercise 5.

Read the following example for clarity, then complete the exercise.

Directions: Which item in Column II goes with each one in Column I?

	Column I	Column II
______	1. Fear of closed places	A. Acrophobia
______	2. Fear of contamination	B. Agoraphobia
______	3. Fear of crowds	C. Claustrophobia
______	4. Fear of darkness	D. Mysophobia
______	5. Fear of high places	E. Ocholophobia
______	6. Fear of open places	

Revise the directions so that the task of matching phobias and definitions is clear.

____

____

Compare these directions with your own. *On the space to the left of each definition in Column I, write the letter of the phobia in Column II. You may use each letter in Column II more than once, or not at all.*

In Exercise 5, because the matching task involves associating names of phobias with their definitions, your revised directions should specify this relationship as the basis of matching premise with response. Also, add to directions that spaces for responses appear to the left of the premises. Finally, the revised directions tell students whether they may use response choices more than once. Permitting students to use the same response more than once usually reduces guessing.

Guidelines for Writing Directions

- ☐ **Specify the basis for matching premise and response.**
- ☐ **State whether responses can be used more than once.**
- ☐ **Indicate where to write answers.**

Check the directions you have written on your **gray sheets**, pages 224-225.

IV. WRITING PREMISES AND RESPONSE CHOICES

Here are five guidelines which will help you in writing premises and response choices.

Guideline 1: Select Homogeneous Premises and Response Choices.

Exercise 6.

This item was written to test student knowledge of the geographical location of European countries. Column II provides two alternative lists of responses. Complete the exercise by selecting the more appropriate list.

Directions: On the line to the left of each location in Column I, write the letter of the country described in Column II. Each country in Column II may be used more than once.

Column I	Column II	
	List (a)	**List (b)**
_____ 1. Bounded to the north by Czecho-slovakia and to the south by Yugoslavia	A. Austria	A. Austria
	B. Bulgaria	B. Brussels
_____ 2. Has been a buffer state between Russia and Germany	C. Finland	C. Berlin
	D. Hungary	D. Finland
_____ 3. An independent nation to the northwest of Russia	E. Latvia	E. Hungary
	F. Poland	F. India
_____ 4. Separates Italy and Germany	G. Rumania	G. Paris

Indicate the more appropriate list: _____ List (a) _____ List (b)

List **a** is more appropriate because it contains only names of European countries called for by the set of premises. List **b** contains the names of countries, European and Far Eastern, as well as the names of cities.

Such choices are not acceptable because they are implausible. Homogeneous items make all choices plausible and also reduce the opportunity for guessing by students who have not mastered the objective being tested. Before writing response choices, review your objectives, then decide what should be tested, and set up a consistent pattern among the choices.

Exercise 7.

Applying the principle of homogeneity, read the examples and complete the exercise.

Directions: Column I lists basic provisions of several acts enacted during the U.S. Colonial Period (1763-1775). Match these provisions with the names of acts listed in Column II. The name of an act may be used more than once. Mark your answers on the answer card.

Column I	**Column II**
1. Taxed newspapers, legal papers, calendars	A. Intolerable Acts
2. Taxed import goods	B. Navigation Acts
3. Regulated Colonial trade	C. Stamp Act
4. Called for enforcement of the Navigation Acts	D. Townshend Acts
5. Took right of self-government away from Massachusetts	

Directions: The following items refer to the Pre-revolutionary period in United States history (1763-1775). Match the information given under I with the appropriate information given under II. An answer may be used only one time. Mark answers on the answer card.

Column I	**Column II**
1. Regulated colonial trade	A. Parliament
2. Frontier closed by proclamation	B. Navigation Acts
3. English legislative body	C. 1763
4. British troops raided Lexington and Concord	D. Stamp Act
5. Taxed newspapers, legal papers, and calendars	E. 1768
	F. 1775

The example that best illustrates homogeneity is the ____ First ____ Second example.

The first example best illustrates homogeneity. All premises require some Colonial Act for the matching response. In the second example, acts, dates, and institutions are intermixed, allowing students considerable opportunity to guess by eliminating implausible choices. Homogeneity of premises and responses makes the matching task less susceptible to guessing and more a measure of actual knowledge of relationships.

Turn to your items on the **gray sheets**, pages 224-225, and apply the guideline of homogeneity. If your items have more than one basis for matching, rewrite them so that they are homogeneous.

Guideline 2. Keep the Length of Matching Entries Brief.

Exercise 8.

By keeping items brief and easy to read, you will increase the likelihood of measuring student learning, rather than reading ability. Examine the premises in the example and complete the exercise.

Directions: Descriptions of levels of knowledge are listed in Column I. Match these descriptions with names in Column II. Mark your answers on the answer card.

Column I	Column II
1. The lowest level of *understanding* involves a type of understanding that permits an individual to know what is being communicated and to use that information in a limited way.	A. Analysis B. Application C. Comprehension
2. The quantitative and qualitative cognitive value judgments about real world material and methods, use of a standardized appraisal process, utilization of criteria.	D. Evaluation E. Knowledge
3. The recalling of specific or general information, or the recalling of patterns, structures, or settings.	
4. The breaking down of a communication into its many parts and understanding the relationship between these parts.	

Revise premises 1 and 2 to be brief and easy to read.

1.____

2.____

The first premise can be shortened to: *The lowest level of understanding . . .*
The second premise is more difficult to revise. By rearranging the words, you can develop a brief, more readable statement. Here is one way to revise premise 2:
Qualitative and quantitative judgments about how the material and methods satisfy criteria.

Check your items on the **gray sheets**, pages 224-225, against this guideline.

Guideline 3: Keep the Number of Items Low.

The emphasis should be on simple and direct testing of what the student has learned. Long lists can be confusing.

Exercise 9.

Compare the two versions below, then complete the exercise.

1. Directions: Match the *symbols* in Column II with the chemical elements in Column I by placing the correct *symbol* on the blank space in front of each number in Column I.

Column I		Column II	
______ 1. Oxygen	______ 7. Hydrogen	A. Na	G. Fe
______ 2. Iron	______ 8. Nitrogen	B. H	H. Ni
______ 3. Sodium	______ 9. Gold	C. Au	I. K
______ 4. Carbon	______ 10. Nickel	D. I	J. P
______ 5. Chlorine	______ 11. Iodine	E. C	K. N
______ 6. Potassium		F. O	L. Cl

2. Directions: Match the *symbols* in Column II with the chemical elements in Column I by writing the correct *symbol* on the blank space in front of each number in Column I.

Column I	Column II	Column I	Column II
______ 1. Oxygen	C	______ 6. Potassium	Au
______ 2. Iron	Cl	______ 7. Hydrogen	C
______ 3. Sodium	Fe	______ 8. Nitrogen	H
______ 4. Carbon	I	______ 9. Gold	I
______ 5. Chlorine	Na	______ 10. Nickel	K
	O	______ 11. Iodine	N
			Ni

Which version do you prefer? ___ First Version ___ Second Version.

Version 2, in which the eleven premises are divided into two separate tests, is preferred. Two completely separate forms would probably be even less confusing. Check your own items on the **gray sheets**, pages 224-225, with respect to how well you observed this guideline. Have you formed short, simple statements that are easy to read and have a range of 4-7 entries? If not, take a few minutes to revise your items.

Guideline 4: Present the Elements of the Test Items in Logical Order.

A logical order can be arranged by listing choices alphabetically, numerically, or chronologically.

Exercise 10.

Read the two examples and choose the one you think is more logically written.

Directions: On the line to the left of each space accomplishment in Column I, write the letter of the date in Column II when the accomplishment took place. Each date in Column II may be used more than once.

	Column I	Column II
______	1. First space vehicle to reach Venus	A. 1960
______	2. First communications satellite placed in orbit	B. 1961
______	3. First landing of men on the moon	C. 1962
______	4. First American in space	D. 1965
		E. 1968
		F. 1969

Directions: On the line to the left of each space accomplishment in Column I, write the letter of the date in Column II when the accomplishment took place. Each date in Column II may be used more than once.

	Column I	Column II
______	1. First space vehicle to reach Venus	A. 1969
______	2. First communications satellite placed in orbit	B. 1962
______	3. First landing of men on the moon	C. 1961
______	4. First American in space	D. 1968
		E. 1960
		F. 1965

Which example is easier to understand? Indicate your answer in the space provided.

______ **First Example** ______ **Second Example**

The first example is easier to read and understand because the alternative responses are written in chronological order. When the matching entries are logically ordered, students can more easily follow the sequence and match date with event, without having to re-order the lists.

Exercise 11.

The example below has poorly organized items. Read it, then complete the exercise.

Directions: Match the styles of architecture in Column II, with the structures by placing the appropriate letter before each number. Answers may be used only once.

Column I	Column II
____ 1. The cathedral of Rheims is an example of . .	A. Moslem architecture
____ 2. The Lincoln Memorial in Washington D.C. reflects the influence of . . .	B. Byzantine architecture
____ 3. The Church of St. Sophia is the finest example of . .	C. Baroque architecture
	D. Greek architecture
	E. Gothic architecture

Re-order the set of premises and list of alternatives above more logically.

Column I	Column II
1.________________________________	A.____________
__________________________________	B.____________
2. ________________________________	C.____________
__________________________________	D.____________
3. ________________________________	E.____________

The example can be improved by listing the premises in the chronological order of the dates when the structures were built (St. Sophia, Rheims, Lincoln) and by listing the choices alphabetically (Baroque, Byzantine, Gothic, Greek, Moslem).

Check the matching items you have written on the **gray sheets**, pages 224-225. Do your items follow special sequences, such as alphabetical, numerical, or chronological? Is there a logical order to your list of premises or choices? If you have constructed your lists in random order, reorder them so that they follow a logical sequence.

Guideline 5: Provide Unequal Number of Response Choices in Relation to Premises.

Exercise 12.

Read these examples, then complete the exercise.

Directions: Match the behavioral descriptions in Column I with the type of personality in Column II. Personality types may be used only once. Write your answers on the attached answer sheet.

Column I	Column II
1. Alternating elation and sadness	A. Asthenic personality
2. Physically and verbally aggressive	B. Cyclothymic personality
3. Self-pitying with low vitality	C. Explosive personality
4. Suspiciousness coupled with excessive self-importance	D. Paranoid personality

Directions: Listed in Column II are structural parts of the eye. Please match these parts with their description that is listed in Column I. Parts may be used only once. Write your answers on the attached answer sheet.

Column I	Column II
1. Area containing "cones"	A. Fovea
2. Central region of the eye	B. Iris
3. Elastic connective tissue	C. Retina
4. Light receptor tissue	D. Sclera
	E. Vitreous humor

Apart from content variations, write down the major difference.

The major difference is ______________________________

____

The major difference between the two examples is the number of response choices. The first example has the same number of responses and premises. The second example has more response choices than premises. This difference becomes critical in the case where choices can be used only once. Having the same number of choices as premises increases the likelihood that students can choose the correct answer by elimination. To reduce elimination or guessing, either have an unequal number of choices with respect to premises, or make some choices fit more than one premise.

Exercise 13.

Read the example and complete the exercise.

Directions: Place the letter of the English preposition in Column II to the left of the French translation that means the same thing in Column I. Prepositions in Column II may be used only once.

Column I	Column II
______ 1. a	A. by
______ 2. avec	B. for
______ 3. par	C. to
______ 4. pour	D. under
______ 5. sous	E. with

Revise the example so that guessing by elimination is reduced.

Directions: Place the letter of the English preposition in Column II to the left of the French translation that means the same thing in Column I. Prepositions in Column II may be used only once.

Column I	Column II
____________	____________
____________	____________
____________	____________
____________	____________
____________	____________

Suggested Revisions:

- ☐ Add more prepositions to the list of choices.
- ☐ Add or delete a French preposition thus making the list of premises and choices unequal in number.
- ☐ Revise the premises and choices to permit choices to be used more than once.

Return to your **gray sheets**, pages 224-225, and determine whether your items meet this guideline.

V. SUMMARY OUTLINE

I. COMPONENTS OF MATCHING TEST ITEMS

Introductory statement
Set of premises
List of response choices

II. TYPES OF RELATIONSHIPS IN MATCHING

Recall of knowledge
Application of knowledge

III. WRITING CLEAR DIRECTIONS

Specify the basis for matching premise and response
Tell whether responses can be used more than once
Indicate where to write answers

IV. WRITING PREMISES AND RESPONSE CHOICES

Select homogeneous premises and response choices
Keep the length of matching items brief
Keep the number of items low
Present the elements of test items in logical order
Provide unequal number of response choices in relation to premises

VI. REVIEW TEST

Read each of the following examples of matching items. If the example violates one or more of the stated guidelines, write down the violations. If the example does not violate any of the guidelines, put a check in the OK column. Answers are at the end of the exercise.

I. Guidelines for Writing Directions

1. Specify the basis for matching premise and response.
2. Tell whether responses can be used more than once.
3. Indicate where to write answers.

II. Guidelines for Writing Premises and Response Choices

1. Select homogeneous premises and response choices.
2. Keep the length of matching entries brief.
3. Keep the number of items brief.
4. Present the elements of test items in logical order.
5. Provide unequal numbers of response choices in relation to premises.

1. **Directions:** On the line to the left of each space accomplishment in Column I, write the letter of the date in Column II when the accomplishment took place. Each date in Column II may be used more than once.

Column I	**Column II**
_____ 1. First space vehicle to reach Venus	A. 1969
_____ 2. First communications satellite placed in orbit	B. 1962
	C. 1961
_____ 3. First landing of men on the moon	D. 1960
_____ 4. First American in space	E. 1965

Violations: __________

OK ______

2. **Directions**: The following is a list of incomplete statements. Select the word or words from the list on the right that best describes or completes the phrase.

Column I

_____ 1. The belt of calm air nearest the equator is called . . .

_____ 2. Climate characterized by clear skies, dry air, and little rainfall is found in the area of . . .

_____ 3. The wind belt immediately north or south of the doldrums is called . . .

_____ 4. Most of the United States lies in the belt of winds known as . . .

Column II

A. Doldrums

B. Horse latitudes

C. Prevailing easterlies

D. Prevailing westerlies

Violations: ________ OK ___

3. **Directions:** Listed in Column II are structural parts of the eye. Match these parts with the description that is listed in Column I. Parts may be used only once. Write your answers on the attached answer sheet.

Column I

_____ 1. Area containing *cones*

_____ 2. Central region of the eye

_____ 3. Elastic connective tissue

_____ 4. Light receptor tissue

Column II

A. Fovea

B. Iris

C. Retina

D. Sclera

E. Vitreous humor

Violations: ________ OK ___

4. **Directions**: Match the following symbols in Column II with the chemical elements in Column I by placing the appropriate *letter* on the blank space in front of each number in Column I.

Column I	Column II
______ 1. Oxygen	A. Na
______ 3. Sodium	C. Au
______ 4. Carbon	D. I
______ 5. Chlorine	E. C
______ 6. Potassium	F. O
______ 7. Hydrogen	G. F
______ 8. Nitrogen	H. Ni
______ 9. Gold	I. K
______ 10. Nickel	J. P
______ 11. Iodine	K. N
	L. Cl

Violations: ________ OK ___

5. **Directions:** Listed below under Column I are the basic provisions of several acts enacted during the Colonial Period (1763-1775) of the United States. Match these provisions with names of the acts listed under Column II. Remember that the name of an act may be used more than once. Mark your answers on the answer card.

Column I	Column II
1. Taxed newspapers, legal papers, calendars	A. Intolerable Acts
2. Taxed import goods	B. Navigation Acts
3. Regulated Colonial trade	C. Stamp Act
4. Called for enforcement of the Navigation Acts	D. Townshend Act
5. Took right of self-government away from Massachusetts	

Violations: ________ OK ___

6. **Directions**: The following items refer to the Pre-Revolutionary period in United States history (1763-1775). Match the information given under Column I with the appropriate information given under Column II. An answer may be used only one time. Mark answers in the space below to the left of Column I.

Column I	Column II
_____ 1. Regulated colonial trade	A. Parliament
_____ 2. Frontier closed by proclamation	B. Navigation Acts
_____ 3. English legislative body	C. 1763
_____ 4. British troops raided Lexington and Concord	D. Stamp Act
	E. 1768
_____ 5. Taxed newspapers, legal papers, and calendars	F. 1775

Violations: ________ OK ___

7. **Directions**: Match the behavioral descriptions in Column I with the type of personality in Column II. Personality types may be used only once. Write your answers on the attached answer sheet.

Column I	Column II
1. Alternating elation and sadness	A. Asthenic personality
2. Physically and verbally aggressive personality	B. Cyclothymic personality
	C. Explosive personality
3. Self-pitying with low vitality	D. Paranoid personality
4. Suspiciousness coupled with excessive self-importance	

Violations: ________ OK ___

8. **Directions**: In Column I are descriptions of geographic characteristics of wind belts. For each statement find the appropriate wind belt in Column II. Record your answer in the appropriate space below. Answers may be used more than one time.

Column I	Column II
_____ 1. Region of high pressure, calm, and light winds	A. Doldrums
	B. Horse latitudes
_____ 2. The belt of calm air nearest the equator	C. Polar easterlies
	D. Prevailing easterlies
_____ 3. A wind belt in the northern hemisphere typified by a continual drying wind	E. Prevailing westerlies
_____ 4. Most of the United States is found in this belt	Violations: ________OK ___

9. **Directions:** Listed below under Column I are descriptions of levels of knowledge. Match these descriptions with names of levels under Column II. Remember that the name of a level may be used more than once. Mark your answers to the left of Column I.

Column I	Column II
_____1. The lowest level of "understanding" involves a type of understanding which permits an individual to know what is being communicated and to use that information in a limited way.	A. Comprehension B. Application C. Analysis D. Knowledge
_____2. The quantitative and qualitative cognitive value judgments about real world material and methods, use of a standardized appraisal process, utilization of criteria.	E. Evaluation
_____3. The recalling of specific or general information or the recalling of patterns, structures, or settings.	
_____4. The breaking down of a communication into its many parts and understanding the relationship between these parts.	Violations: ________OK ___

Answers: (1) II-4 (2) I-1, 2, 3; II-5 (3) OK (4) II-3 (5) OK (6) II-1 (7) II-5 (8) OK (9) II-2.

REFERENCES AND RESOURCES

Cangelosi, James S. **Evaluating Student Achievement.** White Plains, NY: Longman, 1990.

Cross, K. Patricia and Thomas A. Angelo. **Classroom Assessment Techniques.** Ann Arbor, MI: University of Michigan, National Center for Research to Improve Postsecondary Teaching and Learning, 1988.

Ebel, Robert L. and David A. Frisbie. **Essentials of Educational Measurement.** (4th ed.) Englewood Cliffs, NJ: Prentice-Hall Inc., 1986.

Erickson, Richard C. **Measuring Student Growth.** Boston: Allyn and Bacon Inc., 1976.

Gronlund, N. E. **How to Construct Achievement Tests.** Englewood Cliffs, NJ: Prentice-Hall Inc., 1987.

Gronlund, N. E. and Robert L. Linn. **Measurement and Evaluation in Teaching.** (6th ed.) New York: Macmillan, 1990.

Hopkins, Kenneth D., Julian C. Stanley, and B. R. Hopkins. **Educational and Psychological Measurement and Evaluation.** (7th ed.) Englewood Cliffs, NJ: Prentice-Hall Inc., 1990.

Popham, W. James. **Modern Educational Measurement.** (2nd ed.) Englewood Cliffs, NJ: Prentice-Hall Inc., 1990.

Sax, Gilbert. **Principles of Educational and Psychological Measurement and Evaluation.** (3rd ed.) Belmont, CA: Wadsworth Publishing Company, 1989.

VII. APPLICATION EXERCISE

A. Select Relationships for Matching Test Items.

Use the following spaces to list two relationships between a set of premises and a list of response choices you treat in one of your courses. Keep the distinction between recall and application in mind when you specify each relationship. The relationships will form the bases of the matching items you will be writing in the remainder of this exercise.

RECALL RELATIONSHIP:________________________________

____

APPLICATION RELATIONSHIP:____________________________

____

- -

B. Write a matching test item based on the Recall Relationships you stated above.

Directions:

Column I

Column II

C. Write a matching test item based on the Application Relationship in A.

Directions:

Column I	**Column II**

ITEM ANALYSIS ON OBJECTIVE TESTS

Module Developers:	Philip C. Seyer Ron J. McBeath
Editorial Associates:	Oswald B. Carleton Jerrold E. Kemp Carole R. Smith
Editorial Consultant:	Richard B. Lewis

ITEM ANALYSIS ON OBJECTIVE TESTS

This module will help you determine the effectiveness of multiple choice tests in two ways:

- Identify items that seem to be inconsistent with the test as a whole
- Improve the reliability of your tests

These procedures are for norm referenced tests which are designed to rank individuals within a group and to discriminate between high and low achievers. Much of the discussion later in this module relates to types of information you may receive when an objective test has been computer graded and you are provided with a statistical analysis of the results. This module will prepare you to interpret and use the data provided in the choice analysis printout.

The module is organized under these headings:

I. DIFFICULTY LEVEL OF A TEST ITEM

The difficulty level of an item is indicated by the percentage of students who answer an item correctly. Suppose 10 of your students take an examination and 8 of them answer an item correctly; in this case we say that the difficulty level of the item is 80%.

High and Low Difficulty Levels

Number Correct	Class Size	Difficulty Level
40	50	80 (low)
18	60	30 (high)
14	20	70 (low)

An item with a difficulty of 70% or *above* is usually referred to as a *low* difficulty item since over two thirds of the class are able to answer it correctly. An item with a difficulty level of 30% or *below* is usually referred to as a *high* difficulty item since less than one third of the students answered it correctly. Thus, a *high number* means a *low difficulty* item, and vice versa; this is standard terminology.

Exercise 1.

What factors might account for the low difficulty level and high scores in the test items below?

____

____

____

____

____

Difficulty Level of Test Items

Item	Difficulty Level%
1	85
2	90
3	80
4	70
5	80
6	95
7	98
8	60
9	25
all items	76

The high scores could be due to such factors as:

- ☐ **The students were well above average in intelligence.**
- ☐ **The students studied the material extensively and mastered the content.**
- ☐ **The text and related materials were well organized.**
- ☐ **The content was well presented in terms of the objectives.**
- ☐ **The test was too easy.**

The fact that items have a *low difficulty level* does not necessarily mean that they are too easy. Similarly, items that have a high difficulty level are not necessarily too difficult for use in a test.

Study the example below and complete Exercises 2, 3, and 4.

Compare the difficulty level of items used on a Pre-test and Post-test.

	Difficulty Level	
Item	Pre-test	Post-test
1	20	85
2	15	90
3	10	80
4	57	70
5	40	80
6	50	95
7	40	98
8	50	60
9	10	25
10	05	78

Exercise 2.

Assuming that all the students carefully studied the assignment, does it seem to you that students are learning well from the assigned reading?

______ Yes ______ No ______ Can't Tell

It seems that the students are learning well from their assigned reading if the changes in difficulty levels between the pre-test and post-test are a true indication.

Exercise 3.

Assuming that each of the previous questions is properly testing for the acquisition of a single concept, which concepts are not being learned well from the assigned reading?

______	Item 1	______	Item 6
______	Item 2	______	Item 7
______	Item 3	______	Item 8
______	Item 4	______	Item 9
______	Item 5	______	Item 10

Apparently, the students have not satisfactorily mastered the concepts in Items 8 and 9. 50% of the class got Item 8 right even before studying the text, and only 60% got it right after studying. In Item 9 the shift from 10% to 25% indicates a limited learning improvement.

Exercise 4.

The next time the professor gives this course, knowing that former students had difficulty with the concepts in Items 8 and 9, what could he do to help them to better grasp the concepts? Assume that the test items are well written and do not need revision.

____

____

____

Knowing that students tend to have trouble grasping concepts in Items 8 and 9, the professor might conclude that different teaching strategies should be tried. He might discuss the concepts before assigning the chapter to familiarize the students with the key points where difficulties might arise. Another instructional resource such as a film or videotape to study along with the text could be used.

The important point is that by examining the difficulty level of test items, it is possible to identify what students find difficult. Appropriate additions or changes can then be made in the teaching program or the formulation of the test items.

Study the example below, then complete Exercises 5 and 6.

Compare the data from another of the professor's tests.

	Percent Correct	
Item No.	**Pre-test**	**Post-test**
1	50	25
2	45	85
3	95	97
4	20	95
5	15	75

As previously noted, an item may not necessarily be too easy just because it has a low difficulty level in a post-test analysis. Pre-test data may help identify reasons for high scoring.

Exercise 5.

Which item on the pre-test above is probably too easy?

______ Item 1 ______ Item 2 ______ Item 3 ______ Item 4 ______ Item 5

Item 3 is probably too easy; 95% of the students got it right with no instruction. Perhaps the item is faulty and gives students an unwarranted clue to the correct answer. The item may be testing for a skill that nearly all students possess. In this case, the professor could review the item and decide whether to change or remove it.

Another way to identify faulty items is to check the change in difficulty level from pre-test to post-test. Look again at the test data in the example above and complete Exercise 6.

Exercise 6.

What other item is suspect based on the pre-test and post-test data?

______ Item 1 ______ Item 2 ______ Item 3 ______ Item 4 ______ Item 5

Something appears to be wrong with Item 1. It is not always clear whether the instructional approach is faulty or whether the item needs revision. In the next part of this module, you'll learn about an item analysis technique that can help you make decisions in these cases.

II. DISCRIMINATION INDEX

The discrimination index is a measure of how well the results on a single item agree with the results of the entire test. It is based upon the difference between the number of students in the upper and lower groups who got the item right. The index can be positive or negative. This measure can help you decide whether an item is faulty or whether instruction needs to be changed.

An English instructor gave a 10 item test to find out if students could identify figures of speech. Review the results and complete Exercises 7 and 8.

Results from a 10 item test

Students	Test Items										% Correct
	1	2	3	4	5	6	7	8	9	10	
Rogers	x										90%
Smith	x			x							80%
Trent	x		x		x						70%
Adams			x		x			x	x		60%
Brown		x	x		x			x	x		50%
Carson		x	x	x		x	x		x		40%

Students listed in rank order, highest scoring student first. An *x* shows an item was answered incorrectly.

Exercise 7.

Suppose the instructor had given only test item number 1.

Who would have been the three top scoring students?

_______________ _______________ _______________

Who would have been the three lowest scoring students?

_______________ _______________ _______________

Adams, Brown, and Carson would have been at the top of the class; Rogers, Smith, Trent at the bottom.

Exercise 8.

According to the results from the entire test (all 10 items):

Who are the three top scoring students?

_______________ _______________ _______________

Who are the three lowest scoring students?

_______________ _______________ _______________

According to the results of the test as a whole, Rogers, Smith, and Trent are at the top of the class; Adams, Brown, and Carson, at the bottom. Clearly, the results of Item 1 do not agree with those of the total test: in fact, the results are just the opposite. When the data from a single item disagree with the results from the total test, an item is said to be negatively discriminating. In this case, the discrimination index is – 100%, a strong indication that Item 1 may be faulty.

A discrimination index can run from – 100% (complete disagreement), as in Item 1, to 100% (complete agreement), as in Item 10.

III. CALCULATING THE DISCRIMINATION INDEX

1. **Score test as usual.**
2. **Rank students from highest to lowest on the basis of their test scores.**
3. **Identify the top scoring students and an equal number of the lowest scoring students. (Approximately 20% of class for each group is sufficient.)**
4. **Compute the % of top scoring students who answered the item correctly.**
5. **Compute the % of low scoring students who answered the item correctly.**
6. **Subtract the % in step 5 from the % in step 4 for the discrimination index.**

Exercise 9.

Compute the percentage of the top scoring students who answered item 2 correctly. The first three steps for computing the discrimination index for the items are completed below. Now complete step 4 for test item 2. An *x* shows items answered incorrectly.

Students	Test Items										% Correct
	1	2	3	4	5	6	7	8	9	10	
Rogers	x										90%
Smith	x			x							80%
Trent	x		x		x						70%
Adams			x		x			x	x		60%
Brown		x	x		x			x	x		50%
Carson		x	x	x		x	x		x		40%
% of top scorers answering correctly											

↑ Write the result of Step 4 here.

Answer: 100%, since Rogers, Smith, and Trent all answered Item 2 correctly.

Use the steps above for calculating the discrimination index in Exercises 9, 10, 11, and 12.

Exercise 10.

Compute the percentage of low scoring students who answered Item 2 correctly. Write the result for Item 2 in the proper place on the chart.

An *x* shows that an item was answered incorrectly.

Students	Test Items										% Correct
	1	2	3	4	5	6	7	8	9	10	
Rogers	x										90%
Smith	x			x							80%
Trent	x		x		x						70%
Adams			x		x			x	x		60%
Brown		x	x		x			x	x		50%
Carson		x	x	x		x	x		x		40%
% of top scorers answering correctly		100									
% of low scorers answering correctly											

Write the result for step 5 here.

Answer: 33%, since only one of the three low-scoring students (Adams) answered Item 2 correctly.

Exercise 11.

Compute the Discrimination Index.

Subtract the % in step 5 from the % in step 4. Write the Discrimination Index for Item 2 in the proper place on the chart.

An *x* shows that an item was answered incorrectly

Students	Test Items										% Correct
	1	2	3	4	5	6	7	8	9	10	
Rogers	x										90%
Smith	x			x							80%
Trent	x		x		x						70%
Adams			x		x			x	x		60%
Brown		x	x		x			x	x		50%
Carson		x	x	x		x	x		x		40%
% of top scorers answering correctly		100									
% of low scorers answering correctly		33									
Discrimination Index											

↑ Write the value for step 6 here.

Answer: 67% the difference between 100% and 33%

Exercise 12.

Calculate the Discrimination Index.

Write the correct values for Items 4 and 6. Complete the remaining items and check with the answers shown in Exercise 13. An *x* shows that an item was answered incorrectly.

Students	Test Items										% Correct
	1	2	3	4	5	6	7	8	9	10	
Rogers	x										90%
Smith	x			x							80%
Trent	x		x		x						70%
Adams			x		x			x	x		60%
Brown		x	x		x			x	x		50%
Carson		x	x	x		x	x		x		40%
% of top scorers answering correctly		100									
% of low scorers answering correctly		33									
Discrimination Index		.67									

Write the computed values here  

Item 4 has a discrimination index of zero since the same percentage of top and low scoring students got the correct answer.

Item 6 has a discrimination index of 33%, the difference between the difficulty level of 100% for the top scorers and 67% for the low scorers.

Exercise 13.

Find the item with the most desirable Discrimination Index in the chart below.

An *x* shows that an item was answered incorrectly.

It is item_________

Students	Test Items										% Correct
	1	2	3	4	5	6	7	8	9	10	
Rogers	x										90%
Smith	x			x							80%
Trent	x		x		x						70%
Adams			x		x			x	x		60%
Brown		x	x		x			x	x		50%
Carson		x	x	x		x	x		x		40%
% of top scorers answering correctly	0	100	67	67	67	100	100	100	100	100	
% of low scorers answering correctly	100	33	0	67	33	67	67	33	0	100	
Discrimin-ation Index %	-1.0	.67	.67	0	.33	.33	.33	.67	1.0	0	
Difficulty Level %	50	67	33	67	50	83	83	67	50	100	

Item 9 has the best discrimination index (1.00). All high scorers answered the item correctly while all the low scorers were wrong.

IV. DETERMINING THE VALUE OF A TEST ITEM

When determining the value of a test item for a norm referenced objective test, it is important to look at both its difficulty level and discrimination index. A good rule of thumb is: *Items with a difficulty level between 30% and 70% can be expected to have a relatively high discrimination index, that is, at least 30% or above.*

The items with difficulty levels below 30% or above 70% cannot be expected to have a high discrimination index. This is an important point to remember when you examine test data. If an item has a difficulty level that lends itself to a high discrimination index, and yet has a low discrimination index (that is, below 30%), this is a strong sign that this item should be revised, or possibly discarded. Examine the example below and then complete Exercise 14.

Difficulty Level and Discrimination Index of a 7 Item Test

Item No.	Difficulty Level	Discrimination Index
1	85	.05
2	10	.10
3	50	.10
4	45	.40
5	70	.30
6	30	.30
7	40	.20

Exercise 14

Check the items most likely to need revision.

___ Item 1 ___ Item 2 ___ Item 3 ___ Item 4 ___ Item 5 ___ Item 6 ___ Item 7

Items 3 and 7 need review. Item 3 has a difficulty level of .50. With this difficulty level we would normally expect a rather high discrimination index. The low discrimination index of .10 strongly suggests that item 3 needs work. The same is true for Item 7; although its discrimination index of .20 is slightly better, it is still not acceptable in view of its difficulty level.

Items 1 and 2 are acceptable even though each has a low discrimination index. That is because a high discrimination index is impossible when difficulty levels are above .70 or below .30. Some discrimination should be expected however, except when all students answer a question correctly or incorrectly.

FLOW CHART TO INDICATE THE VALUE OF A TEST ITEM

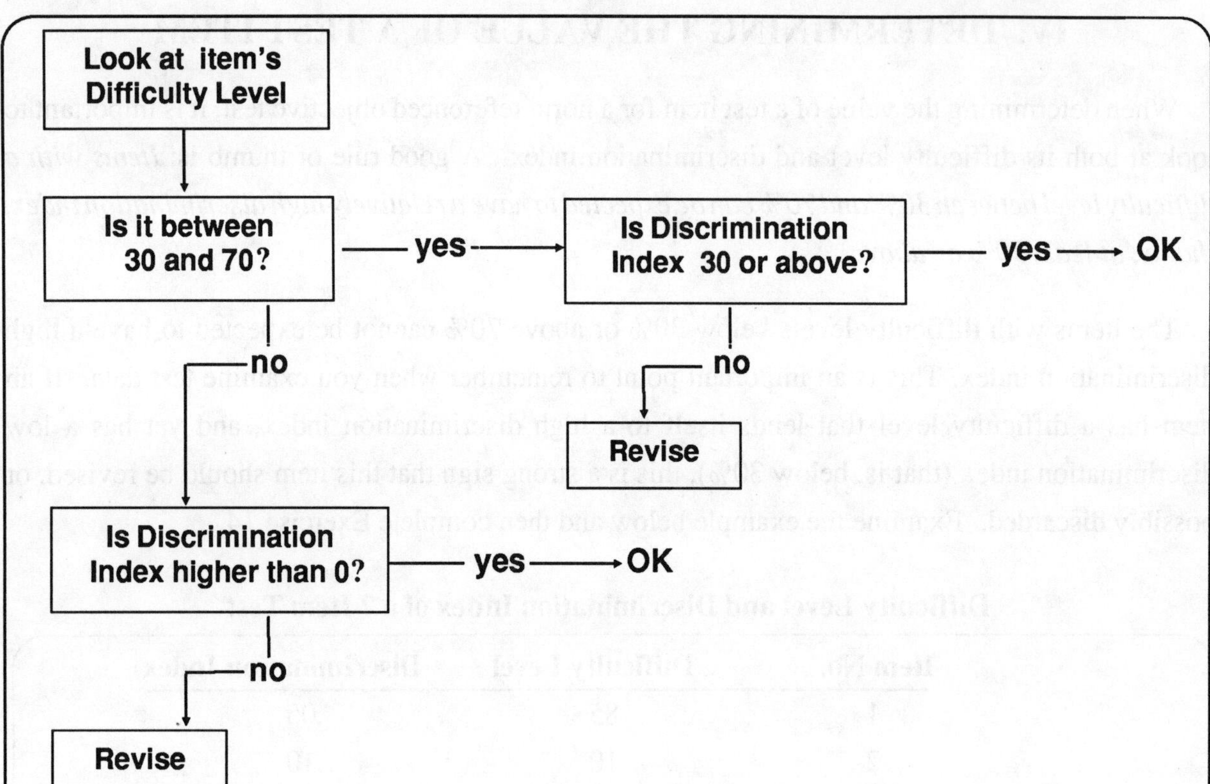
Look at item's Difficulty Level
Is it between 30 and 70?
yes
Is Discrimination Index 30 or above?
yes
OK
no
no
Revise
Is Discrimination Index higher than 0?
yes
OK
no
Revise

Exercise 15.

Use the Flow Chart above to determine the items needing revision.

Item No.	Difficulty Level	Discrimination Index
1	90	−.10
2	50	.75
3	60	.35
4	10	.15

_____ **Item 1** _____ **Item 2** _____ **Item 3** _____ **Item 4**

Item 1 should be revised because it has a negative discrimination index. For Items 2 and 3, both the difficulty level and discrimination index are acceptable. Item 4 has a high difficulty level and the discrimination index is low but positive, so the item does not need revision.

You may find a number of *borderline items*, particularly those items that have a **discrimination index** just under .30 and a **difficulty level** between 30 and 70. It is not necessary to revise such items.

V. USING DATA PROVIDED BY COMPUTER ANALYSIS

One main purpose of this module is to enable you to make effective use of the choice analysis data. The example below is part of a computer printout from a 26-item multiple choice test.

QUESTION	FREQUENCY						PERCENT						DISCRIMINATION INDEX
	A	B	C	D	E	O	A	B	C	D	E	O	
1	16	3	25*	1	0	2	34	6	53*	2	0	4	.19
2	13*	17	6	4	0	7	27*	36	12	8	0	14	.29
3	3	16*	20	3	0	5	6	34*	46	6	0	10	.12

Number of students picking each response

Percentage of students picking each response

16 students picked choice A for item 1

Number of students omitting item

Percentage of students omitting an item

Note that the discrimination index for each item is given in the far right column. Also, note the printout shows the number and percentage of students picking each response option in each item. The correct answer to each item is marked with an *asterisk*. For example, in Item 1, look at column A under *Frequency*. The 16, opposite Item 1, means that 16 students picked choice **A** for question 1. Three students picked choice **B**; 25 students picked choice **C**, *the correct answer*; and one student picked choice **D**. Two students omitted the question.

The percent columns in the data table tell us that 34% picked **A**; 6% picked **B**; 53% picked **C**; and 2% picked **D**. Now try Exercise 16.

Exercise 16.

The difficulty level for each item is given above. What is it for question 1?__________

According to the criteria set up for item analysis, would you have reason to believe that Item 1 needs rewriting? ______Yes______No______Can't tell

The difficulty level is the 53%, since 53% of the students picked choice **C**, the correct answer. The second answer is *yes*. Item 1 needs rewriting since the discrimination index is only .19. With a difficulty level of 53%, a discrimination index of at least .30 can be expected.

VI. ITEM COMPARISON ON CRITERION REFERENCED TESTS

The *criterion referenced test* is designed to measure the level of competency a student has achieved in mastering specified learning skills under specified conditions. The skills will range from low to high levels of intellectual competence according to criteria established by the instructor. This is *different* from the purpose of a *norm referenced test* which discriminates between the high achieving and low achieving students by ranking them relative to each other.

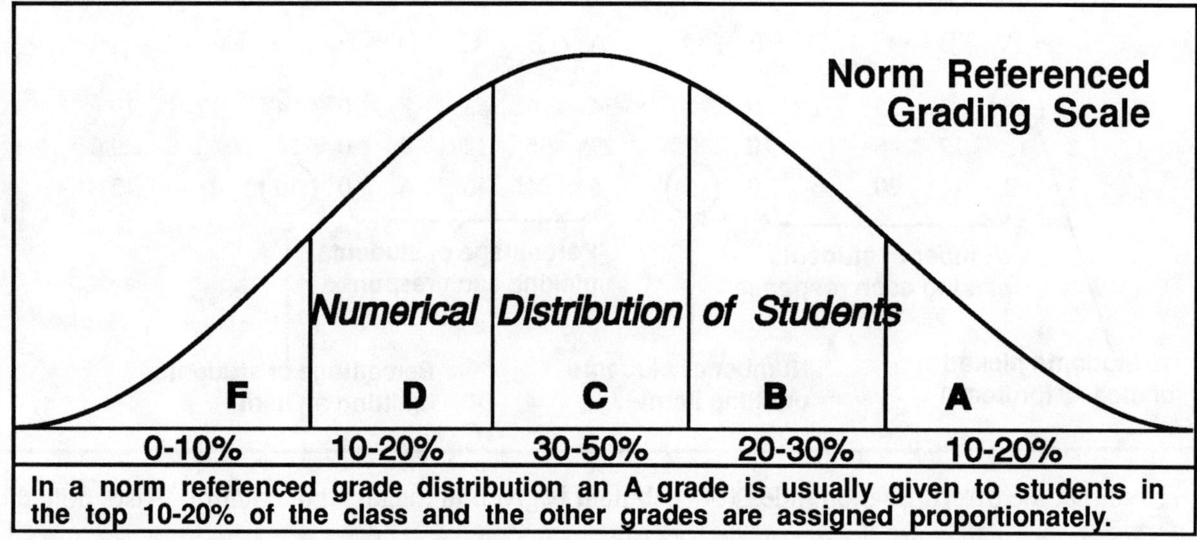

In a norm referenced grade distribution an A grade is usually given to students in the top 10-20% of the class and the other grades are assigned proportionately.

The purpose of ***criterion referenced instruction*** is to have all students reach specified levels of mastery, and the ***criterion referenced tests*** are designed to find out if this has been achieved. The instructional program is designed to help all students reach the highest level possible. Grades are assigned in an absolute rather than a relative manner.

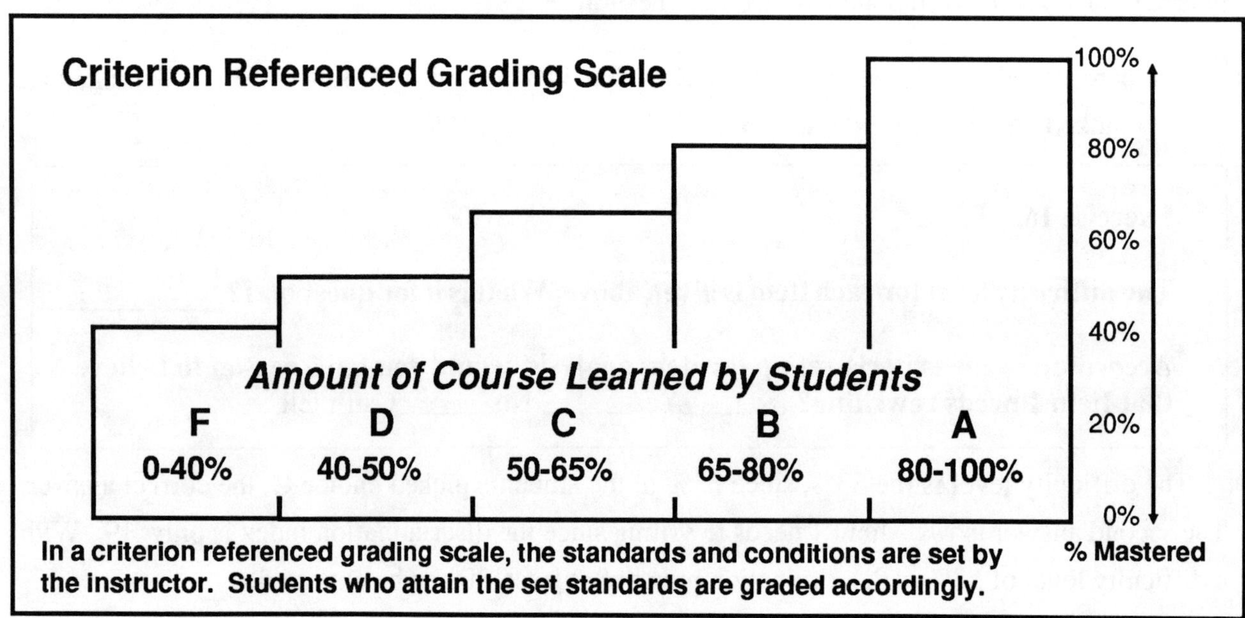

In a criterion referenced grading scale, the standards and conditions are set by the instructor. Students who attain the set standards are graded accordingly.

It will be expected therefore that most students will pass on most questions, so while the standard item analysis procedure for determining difficulty and discrimination indices can be used, the results cannot be interpreted in the same way for item selection. The Discrimination Index will probably be of much more value than the Difficulty Index. With the Discrimination Index, you will know that some changes in instruction or in the test item may be needed if most of the low scoring students get an item correct and the high scoring students get it wrong.

Pre-test and Post-test Item Comparison

The difficulty level and value of criterion referenced tests can be determined better by using a pre-test and post-test comparison of the questions. This comparison is more valuable when each item is categorized against such levels as those Bloom outlined in his Taxonomy. The questions should range through the six levels from Knowledge through Comprehension, Application, Analysis, Synthesis to Evaluation at the highest level. The number of questions you develop and use at each level will depend on your lesson objectives and the course outcomes you are seeking.

TABLE OF SPECIFICATIONS FOR TEST ITEMS
Levels of Knowledge and Intellectual Skills

	Knowledge	Comprehension	Application	Analysis	Synthesis	Evaluation
Topic 1						
Topic 2						
Topic 3						
etc.						

By having such a range of questions, you are more likely to create an instructional program which will help students to establish a factual foundation, develop concepts, use principles to solve problems, make creative applications of their knowledge and critique both the applications and the implications.

An item comparison check can be used to indicate not only the value of each test item, but also where changes may be needed in instruction, practice exercises, text materials and/or resources. See the module on **Setting Objectives** for further information on Bloom's Taxonomy.

VII. SUMMARY OUTLINE

I. DIFFICULTY LEVEL OF A TEST ITEM

70% or above is low difficulty
30% or below is high difficulty
Factors influencing scoring levels

II. DISCRIMINATION INDEX

Agreement of single item results with total test results
Positive and negative indices

III. CALCULATING THE DISCRIMINATION INDEX

Rank students from highest to lowest
Identify top scoring 20% and lowest 20%
Compute percentage of high and low who answered each item correctly
Subtract low from high to find discrimination index

IV. DETERMINING THE VALUE OF A TEST ITEM

Relating difficulty level and discrimination index
Flow chart on accepting, revising, and rejecting items

V. USING DATA PROVIDED BY COMPUTER ANALYSIS

Example of computer printout on choice analysis

VI. ITEM COMPARISON ON CRITERION REFERENCED TESTS

Pre-test and post-test item comparison
Table of specifications for test items

VIII. REVIEW TEST

After reviewing the printout below, check those items needing revision and question mark the borderline cases.

COMPUTER PRINTOUT OF CHOICE ANALYSIS OF THE 26 TEST ITEMS

QUESTION	FREQUENCY						PERCENT						DISCRIMINATION INDEX
	A	B	C	D	E	O	A	B	C	D	E	O	
1	16	3	25*	1	0	2	34	6	53*	2	0	4	.19
2	13*	17	6	4	0	7	27*	36	12	8	0	14	.29
3	3	16*	20	3	0	5	6	34*	46	6	0	10	.12
4	32*	3	5	0	0	7	68*	6	10	0	0	14	.21
5	14	2	2	27*	0	2	29	4	4	57*	0	4	.33
6	12	28*	1	2	0	4	25	59*	2	4	0	8	.38
7	4	38*	1	0	0	4	8	80*	2	0	0	8	.31
8	21	2	15*	6	0	3	44	4	31*	12	0	6	.43
9	8	22*	0	14	0	3	17	46*	0	29	0		.34
10	9	19*	4	7	0	8	19	40*	8	14	0	17	.59
11	4	6*	1	25	0	11	8	12*	2	53	0	23	.27
12	13	1	23*	2	0	8	27	2	48*	4	0	17	.37
13	12*	5	5	13	0	12	25*	10	10	27	0	25	.44
14	13	11	7	13*	0	3	27	23	14	27*	0	6	.20
15	8	16*	15	5	0	3	17	34*	31	10	0	6	.28
16	3	32*	5	4	0	3	6	68*	10	8	0	6	.32
17	6	34*	2	3	0	2	12	72*	4	6	0	4	.37
18	16	8	4	15*	0	4	34	17	8	31*	0	8	.27
19	0	4*	21	13	0	9	0	8*	44	27	0	19	-.01
20	6	7*	4	19	0	11	12	14*	8	10	0	23	.21
21	7	5	23	5*	0	7	14	10	48	10*	0	14	.23
22	6	18*	8	12	0	3	12	38*	17	25	0	6	.31
23	8	10*	19	8	0	2	17	21*	40	17	0	4	.13
24	5	12	24*	1	0	5	10	25	51*	2	0	10	.45
25	0	8	9	21*	0	9	0	17	19	44*	0	19	.24
26	6	6	12	2*	0	12	31	12	25	4*	0	25	-.01

Compare your answers with those in the next example.

VALUE OF THE 26 TEST ITEMS

QUESTION	FREQUENCY						PERCENT						DISCRIMINATION INDEX
	A	B	C	D	E	O	A	B	C	D	E	O	
1	16	3	25*	1	0	2	34	6	53*	2	0	4	.19 √
2	13*	17	6	4	0	7	27*	36	12	8	0	14	.29
3	3	16*	20	3	0	5	6	34*	46	6	0	10	.12 √
4	32*	3	5	0	0	7	68*	6	10	0	0	14	.21 ?
5	14	2	2	27*	0	2	29	4	4	57*	0	4	.33
6	12	28*	1	2	0	4	25	59*	2	4	0	8	.38
7	4	38*	1	0	0	4	8	80*	2	0	0	8	.31
8	21	2	15*	6	0	3	44	4	31*	12	0	6	.43
9	8	22*	0	14	0	3	17	46*	0	29	0		.34
10	9	19*	4	7	0	8	19	40*	8	14	0	17	.59
11	4	6*	1	25	0	11	8	12*	2	53	0	23	.27
12	13	1	23*	2	0	8	27	2	48*	4	0	17	.37
13	12*	5	5	13	0	12	25*	10	10	27	0	25	.44
14	13	11	7	13*	0	3	27	23	14	27*	0	6	.20
15	8	16*	15	5	0	3	17	34*	31	10	0	6	.28 ?
16	3	32*	5	4	0	3	6	68*	10	8	0	6	.32
17	6	34*	2	3	0	2	12	72*	4	6	0	4	.37
18	16	8	4	15*	0	4	34	17	8	31*	0	8	.27 ?
19	0	4*	21	13	0	9	0	8*	44	27	0	19	-.01 √
20	6	7*	4	19	0	11	12	14*	8	10	0	23	.21
21	7	5	23	5*	0	7	14	10	48	10*	0	14	.23
22	6	18*	8	12	0	3	12	38*	17	25	0	6	.31
23	8	10*	19	8	0	2	17	21*	40	17	0	4	.13
24	5	12	24*	1	0	5	10	25	51*	2	0	10	.45
25	0	8	9	21*	0	9	0	17	19	44*	0	19	.24 √
26	6	6	12	2*	0	12	31	12	25	4*	0	25	-.01 √

* Indicates correct answer

Items which should be considered for revision are checked √, a ? is next to borderline items, and satisfactory items are left blank. The unacceptable items are clearly 1, 3, 19, 25, 26.

Items 4, 15, and 18 are borderline.

The difficulty level for item 4 of 68% is so close to 70% that it is hard to find fault with the discrimination index of .21. Items 15 and 18 have discrimination indices of .28, .27. They should be reviewed for possible changes but not automatically rejected.

REFERENCES AND RESOURCES

Bloom, Benjamin S., George F. Madaus and J. Thomas Hastings. **Evaluation to Improve Learning**. New York: McGraw-Hill Book Company, 1981.

Cangelosi, James S. **Evaluating Student Achievement.** White Plains, NY: Longman, 1990.

Ebel, Robert L. and David A. Frisbie. **Essentials of Educational Measurement** (4th ed.) Englewood Cliffs, NJ: Prentice-Hall Inc., 1986.

Gronlund, Norman E. **Measurement and Evaluation in Teaching** (6th ed.) New York: Macmillan, 1990.

Hopkins, Kenneth D., Julian C. Stanley, and B. R. Hopkins. **Educational and Psychological Measurement and Evaluation.** (7th ed.) Englewood Cliffs, NJ: Prentice-Hall Inc., 1990.

Popham, W.J. **Modern Educational Measurement.** (2nd ed.) Englewood Cliffs, NJ: Prentice-Hall Inc., 1990.

Sax, Gilbert. **Principles of Educational and Psychological Measurement and Evaluation.** (3rd ed.) Belmont, CA: Wadsworth Publishing Company, 1989.

Shrock, Sharon A. and William C.C. Coscarelli. **Criterion-Referenced Test Development.** Reading, MA: Addison-Wesley Publishing Company, 1989.

IX. APPLICATION EXERCISE

Administer a multiple choice test in one of your classes, then use the guidelines and flow chart, or a computer analysis from the Testing Office, to determine the difficulty level, discrimination index, and the value of each test item. The procedures outlined are designed for norm referenced tests. If you wish to complete an item comparison for a criterion referenced test, use the guidelines from Section VI.

CONSTRUCTING AND SCORING ESSAY QUESTIONS

Module Developers:	Carole R. Smith Ron J. McBeath Philip C. Seyer
Editorial Associates:	Oswald B. Carleton Jerrold E. Kemp
Editorial Consultant:	Richard B. Lewis

CONSTRUCTING AND SCORING ESSAY QUESTIONS

This module on constructing and scoring essay questions is organized under seven headings:

I. **Purposes and Characteristics of Essay Tests**

II. **Guidelines for Writing Clear Essay Questions**

III. **Strategies to Offset Subjectivity in Scoring**

IV. **Two Methods of Scoring**

V. **Summary Outline**

VI. **Review Test**

VII. **Application Exercise**

I. PURPOSES AND CHARACTERISTICS OF ESSAY TESTS

Before you start to construct an essay test, it is important to consider whether it is the appropriate kind of test to serve your purposes.

Exercise 1.

For each of the purposes for testing below, check whether an *Essay Test* or *Objective Test* would be most appropriate. If you think insufficient information is given to make a decision, check the column, *Can't Tell.*

		Essay Test	Objective Test	Can't Tell
A	You wish to test students' ability to recall 20 principles.			
B	You want to test students' ability to organize and express ideas.			

An objective test would be appropriate for situation A which emphasizes recall. When you want to test for recall of a large number of items in your course, an objective test is appropriate. An essay test would be more appropriate for situation B which calls for the application of knowledge and requires students to organize and express ideas rather than select appropriate response options.

In taking an essay test, students need sufficient time to think through, organize, and write out their answers. Consequently, an essay test should be used to cover only a small number of concepts, but in greater depth.

Exercise 2.

For each of these situations check whether an *Essay Test* or an *Objective Test* would be most appropriate. If insufficient information is given to make a decision, check the column *Can't Tell*.

		Essay Test	Objective Test	Can't Tell
A	You want assistants to be able to correct the test quickly and objectively.			
B	You want to evaluate students' *overall* approach to real problems they face in their environment.			
C	Your performance objective calls for students to be able to pick an appropriate solution when given certain kinds of situations.			
D	You want to evaluate the students' ability to make qualified judgments on a newspaper editorial.			

An essay test would be appropriate for situations B and D. In an essay test, students have to resolve a problem. There are a minimum of prompts for them to rely upon. They are relatively free to decide what factual information to use, how to organize the response, and how much emphasis to give to each aspect of the answer. The essay question is particularly suited for measuring students' capabilities to apply knowledge by producing, organizing and expressing ideas. Thus, from reading responses to an essay question, you have an opportunity to see their approaches to problem solving. Objective tests are likely to be more appropriate for situations A and C. Objective tests can be scored quickly and objectively. They efficiently measure student knowledge on the breadth rather than the depth of the course.

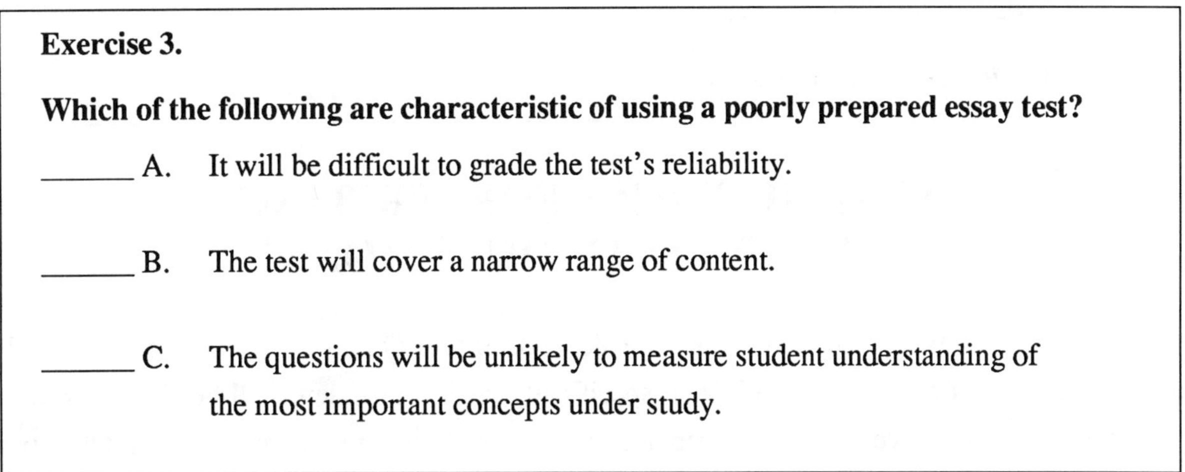

Exercise 3.

Which of the following are characteristic of using a poorly prepared essay test?

______ A. It will be difficult to grade the test's reliability.

______ B. The test will cover a narrow range of content.

______ C. The questions will be unlikely to measure student understanding of the most important concepts under study.

All three are characteristic of using poorly prepared essay tests. Essay tests are used most successfully when well planned and carefully written. But when hurriedly or carelessly prepared, with little thought about what will be considered an acceptable answer, grading will become a difficult and unreliable task. Even carefully written questions, are difficult to grade consistently.

Another difficulty in using poorly prepared essay tests is that they may cover a very narrow range of content and give inaccurate evidence of student knowledge. For example, a professor has covered forty major objectives in a course, and a student has prepared thoroughly on thirty of them. The student could flunk the examination simply because of not studying the few particular concepts included in the test; whereas another student who, by chance, had studied only the topics used in the test, could pass.

Another constraint in using essay tests is that it takes a lot of time and thought to design one that properly measures student understanding of important course goals. It is easy to dash off essay questions, but not so easy to write essay questions that are congruent with course objectives and measure a wide range of thought processes.

Summary of Characteristics of Essay Questions

- ☐ Require careful preparation.
- ☐ Measure ability to organize and apply knowledge.
- ☐ Reveal the process by which students approach and resolve problems.
- ☐ Measure higher order thought processes such as analyzing, synthesizing, solving problems, and making judgments.
- ☐ Cover a narrow range of content, but in greater depth than objective tests.
- ☐ Take a long time to score.
- ☐ Difficult to grade consistently.

II. GUIDELINES FOR WRITING CLEAR ESSAY QUESTIONS

The level of thinking you wish to test for depends entirely on your teaching objectives. By developing a set of objectives which state specifically what the student will be able to do as an outcome of the course, you will have prepared an effective base for constructing tests. Objectives stated in terms of student performance can assist you in developing a range of questions which can be used to test both students' recall and ability to apply knowledge in higher order thought processes.

1. Use Key Words to Specify Thinking Processes

Key or directional words that might be used in essay test questions measuring a wide range of thinking processes are listed below. This list is by no means exhaustive; it merely suggests some of the typical low level and high level cognitive skills that can be measured.

Low Level (Recall)	
Define	List
Name	Enumerate
Describe	State
Explain	Discuss

High Level (Application)	
Apply	Contrast
Organize	Differentiate
Interpret	Appraise
Examine	Predict

Exercise 4.

Classify the following phrases according to the level of thinking processes involved. Write *low* if the phrase involves recall, and *high* if the phrase calls for application of knowledge.

_______ A. Develop inferences

_______ B. Appraise relationships

_______ C. Sequence events

Developing inferences and appraising relationships both require the use or application of knowledge, while sequencing events calls for the recall of knowledge. Key words or phrases specify the range of thinking involved. This is an important aspect to consider when writing essay questions.

Exercise 5.

Which essay question calls for students to use and apply knowledge? Check the appropriate space.

_______ A. List the conditions that influence a person's performance.

_______ B. Predict when an accomplished pianist will perform better, by himself, or in front of an audience. Support your answer with relevant evidence.

Question B requires students to use knowledge. Notice the key word "predict." In this question, students are asked to analyze a situation and predict an outcome. These tasks require higher order thought processes. Question A, on the other hand, asks students to recall from memory some previously learned knowledge. Such a task does not require either analysis or interpretation.

From the list of key words it is apparent that essay questions can be used to assess both higher and lower order thought processes in ways other than asking students to discuss, explain, or summarize. One way is to include basic information which students can respond to and act upon. This technique is especially helpful when the questions simulate real world problems and skills. In a history test, instead of asking students to describe the causes of some historic event, the instructor might give the students an article on the topic and guide them through a critical thinking exercise with the following request.

After reading the accompanying article:

- ☐ Identify the point of view expressed in the article.
- ☐ Compare the view expressed with that given in the textbook.
- ☐ Enumerate any underlying assumptions and critique their validity.
- ☐ Distinguish between facts and opinions in the article.

In a psychology class, instead of asking students to "discuss Miller's theoretical model of displacement," an instructor could present a simulation of a specific event from a case history and then ask students:

- ☐ Explain what happened, on the basis of Miller's theory.
- ☐ If you were X in the situation, what could you do to help?
- ☐ Explain how this action is consistent with Miller's theory.

Exercise 6.

Check the test items which place emphasis on memorization rather than application of knowledge.

______ A. Here is a summary of Schachter's research on affiliation. What steps of the scientific method are illustrated in the summary? Explain by naming each step and writing out the words in the summary that tell you that Schachter carried out that step. What steps, if any, are not clearly mentioned?

______ B. List the major steps of the scientific method in proper sequence. Give as detailed and thorough an answer as possible within the time period.

______ C. Describe the scientific method.

______ D. Here is a report of Mackey's research. Appraise her work according to its adherence to the major steps of the scientific method.

Questions B and C rely principally on memorization skills. Questions A and D test for higher order thought processes. Questions A and D require students to demonstrate their knowledge by working with and responding to some stimulus material. Question A presents students with material and requires that they detect a relationship between real research and the scientific approach by making inferences and picking out significant ideas. Question D requires that students make inferences from actual data, discriminate good research from bad, and give their conclusions about the material. Student responses to B and C ask students to recall knowledge.

Student responses to B and C will not tell you whether a student can analyze actual research and apply the principles and criteria of the scientific method; so while they test for knowledge, they do not give as full a measure of student understanding as questions A and D.

To give you an opportunity to check your own skills in writing essay test questions, turn to the **gray sheet**, page 277, and follow the instructions.

2. State Requirements Clearly

Questions that clearly spell out requirements are preferred to global or ambiguously phrased ones. The more direction and purpose you convey in your question, the easier it is for a well-informed student to respond in the manner expected. Vague, ambiguous phrasing, generally leads to a variety of answers because students interpret the question differently.

Exercise 7.

Which of these questions is preferable? Why?

A. Discuss the causes of the American Revolution.

B. Read this selection on the causes of the American Revolution and write a critique of it in no more than 300 words. You will be graded on how well you meet the criteria discussed in class for critiquing articles. Underline all opinions of the author. Circle any facts the author gives to support his opinions. What point of view is the author taking? Has he left out any important considerations? Do you agree with the author?

I like question ____

Reasons: ____

____

____

____

Question B contains *clear directions* regarding what students are to do. This question consists of a series of specific tasks which call for particular behaviors. Students are asked to apply their knowledge about a statement by critiquing, analyzing structure, and stating their considered opinion. Notice that throughout this exercise students are advised to remember criteria previously discussed in order to judge the adequacy of their answers. Also, students in this question are given explicit directions about length. This helps students to be brief but explicit and forces them to organize their comments.

In contrast, Question A merely presents the topic and lets students structure their answers based on their own perceptions of what is required. Because students may handle the topic in a variety of ways, an instructor would have no common frame of reference for evaluating student responses. This limits the value of this question.

3. Indicate Response Length Expected

This guideline indicates to the student the type of response expected, and enables the instructor to see how well the essential ideas can be organized and expressed in the stated length.

Now check your own questions on the **gray sheet**, page 277, against the three guidelines. Revise your questions so that they state the task clearly, then return here.

4. Set Time Limits

Questions that tell students how much time to spend enable them to pace their writing. This information reduces the chance that a student will be caught with one or more questions to answer when time runs out. It also helps to relieve some test anxiety.

Be sure to review the extent of the task. Doing this will help you decide on an approximate, but realistic, time period for a satisfactory answer. By doing this you can become more aware of the tasks confronting your students and better able to judge their appropriateness.

Exercise 8.

Which of these directions gives students the best idea of how much time should be spent on a question? Check the appropriate spaces.

______ A. You have 2 hours to finish this exam so plan to devote an appropriate amount of time to each question.

______ B. You have 2 hours to finish this exam. The approximate time you should spend on each question is given in parentheses after each question.

______ C. Work as quickly as you can. The proctor will tell you when your time is up.

Direction B is the most explicit set of instructions regarding time requirements. The directions tell the overall time limit and then show the approximate time per question. Direction A also specifies an overall time limit but does not spell out the precise time for each question. From the directions in A, a student may assume each question is equally demanding. This may be a faulty assumption and students may suffer the consequences of poor time management. Item C gives no help about how much time to spend on the questions. These directions encourage students to hurry and probably increase their anxiety.

5. Give Weights to Questions

Another way to help students make time estimates is to show the weight of a question; that is, tell how many points a correct response will get.

The Use of Weighting

(10 points) 1. Identify and discuss several forms of psychological stress that college students face.

(15 points) 2. You are a child psychologist and have been invited to speak to a high school class on the topic "Preparing for Marriage." What would you tell the class regarding pathogenic families and their effect upon children?

Weighting tells students the relative importance of each question and helps them budget their time accordingly. The weight of a question can also be useful in scoring, as you will see shortly, because it establishes maximum points for an acceptable answer. It is helpful to write out an answer in advance to be sure of the breadth of the question and overall importance of the question before you assign the weights.

Strategies for Writing Clear Essay Questions

1. **Use key words to specify thinking processes.**
2. **State requirements clearly.**
3. **Indicate response length expected.**
4. **Set time limits.**
5. **Give weights to questions.**

Examine each of your own questions again on the **gray sheet**, page 277, and check whether you have observed the several suggestions for writing clear and fair essay questions. After reviewing your questions, proceed with the next topic below.

III. STRATEGIES TO OFFSET SUBJECTIVITY IN SCORING

It is difficult to score essay tests with complete reliability. Reliability here refers to the consistency of a student's score after two independent scorings, either by the same grader or by different graders. The greater the subjectivity of scoring, the less reliable the score is likely to be.

Reducing Subjectivity

Two major factors that influence subjectivity are personal preferences and personal inconsistencies over a period of time. Personal preferences are with respect to (1) the students, (2) content, (3) the way the essay is written. Instructor inconsistency in assigning grades over a period of time, is further and significantly influenced by such factors as fatigue, and ability to concentrate. Two particular effects of subjectivity that can be controlled by the use of various scoring strategies are discussed below.

1. Halo Effects.

A halo effect occurs when personal impressions of a student affect an instructor's evaluation of the student's essay responses. The halo effect can be either positive or negative as the cartoons illustrate.

Cartoon 1

Cartoon 2

Cartoon 3

Cartoon 3 shows one way to reduce the chance that a halo effect would bias evaluations.

Here the professor, by scoring anonymous essays, is able to offset subjectivity based on previous knowledge and expectations about particular students.

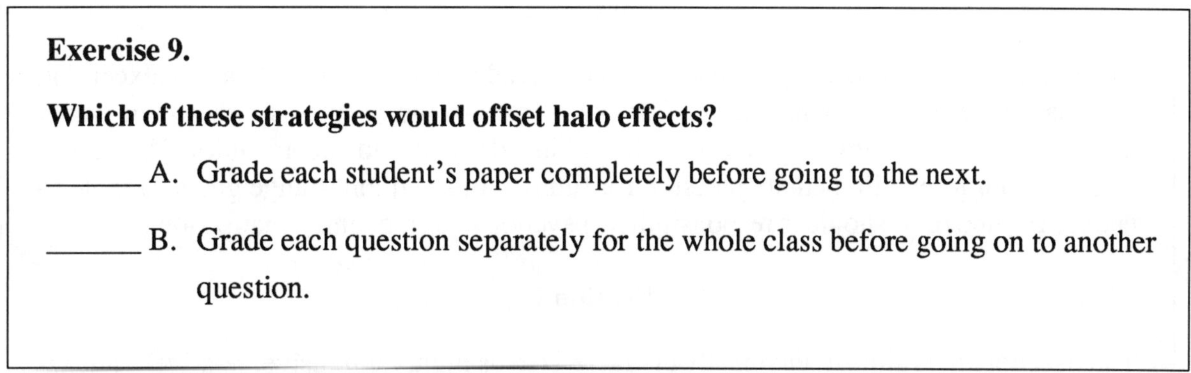

Exercise 9.

Which of these strategies would offset halo effects?

_______ A. Grade each student's paper completely before going to the next.

_______ B. Grade each question separately for the whole class before going on to another question.

Strategy B would more likely reduce halo effects because there is less chance of building an expectation about a student from looking at only one question. Later, when it comes time to grade questions using this technique, be sure to shuffle the papers. This helps to offset order effects, the biasing effects of a paper's placement relative to other papers.

Strategy A could help foster consistency expectations. By reading all the responses of any one student, there would be a greater tendency to see a consistent pattern of responding, whether or not the performance was indeed consistent. This strategy is not recommended if scoring objectivity is desired.

Strategies that Offset Halo Effects

- ☐ **Conceal student names when scoring.**
- ☐ **Score all papers, one question at a time.**
- ☐ **Shuffle papers after scoring each question.**

2. Personal Judgment.

The second area of subjectivity is in regard to your personal judgment of similar responses that are written in different styles.

Style Preference

Which version do you prefer of these two responses to the question: "How would you characterize a psychopath's behavior ?"

Version A

The psychopathic personality is unable to understand and accept ethical values, except on a verbal level. Such persons tend to "act out" tensions and problems rather than worry about them. Psychopaths are prone to thrill-seeking, deviant, and unconventional behavior. They seldom forego immediate pleasure for future gains and long-range goals. Unable to endure routine or to shoulder responsibility, psychopaths frequently change jobs.

Version B

The psychopath is almost universally characterized as highly impulsive, relatively refractory to the effects of experience in modifying his socially troublesome behavior, and lacking in the ability to delay gratification. His penchant for creating excitement for the moment without regard for later consequences seems almost unlimited. He is unable to tolerate routine and boredom. While he may engage in antisocial, even invidious behavior, his outbursts frequently appear to be motivated by little more than a need for thrills and excitement.

Notice that both responses have almost the same content. Version B, is in a flowery style that uses larger and less well-known words. If flowery writing appeals to you personally, you might be tempted to give Version B a higher score. On the other hand, if you prefer straight, factual writing you might give Version A the higher score. Thus, if you are not careful, you might favor one type of response over another even though both are similar in content.

Other factors of personal judgment may account for subjectivity in scoring. The quality of handwriting, the use of a pen rather than a pencil, incorrect spelling, grammatical errors, or prose style, are all factors that may influence your judgment about the quality of the essay.

By being aware of the effects of personal judgment on scoring, and by following some precautionary procedures, you can minimize subjective influences.

Strategies that Offset Effects of Personal Judgments on Essay Scoring

- ☐ **Structure the question so there is little room for subjective interpretation.**
- ☐ **Construct essay tests that contain several questions.**
- ☐ **Construct and use a scoring key.**
- ☐ **Have two independent scorings of a test.**
- ☐ **Avoid optional questions.**

Notice that the strategies listed here draw heavily upon the second guideline for essay construction: Write the question clearly. That is, phrase the question in a manner that lets students know what they must do to answer the question correctly.

This is a good way to minimize subjective scoring because it reduces subjective responses.

A second precaution is to include several essay questions on the test. By increasing the number of questions, the amount of error due to inadequate sampling of course content can be reduced.

Third, use a scoring key because it enables you to score all the responses from a single frame of reference. If you have prepared a tightly structured question (one which communicates to the student what is expected of him), you can prepare a good scoring key.

Fourth, whenever possible, have two independent scorings made of the test. The reliability of a test will be raised considerably if you score the papers twice, preferably with several days intervening, and then take the average of the two sets of scores. Or, even better, you could have one other person score the test beside yourself. This would remove the idiosyncracies of scoring even more and produce scores that are highly reliable.

Finally, avoid the use of optional questions. A common practice is to give students more questions than they are to answer, and give them a choice. Students are usually all for this because they can pick the questions they are better prepared to answer. However, if you are seeking a standard measure of student mastery, using optional questions will give a distorted measure of learning. The assumption that students are equally proficient on the questions they didn't answer may not be true.

Exercise 10.

Which of these directions gives a better measure of what students have learned?

_______ A. Answer all of the questions below.

_______ B. You may answer any four of these six questions.

Note that Direction A gives all students an equal chance to show that they have mastered their instructional objectives. Direction B, because it gives students a choice of question, will not give uniform information about which students have or have not mastered course objectives.

IV. TWO METHODS OF SCORING

Point-Score Method

The point-score or analytic method is considered more reliable than the rating method. In using point-scoring, you write a model answer and devise a scoring key of the essential elements in the answer to guide you in assigning scores. The essential elements include concepts and/or procedures related to course objectives. To make a key, first write down all the probable kinds of responses capable students are likely to give. Then revise them according to how closely they match your objectives. Assign points that correspond to the importance of the elements.

When using this procedure, it is assumed that the questions are written clearly so students who have mastered the skills being evaluated will know what is expected in the answer. Even though students can develop answers in different ways, satisfactory answers should contain a large proportion of the essential components. If you know what a question is supposed to measure, then you should be able to identify the components of a complete answer in a usable scoring key.

An Example of the Point-Score Method

Objective: To demonstrate ability to plan a research project recognizing the theoretical and practical constraints.

Question: As a participant in a research project you are to examine the need for a pre-school nursery center in a new housing development and to make recommendations.

(a) What are the theoretical and practical research constraints you would expect to influence your investigation and findings?

(b) Recognizing the constraints and the purpose of the project, how would you gather and interpret your information?

Model Answer: (a) The social scientist cannot attain the level of objectivity possible in the physical sciences since he is always a part of what is being investigated. The opportunity to get definitive data through experimentation is very limited because it is not possible to isolate and control all the variables. Frequently, investigators have to counter strong prejudicial feelings in gathering data and in presenting their findings. There is limited public support for social research projects.

(b) The data gathering would be made after an approved research design and set of instruments had been developed and tested in a pilot study. The design would include needs assessment, demographic study of the target population, recognition of investigative subjectivity and an examination of the community context. The interpretation should focus on the objectives, be based upon the data, and present alternatives for implementing and evaluating the service.

Point-Score Key

Points		Essential Elements
2	(a)	Social scientist part of his study
2		Prejudicial influences
2		Opportunity for experimentation limited
2		Difficulty in isolating and controlling variables
4	(b)	Project oriented research design
4		Instrument validation
4		Interpret from data base
3	(c)	Organization
2		Language use
25		

The Social Science professor first constructed an essay question which assessed student mastery of a specific course objective. A model answer was then drafted which included the key ideas (components) students should include. This procedure helped the professor to determine how well his question was phrased, and gave him opportunity to check the key ideas. Having identified these key ideas, each was assigned value points. The assignment of points was based upon the importance of these responses in relation to meeting the course objectives.

Notice the professor assigned points for organization and use of language. It was considered important that students could organize their thoughts in a logical fashion, express themselves clearly, as well as present the key ideas necessitated by the requirements. This procedure is acceptable when two conditions are met: (l) students know ahead of time that organization, written expression, and language usage will count toward their total score, and (2) criteria to assess the degree of these abilities are specified for the students before essays are written and scored.

Developing a Scoring Key

Once the key elements are identified, essays can be objectively scored for the presence or absence of these characteristics and corresponding values assigned. The total number of points to be assigned depends on the complexity of the questions and the weight you feel each element deserves. In this question more points were given to higher level thought processes than for information recall. Develop a key which reflects your instructional objectives and which you can use as objectively as possible.

Steps Involved in Using the Point-Score Method of Scoring

- ☐ **Write clear questions that let students know what is expected.**
- ☐ **Draft a model answer.**
- ☐ **Identify essential response elements.**
- ☐ **Revise question wording if necessary to ensure task clarity.**
- ☐ **Assign points to each element corresponding to the importance of the element to the testing objective.**
- ☐ **Read each response and score the test.**
- ☐ **Total the point scores for a final grade.**

Turn to the **gray sheet**, page 278, and follow the instructions.

Exercise 11.

Identify the essential components of the model answer to the question below. Assign points (0-4) for each component in the answer.

Objective: To explain the functions served by the heart as part of the circulatory system of the body.

Question: The human heart, as part of the circulatory system, is a double organ, each part with separate functions. During prenatal life, the heart has an opening between the two auricle chambers. Occasionally this opening persists into adulthood. What effect would you expect this persistence to have on:

a. each of the functions of the heart, and

b. on the individual when exercising strenuously?

Model Answer:

(a) The two heart functions are: (1) systematic — carrying blood to all parts of the body with the exception of the lungs, and (2) pulmonary — carrying blood to the lungs. When the opening persists into adulthood, the systematic function is not affected, but the pulmonary is. The opening between the two auricles permits some blood to flow directly from the right auricle to the left auricle instead of all of it going from the right auricle to the right ventricle and then through the pulmonary artery to the lungs.

(b) When exercising, there is a need for transporting more oxygen from the lungs to the cells of the body. Under the conditions described, less blood may flow to the lungs. Therefore, there is less oxygen to be carried through the aorta to the body. The individual does not have the stamina to engage in strenuous exercises, tiring quickly because oxygen is not being supplied to the body cells as needed for respiration.

Scoring Key

Points	Essential Elements
____	________________________________
____	________________________________
____	________________________________
____	________________________________
____	________________________________
____	________________________________
____	________________________________

Suggested Scoring Key

	Points	Essential Elements
(a)	2	Systematic function satisfactory
	2	Pulmonary function limited
	2	Flow of blood from right auricle to left auricle
(b)	4	Limited amount of oxygen for body cells' respiration
	4	Loss of stamina and tired feeling
	14	

The first part of the answer depends on recall and has been assigned fewer points than the second part, which requires higher level processes of analysis and problem solving.

Rating Method of Scoring

The rating method of scoring is used when it is not practical to draft a model answer; either the responses are so complex or extensive that isolating a host of key elements is cumbersome. These conditions will reduce test reliability. Instead of scoring a response point-by-point with a scoring key, each answer is graded by judging its quality in terms of a previously determined set of rating criteria. These criteria are determined by the testing objectives.

If students were asked to "describe a complete plan for a low-rent housing complex," the rating criteria could include:

- ☐ completeness of the plan (statement of design, assessment of needs, support services, traffic flow, etc.),
- ☐ clarity and accuracy with which the design is described,
- ☐ adequacy of the design,
- ☐ degree to which various parts of the design are properly integrated in the plan.

Typically, about 4 to 7 levels of rating criteria are outlined and given scoring values. Generally, a rating scale with fewer than 4 levels does not provide fine enough distinctions. At the other extreme, using more than 8 levels can be confusing.

When the response is scored, it is assigned a value or a letter grade from the rating criteria. The overall quality of the answer may be rated, or each criterion may be rated separately. The latter procedure provides the most useful information for diagnosing and improving learning and should be used wherever possible. If points are given or taken off for spelling and syntax, students should be told before the assignment.

An Example of the Rating Method

A. "If a society is to strive with any hope of success toward peace and prosperity in a commonwealth, the authority governing that society must not only be able to pass laws and to reassess those laws constantly as circumstances change . . ., it must also be enabled to enforce those laws and to exact penalties for their violation."
B. "Under a government that imprisons any unjustly, the true place for a just man is also in prison."
Assignment: Write an essay on the two passages above in which you answer the following: In what ways are these statements alike and in what ways do they differ? What strong or weak points does each position have? To what extent might a person accept both positions?

Score	Rating Criteria
6	A superior response will be a well-organized essay that does the three things asked for in the assignment. It will compare and contrast the meanings of the two statements. It may explain the meanings by means of comparison and contrast, or it may explain the meanings and compare and contrast them. The best essays will note that while the quotations both say something about government and laws, the first asserts the need for law and order and takes the point of view of the state, while the second affirms the principle of justice as superior to the laws of the state when those laws are unjust, and it is written from the perspective of the individual. The best essays will show consciousness of the possible dangers inherent to the first quotation (that is, it could mean that even unjust laws should be enforced, it says nothing about individual rights, and it emphasizes punishment and authority rather than freedom); and the most perceptive may perceive dangers in an uncompromising position on the second passage. The best papers may show an awareness that the two positions, properly qualified, can both be accepted. An essay getting a score of 6 will show a high degree of competence generally, though it may have minor imperfections.
4-5	These scores apply to responses that concentrate more on one quotation than the other, or that deal with both subjects somewhat less thoroughly than the essays scoring 6. Essays in this group may have minor errors in writing.
2-3	Papers in this category deal with both quotations but may: —be lacking in supporting details, or treat both quotations superficially; —give adequate attention to one but too little to the other; —fail to see that both are concerned with laws and the state but that there are important differences between them; —misunderstand or misinterpret the meaning of either or both; —be primarily critical or argumentative; —have serious faults in writing; —drift away from the topics or display considerable irrelevancy.
1	For any response that is on the topic but suggests incompetence.

In the previous example from Edward White, criteria were established by pretesting the essay with college students. Then responses were classified by quality (e.g., the more complete and comprehensive answer was rated higher). For this particular essay, the highest rating was 6 and the scoring criteria were classified into 4 identifiable groups. Notice that rating criteria are more general than elements on a scoring key; this is a function of the wide range of responses obtainable from the question. From this example, it seems easier to identify specifically what was not said than to apply precisely the criteria that identify a comprehensive and complex response, even when actual responses are available for classification.

Essentially the rating method involves making a series of successive ratings of the papers for each question on a test. The task is neither easy nor rapidly accomplished because several readings are required to place papers in their correct position. For instance, borderline papers in each rating category are re-read to make sure the bottom papers in the *better* category are actually superior to the top papers in the *poorer* category. If necessary, these papers are reclassified.

Scoring by the rating method provides only relative comparisons among a group of students. These comparisons are neither very reliable nor easily explained to students. Moreover, the use of general scoring criteria makes this method highly susceptible to subjective biases. For these reasons, this rating method of scoring is not recommended when the task of the essay question can be precisely specified. If you write essay questions that are broad in scope and definition, you may find the next summary useful.

Steps Involved in Using the Rating Method of Scoring Essay Questions

1. **Write down scoring criteria that cover the testing objectives.**
2. **Classify criteria into 4 to 7 steps and assign a value.**
3. **Read each response and make a quality rating.**
4. **Re-read borderline papers to verify their correct placement.**
5. **Convert rating to letter grades, if desired.**

Turn to the **gray sheet**, page 279, and follow the instructions.

V. SUMMARY OUTLINE

I. PURPOSES AND CHARACTERISTICS OF ESSAY TESTS

Measure ability to organize and apply knowledge.
Reveal student approach to problem solving.
Measure higher order thought processes such as analyzing, synthesizing, and making judgments.

II. GUIDELINES FOR WRITING CLEAR ESSAY QUESTIONS

Use key words to specify the thinking processes expected.
State requirements clearly.
Indicate response length.
Set time limits.
Give weights to questions.

III. STRATEGIES TO OFFSET SUBJECTIVITY

Conceal student names when scoring.
Score all papers, one question at a time.
Shuffle papers after scoring each question.
Structure the question so there is little room for subjective interpretation.
Construct essay tests that contain several questions.
Construct and use a scoring key.
Have two independent scorings of a test.
Avoid optional questions.

IV. POINT-SCORE METHOD

Write clear questions that let students know what is expected in the answer.
Draft a model answer.
Identify essential response elements.
Revise question wording if necessary to insure task clarity.
Assign points relevant to the element's importance.
Read each response and score.
Total the point scores for a final grade.

V. RATING METHOD OF SCORING

Write down rating criteria that cover the testing objectives.
Classify criteria into 4 to 7 steps and assign a value.
Read each response and make a rating.
Re-read borderline papers to verify their correct placement.
Convert rating to letter grades, if desired.

VI. REVIEW TEST

Examine each of the following situations and state whether it supports or overlooks any of the guidelines offered in this module. If you notice anything wrong with the situation, briefly write down the problem. If acceptable, write OK.

1. Students are told: *Write a two-page statement defending the importance of conserving energy. Answers will be evaluated in terms of organization and relevance of the arguments.*

____

2. An instructor gives a high score to a student because: *I am sure this student really knows the material even though he does not express it too clearly.*

____

3. An instructor tells students: *Answer any 4 questions out of a group of 8.*

____

4. Students are told: *Write an essay comparing the Democratic and Republican parties.*

____

5. An instructor writes a scoring key without writing a model answer.

____

6. An instructor reads question 1 of everyone's paper before reading question 2. In between readings, he shuffles the papers.

____

7. An instructor reads an answer to an essay question and then assigns a grade based on his experience of a quality response.

____

8. Students are asked to write an essay: *List the causes of World War I.*

____

Suggested Answers

1. OK.

2. Halo effect biases objective scoring because a student's identity is known.

3. Use of optional questions will not provide standardized measures of mastery.

4. Requirements are not clear enough and there are no time limits nor response parameters, so variation in answers may be quite wide.

5. By developing a model answer and scoring key the professor has a self checking procedure for improving the validity and reliability of the question.

6. OK.

7. No objective criterion is specified so judgments will be susceptible to subjective influences.

8. An inappropriate use of essay testing. Lists are more appropriate in an objective test.

REFERENCES AND RESOURCES

Bloom, Benjamin S., George E. Madaus, and J. Thomas Hastings. **Evaluation to Improve Learning.** New York: McGraw-Hill Book Company, 1981.

Cangelosi, James S. **Evaluating Student Achievement.** White Plains, NY: Longman, 1990.

Ebel, Robert, L. and David A. Frisbie. **Essentials of Educational Measurement.** (4th. ed.) Englewood Cliffs, NJ: Prentice-Hall Inc., 1986.

Gronlund, N. E., and Robert L. Linn. **Measurement and Evaluation in Teaching**. New York: Macmillan, 1990.

Hopkins, Kenneth D., Julian C. Stanley, and B.R. Hopkins. **Educational and Psychological Measurement and Evaluation.** (7th ed.) Englewood Cliffs, NJ: Prentice-Hall Inc., 1990.

Popham, W. James. **Modern Educational Measurement.** (2nd ed.) Englewood Cliffs, NJ: Prentice-Hall Inc., 1990.

Rahmlow, Harold F. and Katheryn K. Woodley. **Objectives Based Testing.** Englewood Cliffs, NJ: Educational Technology Publications, 1979.

Sax, Gilbert. **Principles of Educational and Psychological Measurement and Evaluation.** (3rd ed.) Belmont, CA: Wadsworth Publishing Company, 1989.

White, Edward. **Comparison and Contrast.** Long Beach, CA: California State University and College System, 1974.

VII. APPLICATION EXERCISE

Directions: On this sheet write two essay questions on topics of interest to you or for one of your courses. Write one of the questions to present a simulated situation or provide descriptive material, and require students to respond to it and draw inferences. Keep in mind that essay questions are appropriate for measuring higher order thought processes. Refer back to the list of key words on page 256 for ideas on how to word questions. When you finish, return to the text.

Question 1.

Draft a model answer to the first question you wrote on page 277 using the Point-Score Method.

Model Answer:

Scoring Key

Points **Essential Elements**

Question 2.

Draft a model answer for the second question you wrote on page 277 using the Rating Method.

Score	Rating Criteria
______	______________________________
______	______________________________
______	______________________________
______	______________________________
______	______________________________
______	______________________________
______	______________________________
______	______________________________
______	______________________________
______	______________________________
______	______________________________
______	______________________________
______	______________________________
______	______________________________
______	______________________________
______	______________________________
______	______________________________
______	______________________________
______	______________________________

PERFORMANCE TESTING

Module Developers:	Ron J. McBeath Jeanne Lassen
Editorial Associates:	Oswald B. Carleton Jerrold E. Kemp Peter Pipe
Editorial Consultant:	Richard B. Lewis

PERFORMANCE TESTING

The purposes of this module are to assist you in the development and use of performance tests in a wide range of practical problem-solving situations.

The module is organized under the following headings:

I. **Types and Purposes**

II. **Key Features**

III. **Guidelines for Constructing Tests**

IV. **Guidelines for Using Performance Tests**

V. **Summary Outline**

VI. **Application Exercise**

I. TYPES AND PURPOSES

Types of Tests

Performance tests require that students *demonstrate* their ability to apply knowledge and skills learned. These tests ask students to solve problems, perform tasks, and take actions that are realistic indicators of applied proficiency or competence.

Performance tests can be designed to assess a wide range of competencies. Traditionally, performance tests have been used extensively in technical-vocational education programs. In undergraduate and graduate education, performance tests are now used in many subject areas including: music, art, physical education, foreign language, drama, and the biological, physical, and social sciences.

Many professional programs, such as medicine, psychology, social work, and counseling, use performance testing measures to assess student knowledge, skill, and technique. In the health sciences, for example, performance tests are used continually to test technical and interpersonal skills.

The following examples illustrate several different types of performance where students demonstrate skill in an applied context:

- ☐ In a campus laboratory, a chemistry student conducts an experiment.
- ☐ In a psychology class, two students role-play a therapist and a client in a counseling session.
- ☐ In a business management class, a student writes a cost-effectiveness report.
- ☐ In a hospital, a student nurse gives medication to a patient.
- ☐ In a drama class, students act a scene.
- ☐ In a local history class, a student role-plays an oral history interview with another student who role-plays an historical informant.

The subjects are diverse: chemistry, psychology, business, nursing, drama, history.

The academic levels are diverse: from undergraduate to graduate and professional school level.

The testing conditions are diverse: the student nurse is tested in a hospital. Other students are tested in classrooms and laboratories on a university campus.

The skills which the students demonstrate are diverse: All are demonstrating a range of intellectual competencies, attitudes, and skills. The psychology, nursing, and history students are demonstrating skills in interacting with other people. The chemistry student is using knowledge in conjunction with physical skills to manipulate instruments, equipment, and materials.

The scope of performance testing is broad and far reaching, with applications in many aspects of university education which involve students in intellectual processes beyond memorization. Performance testing measures have application in all levels of education and most subject matter areas.

Performance tests can be used to measure either aptitude or achievement. Aptitude tests measure the potential of an individual to perform a certain behavior. Many beginning students in technical and professional programs are assessed diagnostically for aptitude before they undertake course work. Many non-verbal psychological tests of aptitude are types of performance tests. Achievement testing, however, presumes that the student has prior training, knowledge, or experience. The focus in this module will be on performance tests of achievement that can be predictive of student ability to apply knowledge and skills.

Purposes of Performance Tests

A well-developed performance test has three major purposes:

- ☐ **To measure individual competence against a specified standard.**
- ☐ **To provide direct feedback to the student regarding progress in learning.**
- ☐ **To predict the degree of success in future situations.**

1. Measuring Each Individual's Competence Against a Specified Standard

Performance tests, which are given individually, can add to traditional group testing by providing an alternative type of assessment. In taking a performance test, each student is *competing*, not with other students, but only with himself or herself against predetermined standards. Success or failure to achieve the objectives of the test is based on individual performance relative only to the specified standards for success, not relative to the performance of others.

2. Providing Feedback Regarding Progress in Learning

The test situation and its results assist learning by providing information directly to the student about success or failure to reach specified objectives. A well-structured test also helps the student identify which steps in the total performance need further practice or study.

Through the use of media, such as audio or video tape recorders, a performance test can be recorded. Instructors can use these results for subsequent discussion and direct feedback to guide students in specific directions for individual improvement.

3. Predicting Success in Future Situations

Performance tests measure and predict student abilities to transfer knowledge and skill to practical situations. Tests used in a nursing course may seek to predict successful transfer of relevant skills to future professional situations such as may be met in hospitals or clinics. The predictive quality of the test depends upon the accurate identification of:

1. The situation(s) to which learning will be transferred.

2. The skills necessary for an individual to succeed in the situation(s).

It is the *demonstrable* aspect of performance tests which differentiate them from other types of tests used in university education. Objective tests, such as multiple choice or true/false, and subjective tests, such as essay, ask for descriptions and applications of learned information, knowledge, skill, processes, or solutions to problems. The performance test asks for an observable demonstration of specific knowledge or skill in a realistic testing situation.

II. KEY FEATURES

There are four key features shared by all types of performance tests:

1. **Observable performance**
2. **Domains of performance**
3. **Standards for performance**
4. **Conditions for the performance**

1. Observable Performance

The performance of the student is active and participatory, involving an observable process and often an observable final product. The performance involves demonstrable action, *not* a description of actions.

The student who role-plays a therapist is demonstrating what a therapist does by talking, by listening, by interacting with another student who role-plays the client. These behaviors can be observed. The chemistry student is demonstrating specific observable laboratory skills necessary for competence in chemistry.

The business student who writes a report demonstrates selected abilities necessary for success as an administrator in the field. The ability to write acceptable reports is among the competencies required of a business administrator.

The type of student participation and test format selected depend upon objectives of the course, the subject matter and the standards for successful performance established by the instructor. If applied skills in the discipline demand an oral performance, as would be appropriate in drama, psychology, or history, then that is the basis around which the test is structured.

Actual performance will be observed as:

- ☐ **verbal** — involving oral or written activities
- ☐ **non-verbal** — involving expressions, gestures, or listening
- ☐ **fine motor skills** — as in handling small objects
- ☐ **gross motor skills** — as in bodily movements
- ☐ **a combination of these**

Developing required levels of mastery in a course involves having skills in more than one of these areas, usually in all of them. However, no single test should be expected to cover a complete range of skills. In order to measure and record student achievement of test objectives, the performance is described in observable terms that are active and can demonstrate learning.

Exercise 1.

Check *Yes* or *No* for each example to indicate whether or not it is an active performance.

1. Nursing Student

______ A. Records an oral temperature on a patient's chart.
______ B. Understands the need to make patients comfortable during an examination.
______ C. Selects a vein in a patient's arm from which to draw a blood sample.

2. Drama Student

______ A. Grasps the difference between theme and plot.
______ B. Knows how to operate stage lights.
______ C. Quotes the soliloquy from Hamlet.

3. Business Student

______ A. Calculates a list of expenditures.
______ B. Categorizes financial data into net and gross receipts.
______ C. Understands the procedures in compiling financial reports.

4. Chemistry Student

______ A. Appreciates the importance of safety precautions in laboratory work.
______ B. Measures specified chemicals.
______ C. Considers the composition of a chemical compound.

Performance descriptions should make clear what actions are expected of the student. Some of the examples in Exercise 1 state an active, observable performance, while others do not.

Check your response for **active performance** in Exercise 1 against the following answers:

1. Nursing Student

YES A. Records an oral temperature on a patient's chart.

NO B. Understands the need to make patients comfortable during an examination.

YES C. Selects a vein in a patient's arm from which to draw a blood sample.

2. Drama Student

NO A. Grasps the difference between theme and plot.

NO B. Knows how to operate stage lights.

YES C. Quotes the soliloquy from Hamlet.

3. Business Student

YES A. Calculates a list of expenditures.

YES B. Categorizes financial data into net and gross receipts.

NO C. Understands the procedures in compiling financial reports.

4. Chemistry Student

NO A. Appreciates the importance of safety precautions in laboratory work.

YES B. Measures specified chemicals.

NO C. Considers the composition of a chemical compound.

The terms which do *not* state action and therefore do not clarify what is expected of the student in the test are words such as:

understands, grasps (cognitively), knows, appreciates, considers.

These terms are descriptions of internal qualities which cannot be directly observed or measured. They may be appropriate as goals or outcomes of instruction, but in a performance test they could not sufficiently specify the actions to be demonstrated.

In the nursing example, *understands the need to make patients comfortable* does not specify what the student must do to demonstrate understanding. *Stating the procedural techniques which have been previously taught to ensure patient comfort* would more clearly convey an active performance.

2. Domains of Performance

Depending on the specified objectives of a test, instructors may choose to concentrate observation in one domain of learning or test student performance in all three domains: *cognitive, affective,* and *psychomotor*.

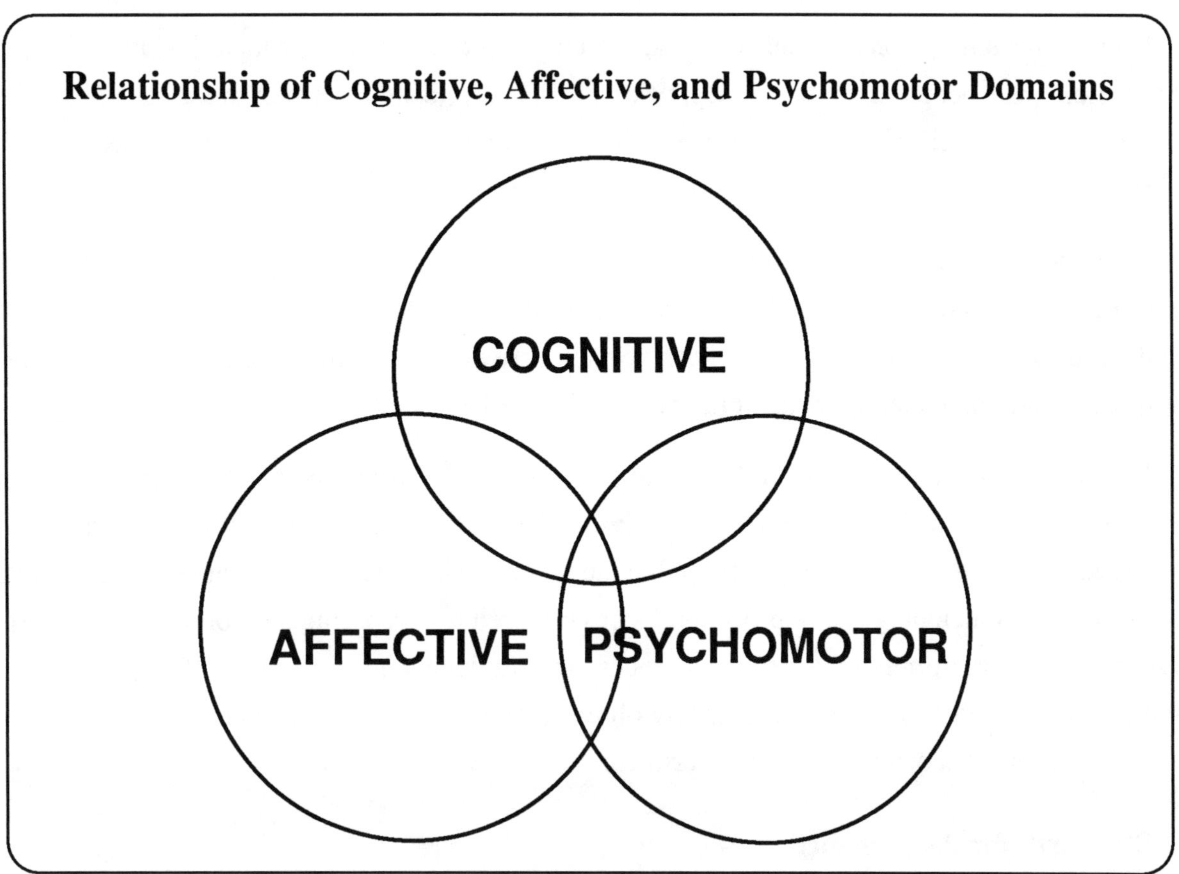

Cognitive learning is demonstrated by knowledge recall and the intellectual skills: comprehending information, organizing ideas, analyzing and synthesizing data, applying knowledge, choosing among alternatives in problem-solving, and evaluating ideas or actions.

Affective learning is demonstrated by behaviors indicating attitudes of awareness, interest, attention, concern, and responsibility, ability to listen and respond in interactions with others, and ability to demonstrate those attitudinal characteristics or values which are appropriate to the test situation and the field of study.

Psychomotor learning is demonstrated by physical skills: coordination, dexterity, manipulation, grace, strength, speed; actions which demonstrate the fine motor skills such as use of precision instruments or tools, or actions which evidence gross motor skills such as the use of the body in dance or athletic performance.

The instructor who tests the chemistry student will be concerned typically with the cognitive and psychomotor abilities of a student in performing a chemical experiment, but may also be interested in evaluating student attitudes regarding the experiment, particularly those behaviors that show concern for safety and accuracy. The psychology instructor and the history instructor may be principally concerned with observing and evaluating the attitudes of their students in role-playing.

In either the simulation of a counseling session or the process of an oral historical interview, the interaction with people demands a degree of proficiency in areas which are clearly affective. Abilities are required which demonstrate skill in listening and responding appropriately, skill in setting the client at ease, and skills of questioning which will not alienate or threaten.

There are instances where performance tests attempt to give equal emphasis to all domains of learning simultaneously. A student nurse might be tested on cognitive knowledge of giving medication to a patient; affective skill (bedside manner) evidenced in the process; and psychomotor skill using and manipulating medical instruments, as well as handling the patient physically.

In the case of a psychology student or a drama student, the instructor observes process and sequence of steps in the role-playing or activity. The business student may not necessarily be observed in the process of writing a report, but the report itself is evaluated because it demonstrates numerous skills including use of procedural steps required for preparing a report. In some cases, a test will require performing the steps in a process and producing an end product. The performance of a chemistry student may be evaluated by observation during the test and also by the quality or accuracy of the final outcome of the experiment.

3. Standards for Performance

Depending on the objectives of the test, standards for success might include some or all of the following:

- ☐ The level of accuracy required in a ***final product***, such as a written report, or the correct end product of a chemical experiment.
- ☐ The level of accuracy in performing each of the various ***steps of a process*** to be followed, such as the process of a student nurse giving medication to a patient, or a history student conducting an interview.
- ☐ The necessity for a ***proper sequence of actions*** or ***steps in a process***, as in conducting a chemical experiment or in role-playing a therapist.
- ☐ The necessity to perform the test within a ***specific time limit***, as in a physical education test in track or field sports, or in a role-playing test.

Once the objectives and tasks for learning are established, the levels of mastery required can be specified.

In the chemistry test, both the correct sequence of steps and the need for 100% accuracy in measuring could be important standards for success. The consequences of inaccuracy in measurement, or the improper order of chemicals in combination, could be dangerous. Speed or time as standards probably would not be appropriate in giving a test of this nature.

In the case of the psychology student in a role-playing situation, one realistic standard to use could be a time constraint. Psychologists usually limit their time with each client. A performance test that seeks to represent transactions between therapist and client should have a realistic time limit for the role-playing exercise.

A test should require the type of performance representing application of skills in a specified context of a practical nature. Consider a test that requires a business student to write a cost effectiveness report. The test standards should be based upon a realistic assessment of standards that, in a professional environment, govern the writing of a cost effectiveness report. The instructor, therefore, designs a procedure that instructs and then tests students in writing such a report. One performance standard might specify the accuracy required in using data for the report. Another could be the appropriate sequence of steps taken to ensure that the data will be presented in a well organized, structured format. Proper grammatical construction of the report and clarity of written expression would also be realistic standards to apply to this type of test.

Standards specify how well a student must carry out the stated performance to achieve the objectives. A standard may be singular, such as *only* accuracy or *only* speed, or multiple.

In the next exercise there are several examples of objectives which state an appropriate single standard, multiple standards, or which do not include a sufficient statement of standards.

Exercise 2.

Check each example and indicate whether the statement describes a single standard, multiple standards, or is an incomplete statement of standards.

	The student will . . .	Single Standard	Multiple Standards	Incomplete Standards
1.	Record an oral temperature on a patient's chart accurately to the nearest 1/10 of a degree.			
2.	Calculate a list of expenditures with no mathematical errors in 3 minutes.			
3.	Type 75 words per minute for 5 minutes.			
4.	Measure the following specified chemicals in equal amounts in sequence as stated in the text.			
5.	Translate (verbally) the following paragraph from English to Spanish.			
6.	Demonstrate in order the 5 specified steps required to set up audio equipment correctly for an oral interview.			

1. The standard in this example is *accurate to the nearest 1/10 of a degree*. It demands only a single standard — the accuracy of the recorded temperature.

2. The phrase *with no mathematical errors in 3 minutes* describes multiple standards of accuracy and speed.

3. In this example, the statement is incomplete. Standards of speed and time, *75 words per minute for 5 minutes* are given, but the appropriate concurrent standard of accuracy such as *with fewer than five errors*, or *with no errors*, is lacking. In this case, speed alone is not meaningful without a standard of accuracy.

4. The phrase *in equal amounts in sequence as stated in the text* describes multiple standards of accuracy and sequential order.

5. In this example, there is no statement of standards for grammar or pronunciation. A maximum time in which to translate the selection could also be an appropriate specified standard.

6. Multiple standards are stated in this example. A standard dealing with sequence is expressed by the terms *in order* and *5 specified steps*. A standard of accuracy is specified by the need to perform these actions *correctly*.

Standards are realistic when they represent situations in which skills are to be applied. In a nursing program, skills are taught based on their ultimate applied use in a hospital, clinic, doctor's office, or other professional setting. Those settings give nursing instructors guidance in determining what their students need to be able to know and do, to function competently in such situations. The subject matter and skills that are included in various types of performance tests give student nurses practice in developing skills they have studied and will be required to perform in the future.

4. Conditions for the Performance Test

The conditions for a performance test should also simulate or reflect the essential aspects of practical situations. For a chemistry student to demonstrate skill in conducting experiments, the appropriate physical setting must be available: a laboratory with necessary equipment, chemicals, and instruments requisite to the experiment. The conditions also should include any data, guidelines, or instructions which are necessary to the procedure.

For the psychology student to role-play a therapist, the physical conditions should approximate the office environment: appropriate chairs or other furniture which *set the scene* for a realistic interaction between two students as *psychologist* and *client*. The instructor will need to specify all the essential elements of the exercise, the characterization of the client, the problem which brings the client to the therapist, the purpose of the meeting, the goals of the client, the goals of the therapist, and essential information and guidelines which the students need to guide them in their interaction.

Conditions refer to *all* the elements which will enable the student to carry out the required performance in a simulated environment:

- ☐ **The appropriate physical environment**
- ☐ **The necessary equipment, materials, supplies, instruments, tools**
- ☐ **The necessary guidelines, data manuals, audiovisual media**
- ☐ **Any necessary involvement of other people**
- ☐ **The statement of the purpose of the test and performance required**
- ☐ **The statement of the standards for successful performance**

Tests in Simulated Conditions. Most performance tests take place under simulated conditions in a classroom, laboratory, learning center, gymnasium, or some other physical environment within a university. The conditions simulate situations only to the extent needed for the student to perform a particular skill or task.

Depending on the objectives of the test and the particular subject, tests may involve things or people or both. Things such as materials, instruments, equipment, or tools are often necessary. It is essentially the nature of the test objectives that dictate whether test conditions need be simple or complex, inexpensive or costly. Some tests involve highly elaborate or sophisticated simulation equipment. Courses in business make extensive use of many types of office machines to test students' skills. Medical fields, such as nursing, often use equipment and materials which replicate those items used in hospital settings.

In various types of role-playing tests, students other than the student being observed and tested may be involved. The example of the psychology role-playing exercise involves two students, only one of whom may be evaluated. In other fields, such as drama or physical education, students may be participating in testing exercises or activities which involve one or several other people who, while not being tested themselves, are an essential part of the conditions of the test.

One type of role-playing test, the *work sample* test, provides a simulation of a task or problem relevant to a particular kind of job. One example is the "in basket" test which simulates one or several tasks involving administrative decisions. The student is presented with simulated memos, letters, reports, all problem oriented, designed to assess how the student would perform in choosing among alternative courses of action. The principle behind the work sample type of test is readily transferable to other subjects, where solving a specific problem or mastery of a particular task is required.

A statement of the conditions of the test specifies the essential aids which will be available or the limitations which will be imposed on performance. Two quite different types of performances are required in view of the two different sets of conditions *italicized* below:

1. *Given a standard calculator*, the student will calculate a list of expenditures with no mathematical errors.

2. *Without the use of a calculator or other aids*, the student will calculate a list of expenditures with no mathematical errors.

Exercise 3.

In the following examples, underline those words or phrases which indicate the conditions under which the student will perform.

1. Without the use of instructions the student will correctly insert a cartridge typewriter ribbon in 2 minutes.
2. Using six previously composed questions, the student will conduct an interview lasting no longer than 30 minutes.
3. The student will play a selected piece of music on the piano with no more than three errors.
4. Given the instruments listed on the instruction sheet, and following the sequence as outlined, the student will dissect a frog leg.
5. Without the use of references, the student will compose a Haiku poem with the correct number of syllables per line.

1. The conditions are indicated by *without the use of instructions*. You may have chosen another phrase such as *in 2 minutes*. This is a standard rather than a condition.

2. In this example *using six previously composed questions* describes the conditions.

3. This example does not adequately outline the conditions; *on the piano* stipulates a partial condition, but further clarification is needed, such as *from memory* or *given sheet music*.

4. *Given the instruments listed on the instruction sheet* tells the student what aids will be provided in the conditions of the test.

5. The phrase *without the use of references* indicates the limits of the test conditions.

Tests in Natural Conditions. In some cases, simulated conditions are not necessary. Test performances take place under actual conditions in the *natural* environment. The student nurse giving medication to a patient in a hospital is being tested under *natural* conditions. The instructor in this case observes and evaluates performance in the natural environment.

In professional situations, particularly where students are dealing with other people, clients, patients, and pupils, their test performances take on special significance. Each performance of a student has consequence for other people, in ways that are lacking in test performance in the classroom. In the classroom, students are responsible only to themselves.

- ☐ In some natural test situations the student's interaction with people puts the student in a position of responsibility with others.
- ☐ The student represents a professional in that field, and must interact with others according to the standards of that profession.
- ☐ Before being placed in such a situation, each student should have been familiarized with the expected standards of conduct.

Concerns related to testing in natural conditions

(1) **The problem of reliability**: Situations in real life cannot be controlled as they can be in a classroom. An instructor who observes two student teachers in two different classrooms, or two medical interns with two different patients, is observing performance taking place under markedly different circumstances. The human variables involved cannot be controlled or replicated. Reliability is lost, but realism is gained.

- ☐ Limited control of the situation with many interfacing variables.
- ☐ Reliability is reduced as realism is gained.

(2) **The problem of instructor or observer presence**: The situation takes on an artificial quality because of the presence of the examiner. This problem can be partially overcome by observation over a period of time, so the pupils, patients, or clients involved may come to accept the presence of the examiner. In some instances, as in observing therapeutic performance, videotapes or one-way mirrors may be used instead of direct on site observation.

- ☐ Observer changes the nature of the situation.
- ☐ Acceptance of the observer may improve over a period of time.
- ☐ Videotape may be preferable to direct observation.

Summary: Domains, Standards, and Conditions

The Performance Domains

- ☐ **Can be observed and evaluated through a variety of performances: verbal; non-verbal; and fine or gross motor skills.**
- ☐ **Reveal a wide range of skills and abilities in the three domains of learning, cognitive (knowledge), affective (attitudes), and psychomotor (skills).**

The Standards

- ☐ **Reflect a practical, future situation.**
- ☐ **State the required level of the performance.**
- ☐ **State the standards for the levels of performance quality.**

The Conditions

- ☐ **State the circumstances under which the student must perform.**
- ☐ **Simulate a natural situation only to the extent required for a specified performance.**

III. GUIDELINES FOR CONSTRUCTING TESTS

Well constructed performance tests are based on assessing needs, identifying the learning tasks, writing the performance objectives, developing an evaluation plan and determining the support materials required.

1. Assess the Situation in Which Learning Will Be Applied

The situation may be in a classroom or completely beyond the instructional environment. In order to plan a well designed, predictive performance test, it is necessary to consider first the situation where future application of knowledge and skills will take place.

In the case of a beginning chemistry course, the situation to which students will transfer what they have learned is a similar laboratory facility where they will be required to conduct experiments independently and in a responsible manner. Considering the relative inexperience of students in conducting unsupervised experiments, the instructor sees the need for students to learn and be tested on a series of essential basic skills such as:

- ☐ recognizing laboratory materials and equipment
- ☐ developing attitudes which will guide them in the safe use of chemicals
- ☐ manipulating the required instruments necessary for experimentation

Unless students have mastered skills in these areas, the instructor will not assign them to unsupervised laboratory work. Instructional activities which give students practice with the required skills and a performance test which measures their levels of competence are needed. Students will need to be able to transfer the skills they have mastered to the future situation of the unsupervised laboratory.

The particular levels of knowledge, types of skills, and necessary attitudes to be assessed by a performance test can be determined effectively when the following considerations about the future situation are examined:

- ☐ The physical and human characteristics of situations to which learning is to be transferred.
- ☐ The nature of the particular field and the unique kinds of skills which are necessary for the level of competence required.
- ☐ The type of course, beginning, advanced, professional, which determines the appropriate levels of learning and skill.

Situations beyond the school may be more complex than those in a classroom, and, because of changing conditions, require continuing examination. New policies, processes, and techniques all have an impact on the future situation in which students eventually must perform. It is very easy for instructors to get out of touch with working conditions outside school. By current assessment of the situation you will be better able to specify your test objectives with reasonable assurance of their being relevant.

Turn to the **gray sheet,** page 316, and complete Items 1 and 2.

2. Identify the Learning Tasks

Test performances are comprised of many separate actions that demonstrate the various levels of skills which have been learned in a course. Analysis of the learning tasks will aid instructors in identifying the components of a performance. These can be listed in sequence as the major steps to observe and record.

In developing a description of learning tasks, you are identifying the actions to be observed in a performance test. You may want to go through the steps of a procedure yourself and itemize them, or observe a competent person perform them.

The format for describing the task may be a list or narrative summary. Below is an example of the steps to set up equipment for a filtration procedure in a chemistry laboratory.

Major steps to be performed in sequence

1. Attach ring to ring stand.
2. Place funnel in ring.
3. Place beaker below funnel.
4. Fold filter paper.
5. Place filter in funnel.
6. Wet filter with distilled water.

Such a list of steps identifies the observable performance required in the test. Next, the indicators of success are specified for the most critical steps in the process:

Major Steps	Critical Indicators
1. Attach ring to ring stand.	Clamp attached tightly
2. Place funnel in ring.	
3. Place beaker below funnel.	Tip of funnel touches side of beaker
4. Fold filter paper.	Folded in 1/2, creased folded in 1/4, creased
5. Place filter in funnel.	Open to make a funnel shape with 3 thicknesses on one side
6. Wet filter with distilled water.	Wet, but not dripping

The necessary equipment, or conditions required for the task, are now determined. The following items would be necessary to perform the example procedure.

Beaker
Ring
Ring stand
Funnel
Filter paper
Distilled water

In the previous example, all the learning activities are measurable through performance tests.

However, not all learning in an instructional sequence can be evaluated through this method. In the case of instructing students in a local history class, on the steps involved in conducting an oral history interview, not all the activities need to be, nor can be, individually observed.

Professor X teaches a course in local history and has instructed students in procedures which are necessary for planning, conducting, and following up oral interviews with local experts and resource people.

Exercise 4.

Of the instructional activities listed below, which ones would be necessary to observe directly through the use of a role-playing performance test?

Check those items which you think appropriate for inclusion:

______ 1. Establish the objectives for an interview.

______ 2. Write questions appropriate to the purpose of the interview.

______ 3. Make contact with prospective resource people to arrange an interview.

______ 4. Conduct the interview in a friendly and professional way.

______ 5. Operate audio equipment to record the interview.

______ 6. Follow up the interview with a written transcript of the process for the interview.

In a role-playing test, Items 4 and 5, *conduct the interview* and *operate audio equipment*, are the most essential skills to be directly observed. The instructor could spend time with individual students to evaluate their progress with the pre-interview planning steps 1, 2, 3, and post-interview follow-up step 6, but to observe the actual performance of these steps in a role-playing context would not be necessary.

The conduct and recording of the interview are procedures which will be expected to transfer to a real interview situation. The role-playing test will give practice with the required skills which have been taught as preparation for conducting an interview. The test will also give the instructor a direct indication of mastery of essential interviewing and recording procedures and readiness to attempt an interview outside of class.

In the case of the oral history interview, the instructor wants direct and observable evidence through the use of a performance test that students can conduct an interview *in a friendly and professional way*. How do you think students can be evaluated on criteria such as this?

Evaluating the performance of skills such as are required in an oral history interview is complex. What is *a friendly and professional way*? This type of standard is open to much more interpretation than, the requirement in the previous example, that the filter paper be *folded in half*. It is possible and appropriate to stipulate standards for friendly and professional interviewing in a role-playing test. The critical issue in requiring a demonstration of necessary attitudes is the coverage of these requirements during instruction. You and your students must establish common understanding as to ways that these attitudes and indicator behaviors can be identified and subsequently demonstrated. These should be discussed, agreed upon, and practiced with as much emphasis as is necessary, for successful performance.

Turn to the **gray sheet**, page 316, and complete Item 3.

3. Write the Performance Objectives

(a) Specify the Performance: State what the student must do in the test situation in terms which are active, observable, and measurable. The performance must demonstrate the student's knowledge and skill learned through prior instructional activities. It is critical to use *action* verbs to describe what is expected in mastery of the objectives. For example, the chemistry instructor has set a goal for students to be able to recognize the equipment and materials in the laboratory as the first step toward using this equipment in an experiment. To ask that they *recognize*, does not describe what they must *do* to demonstrate that recognition. In the objective, they should be asked to name, list, or label the equipment and materials. Thc processes of naming, listing, or labeling involve actions, oral or written, which the instructor can observe.

The instructor also wants to know that the students have developed attitudes of safety and caution in working with the laboratory equipment and supplies. The instructor must therefore list the kinds of actions which will indicate that those attitudes are present. Behavior indicators would include *return* the chemicals to a central area, or *turn off* gas burners, or *wipe up* any spilled chemicals, or *replace* all lids or stoppers on containers.

Following are four lists of action verbs ranging from simple to complex which depict knowledge, attitude, and physical processes. Some verbs state physical action specifically whereas others may need further qualification to indicate observable action, such as in writing, expressing orally, or pointing out.

Action Verbs for Performance Objectives			
1.	**2.**	**3.**	**4.**
grasp	**arrange**	**anticipate**	**adapt**
insert	**categorize**	**calculate**	**devise**
label	**compare**	**construct**	**diagnose**
list	**characterize**	**design**	**compose**
measure	**isolate**	**illustrate**	**create**
quote	**match**	**interpret**	**invent**
record	**order**	**organize**	**resolve**
set	**rank**	**solve**	**synthesize**
turn	**select**	**translate**	**predict**

(b) Specify the Standards: State the standards for the test performance in terms which describe how well the student must perform in regard to speed, accuracy or correct sequence of actions.

The student nurse who is giving medication to a patient is expected to follow *a sequence of steps in the specified order*: remove old bandage, clean infected area, medicate the area, apply a new bandage.

Standards are included in the objectives by using phrases such as:

- ☐ in sequential order
- ☐ accurate to the nearest 1/4 inch
- ☐ within five minutes
- ☐ with no errors in calculation
- ☐ including at least four of six possible factors
- ☐ in a friendly professional manner

(c) Specify the Conditions: State the conditions in your test objectives that delineate the circumstances under which the student performs. If there are any aids or equipment to be used, these must be stated. Similarly, if any limitations are imposed on performance, they also need to be described to the student. The conditions clarify for the student exactly what will be available or unavailable in carrying out the expected performance.

Conditions are stated in descriptive phrases, such as:

- ☐ given a valence chart
- ☐ given a calculator
- ☐ without the aid of notes
- ☐ using a driving simulator
- ☐ given a manual of procedures

Turn to the **gray sheet**, page 317, and complete Item 4.

4. Develop Evaluation Plan and Format

Determine What to Observe: A performance test is designed to measure mastery of process skills and final outcome or product. Process evaluation concentrates on observing the quality or accuracy of the steps or procedures in the performance. Product evaluation focuses primarily on the end result or outcome of the performance. Most performances lend themselves to an evaluation of both process and product.

In nursing education, for example, students may be tested and evaluated for both process and product in situations that involve patient care. If test objectives deal with evaluating the rapport of the student with the patient, *bedside manner*, there is clearly no material product involved. Evaluation may be on actions of the student such as: how the medical procedures about to take place with the patient are explained; how clearly questions raised by the patient are answered; what steps are taken to ensure the comfort of the patient.

The product in this case is the outcome or result of the *bedside manner* process: Are the procedures clear to the patient? Have all questions been adequately answered? Is the patient comfortable? There may be a concurrent process and product evaluation in view of the purposes of the examination. If a student is drawing a blood sample from a patient, there are steps involved in that procedure that may be examined for accuracy and sequence. In addition, the blood sample itself is a result of the test and can be measured by standards such as: Was the proper amount of blood drawn? Was it too much or too little, or the exact amount specified in the test?

As with all types of testing, students must be clearly informed in advance of the standards by which they will be evaluated.

Exercise 5.

Each of the following descriptors refers to a test situation in a History course. Stephen is a student role-playing an oral history interview with another student, Susan. These are some of the things the instructor has observed. By checking the appropriate box, identify those descriptions which would be evaluated on the basis of process and those considerations which would be examined as results, outcomes, or products.

		Process	Product
1.	Stephen listens attentively to the responses Susan gives to the questions he has asked.		
2.	He turns the tape recorder on to record, but does not check to see if the microphone is picking up sound before he begins the interview.		
3.	Stephen asks questions which are clear, concise and well thought out.		
4.	As the interview is coming to a close, Susan says she has enjoyed being interviewed and was glad to cooperate.		
5.	As Stephen plays back the tape he finds that the microphone has barely picked up the sound of Susan's voice.		

In this exercise, Items 1, 2, and 3 illustrate the *process* which is occurring during the interview. Stephen's actions are indicating his level of mastery of the various kinds of appropriate interviewing procedures he has been taught. By listening attentively and asking clear and concise questions, he is more likely to ensure the *outcome* exemplified by Item 4: Susan's expression of her willingness to cooperate.

In Item 2, Stephen leaves out an important step in the process of setting up his recording equipment, the *result* or *product* is described in Item 5.

Keep in mind that your students need to be aware of the importance of *both* process and product standards. Consider the chemistry student who achieves the objective of measuring and combining chemicals correctly to produce a specified result but goes about the procedures in a disorganized manner, spilling chemicals, failing to follow the proper sequence of tasks, and leaving the work area in chaos. The end result of the test could be acceptable, but the process which the student followed to achieve it would not be. For the instructor to evaluate the total performance, standards dealing with both process and product need to be specified.

Regardless of the type of performance or the subject matter, tests must be developed to measure performance accurately and objectively by the standards established. Evaluation is by observation, a method not commonly used to assess student performance in traditional group testing situations. The instructor can evaluate or give instructions for improvement immediately following the test, while the student is still involved and motivated. The performance objectives and learning tasks should guide instructors in the determination of what skills are most important to observe and measure. Observation should be confined to those types of behavior or skill which cannot otherwise be adequately evaluated. A limited number of observable tasks in any one test situation should be considered, both for the sake of the instructor who must observe and the student who must perform.

Decide Whether to Record Performance: The test performance can be recorded relatively easily on audio or videotape. Through this process, at a later time or in a different place, the performance can be evaluated with the student or by a group of reviewers. The choice of a medium for recording the performance should be based upon the nature of the performance. If the performance is entirely verbal, as in an interview or speech making situation, then recording on audio tape can be satisfactory.

If visual factors are important, as in human interaction or manipulative skills, then the recording should be on videotape.

Select Method to Record Observations: The types of measurement instruments commonly used in performance testing are of three major types:

- ☐ **Checklists**
- ☐ **Rating scales**
- ☐ **Anecdotal records**

Each type has advantages and disadvantages. The performance, the subject matter, the particular situation and needs of each instructor and the students should indicate which type or types of instruments to use.

Checklists offer only two options, *yes/no*, or *done/not done*. Checklists can be used effectively to observe steps in a procedure or specific isolated actions necessary for successful performance. Checklists are used to assess whether an action was or was not taken. They cannot, however, help the instructor assess the quality of an action as can a rating scale which differentiates levels of acceptable performance.

In developing checklists, the following points may serve as guidelines.

- ☐ Each of the potential actions in performance should be described in specific terms.
- ☐ Common errors in performance, if clearly identifiable, may be designated on a checklist.
- ☐ The appropriate actions or potential errors should be arranged sequentially on the checklist to aid the observer in following the performance.

An Example Checklist Format for Recording Test Performance

Student: ____________________

Instructor: ____________________

Date: ____________

Test Objective: ____________________

Major tasks or skills listed in sequence to be performed	**Performed** Yes	No
1.____________________	______	______
2.____________________	______	______
3.____________________	______	______
4.____________________	______	______
5.____________________	______	______

Rating scales can provide a method by which a specific value is attached to a performance, and the degree of proficiency at a given task can be assessed. The usefulness of a rating scale depends on the clarity of the relationship between the objectives and the behavior under observation. Only behaviors which can be observed and rated objectively should be considered for inclusion in a rating scale.

There are some limitations to using rating scales. Personal bias of the rater may affect the rating. Some observers tend to rate all students alike, whether high, average, or low.

Rating scales have several different formats. The numerical scale is commonly used in many educational settings. Numerical value is assigned to descriptive characteristics or standards of performance, from low to high, such as:

Unacceptable (0). **Acceptable with corrections (l).** **Acceptable (2).**

While descriptive terms like *average*, *above average*, *below average*, *superior*, or *unsatisfactory* are often used, they are more suitable for norm or group referenced tests than individual performance tests. In performance tests, students should not be judged against each other, but against identified standards for performance.

The rating scale should use descriptive phrases which differentiate between achieved levels of a particular behavior essential for successful completion of a task. A rating scale for a business role-playing test involving tasks of supervisory abilities might include these phrases:

- ☐ Individual receives little cooperation from co-workers; work progress blocked.
- ☐ Individual receives adequate cooperation from co-workers; enables work to proceed.
- ☐ Individual receives full support from co-workers; work proceeds with high morale.

For a Discussion Leader a rating scale could use these phrases:

- ☐ Leader has participants respond to the questions raised.
- ☐ Leader has individuals develop and ask questions spontaneously.
- ☐ Leader has the group interacting with its own questions and responses.

Construction Guidelines for Rating Scales

- ☐ The objectives should serve as guides for inclusion of characteristics which are deemed relevant to the performance.
- ☐ The acceptable or unacceptable nature of performance must be consistent with the stated standards for success.
- ☐ Those behaviors which are rated must be suitable for conversion into a scale.
- ☐ Scales themselves should contain a minimum of three points of differentiation and a maximum of seven.
- ☐ If critical, performance should be rated by more than one observer to provide reliable assessment.
- ☐ The listed description of tasks must be clear and concise. Terms that may be interpreted differently where more than one rater is involved, should be avoided.

An Example of a Rating Scale for Recording Performance

Student: ____________________ **0 = Unacceptable**

Instructor: ____________________ **1 = Acceptable, with corrections**

Date: ______________ **2 = Acceptable**

Major skills or procedures listed in sequence to be performed	Rating	Necessary corrections
1	0 1 2	
2	0 1 2	
3	0 1 2	
4	0 1 2	
5	0 1 2	
6	0 1 2	
7	0 1 2	
8	0 1 2	

Any performance can be evaluated through the use of either a checklist or a rating scale. However, depending on the complexity of a performance and the levels or distinctions of acceptability which you think necessary to consider, you may find that one type of measure is preferable over the other.

Exercise 6.

In the examples below, indicate by checking the appropriate box whether the use of a checklist or a rating scale would be most advantageous.

	Checklist	Rating Scale
1. Fold filter paper correctly for a chemical procedure.	______	______
2. Establish and maintain a friendly and professional manner in an oral interview.	______	______
3. Record accurately an oral temperature on a patient's chart.	______	______
4. Present a dramatic interpretation of Hamlet's soliloquy.	______	______
5. Calculate correctly a column of figures.	______	______
6. Compose a Haiku with the correct number of syllables.	______	______
7. Explain to a patient the examination procedures about to take place.	______	______

Items 2, 4, and 7 could involve many degrees or levels of acceptability. These performances would be most meaningfully evaluated by using a rating scale.

Items 5 and 6, call for a correct solution to a mathematical calculation and the correct number of syllables used in composing a poem. A checklist would be appropriate to indicate how the correct answer was calculated, or the correct number of syllables was used. However, if the aesthetic quality of the Haiku composition were to be considered in addition to its technical structure, a rating scale would be more appropriate to use.

While Items 1 and 3 might possibly be measured according to degrees of acceptability by using a rating scale, these items could be adequately evaluated by a checklist.

Anecdotal Records provide an open ended instrument to observe, describe, and evaluate performance in narrative fashion. When used over a considerable period to evaluate representative kinds of performance, anecdotal records can be useful as cumulative performance data. Problems which may arise in using anecdotal records center mainly on difficulties in obtaining enough samples of performance to be representative. Narrative evaluation is time consuming and often impractical with large numbers of students.

Instructor bias may occur when using this format. The actual recording of behavior must be completely factual and kept separate from interpretations and recommendations. Instructors must consider why they are observing a particular behavior and how assessment and evaluation of that behavior will contribute to the student's accomplishment of the instructional objectives. Narrative evaluation does not mean making value judgments. Narrative measures have the same need for objectivity as other measurement devices.

Following is a list of suggestions for using anecdotal records:

- ☐ A determination of *what* behaviors will be observed and *why* should be decided upon and prepared in advance. This step is essential to aid the instructor in focusing attention on the specific and most important behaviors in the test situation.
- ☐ In order to produce reliable evaluative statements, performance should be observed over a period of time in relevant context situations.
- ☐ Anecdotal information should be written down during or immediately following the testing process.
- ☐ Anecdotal observations must be concise and specific. Usually, only one incident or task at a time should be observed and evaluated in a narrative format.
- ☐ A description of the behavior or performance should be recorded separately from any interpretations or recommendations.

An Example of the Anecdotal Format

Student:________________ **Instructor:**____________________ **Date:**______

Test Objective:

Behavior Observed:

Interpretation:

Recommendations:

Overall Assessment:

_____ **Acceptable** _____ **Acceptable with corrections** _____ **Unacceptable**

5. Determine Materials Required

Depending on the nature of the test, the appropriate use of equipment and materials and/or the involvement of other people may be necessary. For the purposes of your test, you might determine a need for some or all of the following:

- ☐ Guidelines or data necessary for problem solving
- ☐ Technical manuals
- ☐ Audiovisual media
- ☐ Materials, supplies
- ☐ Instruments, tools
- ☐ Equipment, real or simulated
- ☐ Involvement of other people

All items necessary for testing should be determined in advance, then organized and made available in a consistent way for each student who takes the test.

Construction Guidelines Summary

1. **Assess the situation in which learning will be applied.**
2. **Identify the learning tasks.**
3. **Write the performance objectives.**
4. **Develop evaluation plan format.**
5. **Determine appropriate materials required.**

Turn to the **gray sheets**, pages 317 and 318, and complete Items 5 and 6.

IV. GUIDELINES FOR USING PERFORMANCE TESTS

1. Be Consistent and Clear

Every performance test requires a form of written instructions, guidelines, or directions for students who take the test or for other instructors who may administer the test. The instructions should clearly and consistently state identical information for each student.

- ☐ The objectives that the student is expected to accomplish.
- ☐ The standards for success in terms of accuracy, sequence, or speed.
- ☐ The conditions under which the student will take the test, with what materials and under what limitations.
- ☐ A checklist of all items which are to be used in the test can further help to clarify administration.

It may be helpful to prepare a brief media presentation, such as an audio tape or an audiovisual aid which delineates the instructions or guidelines for the test. This information in a media format can be presented to the class as a whole or to each individual at the time of the test. This method provides consistent directions and relieves the instructor from verbally stating instructions for each individual taking the test. Any discussion or clarification should be conducted with the entire class, rather than with individual students, thereby establishing necessary consistency and equity.

When test situations demand the use of supplies or equipment, it is necessary to ensure:

- ☐ A consistent set-up for the test, as in the case of a lab experiment, so that each student begins with identical items displayed in identical fashion.
- ☐ Equipment is in working order; check that tape recorders, typewriters, and microscopes are operational.
- ☐ Sufficient expendable supplies so that the student will not run out of the necessary chemicals, paper, or other usable items during the test.

2. Anticipate Common Problems

There are several additional items of concern in administering individualized tests:

The possibility of bias: Observational bias may occur on the part of the instructor. Often superior or inadequate past performance of individuals, *halo effect*, can influence observation.

Circumstances such as whether or not the instructor knows the student well or is favorably or unfavorably disposed toward him or her can also influence rating. It is not possible to be totally unbiased when dealing with individuals in all circumstances. Because of the circumstances of the test situation and the nature of an evaluative relationship between instructor and student, it is important for instructors to be aware of the possible factors other than student performance that can influence assessment.

The problem of multiple observation: If several instructors may be observing test performance, there must be consensus among them on all major aspects of the test, such as the clarity of the objectives, the most critical skills in the test, the specificity of criteria for success, the method of observing and the format for recording performance. By determining consensus on these points well in advance of test administration, instructors can ensure consistency among observers, thereby enhancing reliability.

The problem of memory error: Unless all pertinent observations are recorded at the time of the test, instructors may overlook or forget important aspects of performance. In order to give an accurate and meaningful critique to each student, a systematic method of recording the anecdotal record, checklist, or rating scale, needs to be used consistently.

The difficulty in providing adequate feedback: In order for the student to improve skills assessed by the test, it is essential to give clear information about the performance. Often, and desirably, a critique of the performance is discussed with the student at the conclusion of the test, covering:

- ☐ the overall acceptability of the performance
- ☐ the strong aspects of the performance and the positive accomplishments revealed during the test
- ☐ the skills or steps which need correction or further work
- ☐ the specific methods to improve necessary skills or techniques

Turn to the **gray sheet**, page 318, and complete Item 7.

V. SUMMARY OUTLINE

I. TYPES AND PURPOSES

Types range through all areas of curriculum

Purposes

- Measure individual competence against a specific standard
- Provide feedback regarding progress in learning
- Predict success in future situations

II. KEY FEATURES

Observable performance — verbal, non-verbal, fine and gross motor skills

Domains of performance — cognitive, affective, psychomotor

Standards for performance — level of accuracy, steps, sequence, timing

Conditions for the performance test — simulated, natural circumstances

III. GUIDELINES FOR CONSTRUCTING TESTS

Assess the situation in which learning will be applied

Identify the learning tasks

Write the performance objectives

- Specify the performance
- Specify the standards
- Specify the conditions

Develop evaluation plan and format

- Determine what to observe
- Decide whether to record the performance
- Select the method to record observations
  with checklist, rating scales, anecdotal records

Determine materials required

IV. GUIDELINES FOR USING PERFORMANCE TESTS

Be consistent and clear

Anticipate common problems

- Bias
- Multiple observation
- Memory error
- Feedback difficulties

REFERENCES AND RESOURCES

Bloom, Benjamin S., George F. Madaus, and J. Thomas Hastings. **Evaluation to Improve Learning.** New York: McGraw-Hill Book Company, 1981.

Brown, Frederick G. **Principles of Educational and Psychological Testing.** (3rd ed.) New York: Holt, Rinehart and Winston, 1983.

Cangelosi, James S. **Evaluating Student Achievement.** White Plains, NY: Longman, 1990.

Erickson, Richard C. and Tim L. Wentling. **Measuring Student Growth.** Boston: Allyn and Bacon Inc., 1976.

Gay, L. R. **Educational Evaluation and Measurement.** (2nd ed.) Columbus, OH: Charles E. Merrill Publishing Company, 1985.

Gronlund, N. E. and Robert L. Linn. **Measurement and Evaluation in Teaching**. (6th ed.) New York: Macmillan, 1990.

Hopkins, Kenneth D., Julian C. Stanley, and B.R. Hopkins. **Educational and Psychological Measurement and Evaluation.** (7th ed.) Englewood Cliffs, NJ: Prentice-Hall Inc., 1990.

Popham, W. James. **Modern Educational Measurement.** (2nd ed.) Englewood Cliffs, NJ: Prentice-Hall Inc., 1990.

Sax, Gilbert. **Principles of Educational and Psychological Measurement and Evaluation.** (3rd ed.) Belmont, CA: Wadsworth Publishing Company, 1989.

VI. APPLICATION EXERCISE

1. State the particular competency or skill to be tested in your performance test.

____

____

____

2. What is the future situation in which the students will need to make use of the skills to be assessed by the test?

____

____

____

____

3. State (a) the learning tasks and major steps to be performed, and
   (b) the standards or critical indicators of successful performance.

Major Steps in the Learning Task	Critical Indicators of Success

4. Write the objectives:

a. State what the student must do in active terms. (the performance)

____

____

____

b. State how well, to what standard, the student must perform.

____

____

____

c. State the conditions under which the performance will be carried out.

____

____

____

5. Select the format you will use to observe the performance. Based on the type of format chosen (1. checklist, 2. rating scale, or 3. anecdotal record), outline all information which will be necessary for inclusion on your observational record.

6. List materials, equipment, or supplies which will be necessary to use as part of the conditions of the test. Outline any necessary involvement of other people such as in the role-playing test.

7. Using Your Test:

By reviewing steps 1-6 above, write instructions for your test which will give students all appropriate information to proceed to take the test.

DEVELOPING OPINION, INTEREST, AND ATTITUDE QUESTIONNAIRES

Module Developers:	Philip C. Seyer Carole R. Smith Ron J. McBeath
Editorial Associates:	Oswald B. Carleton Jerrold E. Kemp Jeanne Lassen
Editorial Consultant:	Richard B. Lewis

DEVELOPING OPINION, INTEREST, AND ATTITUDE QUESTIONNAIRES

The objective of this module is to help you develop and use questionnaires to measure student opinions, interests, and attitudes. The module is organized in the following sections:

I. PURPOSES

Before you start developing a questionnaire, decide what kind of information you want to gather regarding students' opinions, attitudes, and interests. Are you looking for information about course requirements or lecture style? Perhaps you want an indication of their interest levels for class activities or a general appraisal of the attitudes held and being developed.

Turn to **gray sheet**, page 346. There are a number of questions under five categories to help you decide what you want to find out from your students. Read them and put a check mark beside any that are relevant to your needs. If you have other questions, for which you would like to obtain responses from your students, write them in the spaces provided under the headings or as separate items at the bottom of the page. As you go through this module, you'll be developing questionnaire items based on these questions.

After deciding what you want to find out, the next step is to select an appropriate format for your questionnaire items. Two categories of formats are described in this module, **fixed response**, and **open response**.

II. FIXED RESPONSE FORMATS

The six formats described in this section include **Adjective Checklists**, **Behavior Checklists**, **General Rating Scale**, **Likert Scale**, **Semantic Differential**, and **Ranking**.

CHECKLISTS

Two basic forms for fixed response format questionnaires are the adjective checklist and the behavior checklist.

Adjective Checklist

A number of adjectives which might express student feelings about a topic or assignment are placed in a checklist. Students are asked to indicate their feelings by underlining or circling their choices.

Underline the words that come close to telling how you feel about the topic . . .

unnecessary	easy
needed	exciting
stimulating	far out
too difficult	right on
too easy	dumb
useful	worthless
useless	boring

Circle each word that tells how you feel about the group projects and oral presentations . . .

interesting	clear
dull	frustrating
exciting	difficult
boring	useful
informative	stimulating
practical	unpleasant
worthless	important

Student responses to an adjective checklist can give the instructor an indication of class feelings about the assignment. This type of checklist is relatively simple to construct. It includes a set of directions and a list of adjectives. The list should consist of 12-15 adjectives that describe possible reactions in terms of the subject being treated. It should use an equal number of positive and negative words in random order.

Guidelines for Writing an Adjective Checklist

1. State directions clearly, indicate the subject and types of responses desired.
2. Include 12–15 adjectives.
3. Use an equal number of positive and negative adjectives in random order.

Turn to **gray sheet**, page 346. Pick a suitable topic for the questions you checked or wrote in. On the **gray sheet**, page 347, complete Exercise A and develop an adjective checklist.

Note the main difference between the adjective checklist examples on the previous page and the behavior checklist below.

Behavior Checklist

During the last semester which of these things, if any, have you done?

______ Used Reader's Guide to Periodical Literature to find a magazine or journal article.

______ Asked a librarian for help in locating a book.

______ Checked out at least one reserved book overnight.

______ Made a copy of one or more pages from a journal article.

______ Used the library for leisure reading.

______ Skimmed or studied material on microfiche.

The difference which is specially significant is that the behavior checklist asks students to describe what they have *done* rather than to indicate how they *feel.* This technique is valuable because the presence or absence of behaviors often gives a strong indication of student interests or attitudes.

Guidelines for Writing Behavior Checklists

1. Specify the time period for the behavior, when appropriate.

2. Specify the behavior in concrete terms so there is no doubt about what you mean.

Exercise 1.

Here are two different ways to phrase the introduction to a behavior checklist. Which one follows the *first* guideline?

______ A. How many books have you read recently on each of these topics?

______ B. During the last semester, how many books did you read on each of these topics?

B is the better answer, because it clearly specifies the time period in which the behavior has happened.

Exercise 2.

Which one of these follows the second guideline for writing behavior checklists?

______ A. During the past 7 days, which of these exercises have you done at least once a day?

______ Sit ups (10 repetitions minimum)

______ Jumping jacks (20 repetitions)

______ 1 mile jog

______ B. Have you had any exercise during the past 7 days?

A follows the second guideline because it names the specific behaviors. In **B** the word *exercise* is probably subject to too many interpretations. One student may consider walking a block as exercise, while another may not consider exercise as anything less than a two mile jog.

Turn to **gray sheet**, page 347, and write a behavior checklist item for students in one of your classes. You may wish to make up a checklist that would enable you to interpret the students' attitude toward your subject matter or perhaps measure their interest in some topic. Refer again to the questions you marked on **gray sheet**, page 346. Examine your behavior checklist item in terms of the guidelines. Did you specify the time period clearly? Did you define the behavior in precise measurable terms? If not, make any needed corrections.

Scoring Checklists

Students can be asked to fill out an adjective checklist both *before* and *after* their involvement in a new topic. A Sociology professor who was concerned about how student attitudes would be affected by the inclusion of a controversial topic in a course obtained the following results from a checklist.

Underline the words that express your feelings about studying the problems relating to the expansion of the Municipal Airport.

	Before	After
unnecessary	20%	15%
useful	5%	5%
useless	40%	60%
important	15%	20%
challenging	10%	15%
waste of time	20%	20%
unimportant	25%	25%
practical	10%	15%
boring	20%	30%
informative	15%	20%

The instructor felt that students were not impressed with this topic as an urban problem and that their attitudes were not appreciably influenced by the lectures. The next semester, the instructor treated the same topic, but now involved students in active participation to a greater degree by including a community survey and a role-playing simulation activity. Again, the adjective checklist was used both as a pre-unit and post-unit measure of student feelings with these results.

1st and 2nd Semester Results Comparison

Underline the words that express your feelings about studying the problems relating to the expansion of the Municipal Airport.

	First Semester		Second Semester	
	Before	**After**	**Before**	**After**
unnecessary	20%	15%	30%	5%
useful	5%	5%	5%	35%
useless	40%	60%	40%	5%
important	15%	20%	10%	50%
challenging	10%	15%	10%	65%
waste of time	20%	20%	30%	5%
unimportant	25%	25%	30%	10%
practical	10%	15%	10%	40%
boring	20%	30%	20%	0%
informative	15%	20%	20%	50%

It is clear that student responses were much more significant in the second semester and indicated a definite shift in attitude. By using the checklist, the instructor recognized that the change in the learning experiences was productive.

Adjective and Behavior Checklists:

Advantages	**Simple to design.** **Easy to use.**
Limitations	**Little room to express degrees of interest, attitude, or opinion.**

RATING SCALES

The next type of fixed response format includes two Rating Scales. First is the **General Rating Scale** which can include any number of rating points; second is the **Likert Scale**, which is a five point scale.

General Rating Scale

By giving students a scale they are not forced to commit themselves to a black and white decision, but are allowed to pick a point on a continuum; this is the chief advantage of a rating scale. This rating scale has a list of *activities,* and students are to rate the activities on a scale from 1 to 4.

General Rating Scale - Activities

Show how interesting you found each of these learning activities. 1 = never interesting 2 = sometimes interesting 3 = frequently interesting 4 = always interesting				
	1	**2**	**3**	**4**
Theatre Games				
Watching Films				
Field Trip 1				
Field Trip 2				
Role-Playing				
Group Discussions				
Debates				
Computer Simulation				

Other topics may be rated. The next example is a three point scale that rates *materials.* In the subsequent example, students are asked to rate *conditions* on a four-point scale.

General Rating Scale—Materials

For this unit, indicate how helpful you feel each of these instructional materials was by checking the appropriate column opposite each item.

	Ratings		
	Very Helpful	**Somewhat Helpful**	**Not Especially Helpful**
Instructional handouts			
Study guide			
Text			
Outside reading			
Audio tape			
Interactive Video			

General Rating Scale—Conditions

Foreign students give these reasons for dissatisfaction with their stay in the USA. Indicate their importance to you.	**Importance**			
	Great	**Some**	**Little**	**Zero**
Separation from family.				
Missing opportunities to converse in native language.				
Eating strange foods.				
Absence of contact with close friends.				
General feeling of being homesick.				
Lack of familiar sports events.				

The Likert Rating Scale

A commonly used rating scale for opinion, interests, and attitudes is the Likert scale. Rensis Likert, a psychologist, first developed this scale for research in attitude assessment. The key feature of the Likert scale is that it asks students to rate various statements, using a *five point* rating scale, ranging from *strongly agree* to *strongly disagree.* This procedure to *identify the level* of agreement is a key feature of the **Likert Scale.**

Read each statement about this course carefully. Show to what extent you agree or disagree with it by checking the proper column.

	Strongly Agree	**Agree**	**Not Sure**	**Disagree**	**Strongly Disagree**
A. This course is poorly organized.					
B. The course topics are relevant.					

Complete Exercise C on **gray sheet**, page 348. Refer to your list of questions on **gray sheet,** page 346, to help you think of appropriate opinion, interest, or attitude statements.

Guidelines for Writing Statements for a Likert Rating Scale

☐ **Write Statements Containing Only One Thought.**

Exercise 3.

Here are two ways to write items for a rating scale. Which version do you prefer?

______ A. The topics in this course are interesting and relevant.

______ B. (1) The topics in this course are interesting.

______ (2) The topics in this course are relevant.

The preferable version is **B**, because *each statement contains a single idea.* If the item is written as in **A**, students will have difficulty responding if they feel the topics were interesting but not relevant, or relevant but not interesting.

☐ **Use Familiar Words and Phrases.**

Exercise 4.

Look at these two statements. Decide which phrasing you prefer.

______ A. Students receive sufficient opportunities to contribute to curriculum design with respect to this course.

______ B. Students have enough say in planning this course.

Statement **B** is preferred because in it *familiar words and phrases are used.*

Exercise 5.

Here are two methods for generating attitude statements. Which might be preferable?

______ A. Make up various statements from your own experience.

______ B. Use tape recordings of student discussions to generate statements.

B is preferred, it draws more directly on the experience of the students and provides the actual words they use. Allow extra time for the development of this type of statement.

☐ **Avoid Proverbs and Clichés.**

Exercise 6.

Here is another pair of attitude statements. Pick the one you prefer.

______ A.The early bird gets the worm.

______ B.I found it helpful to finish my self-paced study early.

The meaning of a proverb is often ambiguous and may be unthinkingly accepted or agreed to by some students. **B** is the preferable statement.

☐ **Write Short, Concise Statements.**

Exercise 7.

Which statement do you prefer?

______ A. I find Prof. Brown's language easy to understand.

______ B. The type of language utilized by Prof. Brown, in the enlightening lectures he presents to the class, is completely comprehensible.

Statement **A** is more concise than **B**. The general rule is write short, concise statements.

As a rule of thumb, try to limit yourself to a maximum of 15 words per sentence. After you write an attitude statement, read it over again to see how many words you can eliminate without destroying the meaning. If you are in doubt about whether a word or phrase is needed in an attitude statement, leave it out.

☐ **Include an Equal Number of Positive and Negative Statements.**

Exercise 8.

Examine the statements in the table below in terms of their order and the proportion of positive to negative statements. Write your comments below.

	Strongly Agree	Agree	Not Sure	Disagree	Strongly Disagree
1. The presentation was well organized.					
2. The visuals helped me to learn.					
3. The handouts were relevant to the presentation.					
4. The objectives were clear.					
5. The quiz was fair.					
6. I felt free to ask questions.					
7. The time seemed to drag.					
8. I wish I had skipped class.					

Comments:____

____

____

In Exercise 8 there are six positive statements and only two negative ones. To ensure that a scale is well balanced, *have an equal number of positive and negative statements.*

☐ Randomize the Placement of Positive and Negative Statements.

One problem in Exercise 8 is that all of the positive statements are grouped together. To prevent students from developing a fixed pattern of responding, *randomize the placement of pro and con statements.*

☐ Assess Usefulness of Statements by Watching Student Reactions.

In addition to following these guidelines, you may tell when you have written useful attitude statements by *watching* students' *responses* while they are completing the questionnaire.

Exercise 9.

Which of these shows that you have written useful attitude statements?

______ a. Some students skip certain items.

______ b. Some students cross out certain items and refuse to answer them.

The answer is ***neither*** situation indicates useful items. If students are skipping items or crossing them off, it shows the items are not relating well to their opinions, interests, or attitudes.

Exercise 10.

Which of these shows that you have written useful attitude statements?

______ a. In talking to you, students say such things as: "I bet you got these statements from John; he's always saying things like this." (John is a well-known, outspoken student.)

______ b. Students seem eager to give you more information or examples related to certain statements.

Both situations show that you have written useful items. If students recognize the wording you have used, it is a sign that you have written in a style to which they can easily relate. If students seem eager to give you more information, you have evidently written items that have stimulated them to think, and that interest them.

Exercise 11.

Which of these shows that you have written useful attitude statements?

______ a. Students quietly fill out the questionnaire and have little to say about it when you bring it up for discussion.

______ b. In discussing the questionnaire, students say it doesn't relate to their interests.

Neither of these situations shows you have written useful attitude statements. Ideally you want students to be stimulated by responding to the attitude statements and to be eager to discuss the issues involved.

Exercise 12.

Which of these shows that you have written useful attitude statements?

_______ a. A large percentage of students (over 25%) pick *uncertain* or *don't know.*

_______ b. Students seem excited by some statements with which they strongly agree or disagree.

The situation described in **b** is desirable. If students get excited as a result of responding to attitude statements, it is because you have written statements that are on target and about issues students consider significant.

If a large percentage of students have a neutral position on an issue, it is likely the item you have written fails to differentiate among students' attitudes.

Review the guidelines for preparing rating scale statements below. Turn to **gray sheet**, page 348, and examine the rating scale statements you wrote in Exercise C. Make any necessary changes.

Guidelines Summary: Rating Scales

- ☐ **Write statements containing only one thought.**
- ☐ **Use familiar words and phrases.**
- ☐ **Avoid proverbs and clichés.**
- ☐ **Write short, concise statements.**
- ☐ **Include equal numbers of positive and negative statements.**
- ☐ **Randomize the placement of positive and negative statements.**
- ☐ **Assess usefulness of statements by watching student reactions.**

Interpreting Rating Scale Responses.

Numerical values can be assigned for scoring favorable statements on a 5—1 weighting, going from *strongly agree* to *strongly disagree*. For unfavorable statements weights must be reversed. An individual's score is a total of all the items and a high score generally indicates a favorable attitude.

Exercise 13.

Suppose you have a Likert scale with ten items. If you use a five point scale, the possible total scores for a single student would range from 10 to 50. Suppose two students have a score of 30. Which statement below is true?

______ a. Both students have about the same attitude.

______ b. Both students feel more or less neutral toward the attitude statements.

______ c. Both

______ d. Neither

The answer is **d.** Neither explanation **a** nor **b** is correct. To find a student's total score on a rating scale, you merely sum his responses to all the items. The interpretation of the total high and low scores is usually clear: a low score shows an unfavorable attitude; a high score, a favorable attitude. However, scores falling in the middle are more difficult to interpret because they can be achieved in different ways: a student may take a neutral position on most or all of the items, or may take a strongly favorable position on some items and strongly unfavorable position on other items. A neutral score resulting from balancing of pro and con judgments may mean that the total score is a combination of two scores relating to *two* quite different attitudes. On the other hand, a neutral score resulting from a consistent checking of *unsure* may mean the student doesn't care one way or another, is simply undecided or uninformed, or has no opinion about the concept.

Rating scales can be used effectively to analyze the types of responses made by the whole class. Tests given early in the semester can be compared with later tests, to see the changes that have occurred. The patterns of responses will also indicate areas of agreement and disagreement.

Advantages and Limitations of Rating Scales

Advantages:
- ☐ **Show intensity of feeling.**
- ☐ **Provide numeric score for individuals and class.**
- ☐ **Useful for early and late semester comparisons.**

Limitation:
- ☐ **Scores in middle range are difficult to interpret.**

SEMANTIC DIFFERENTIAL

The semantic differential scale was developed by Charles Osgood and his associates. It is a combination of both the adjective checklist and rating scale. In this format, the single concept to be rated is written above the scale. Under the concept are a number of **seven point scales**, with **opposing adjectives** or short phrases at each end.

How would you rate the mother in the novel on these scales?
Check appropriate space on each scale.

warmhearted	_____ :_____ :_____ :_____ :_____ :____ :____	coldhearted
selfish	_____ :_____ :_____ :_____ :_____ :____ :____	unselfish
patient	_____ :_____ :_____ :_____ :_____ :____ :____	impatient
competent	_____ :_____ :_____ :_____ :_____ :____ :____	incompetent
introverted	_____ :_____ :_____ :_____ :_____ :____ :____	outgoing
scatterbrained	_____ :_____ :_____ :_____ :_____ :____ :____	sensible
self-assured	_____ :_____ :_____ :_____ :_____ :____ :____	always worried
unhappy	_____ :_____ :_____ :_____ :_____ :____ :____	happy

Constructing a Semantic Differential Scale

When setting up the scales for a semantic differential, randomly place the location of the positive adjective as shown below. If you always put the positive adjective on the right side or always on the left side, students tend to mark all scales in the same way even though they may actually feel differently about specific adjectives.

Give your reaction to the film we had in class on the scales below:

appropriate	_____ :_____ :_____ :_____ :_____ :____ :____	inappropriate
confusing	_____ :_____ :_____ :_____ :_____ :____ :____	clear
boring	_____ :_____ :_____ :_____ :_____ :____ :____	stimulating
accurate	_____ :_____ :_____ :_____ :_____ :____ :____	inaccurate
biased	_____ :_____ :_____ :_____ :_____ :____ :____	authentic

On the **gray sheet**, page 346, pick a question you feel the semantic differential would help you answer. Turn to Exercise D, on **gray sheet** page 349, and design your own semantic differential scale.

Guidelines Summary: Semantic Differential Scale

- ☐ **Adjectives at each end of scale are opposites.**
- ☐ **Separate each pair of opposite objectives by a seven point scale.**
- ☐ **Randomly place location of positive adjectives.**

Scoring a Semantic Differential Scale

In scoring a semantic differential scale, follow the same procedure used for scoring a Likert scale. Assign numerical values from 7—1 going from the positive to the negative on individual items. Some will be in the reverse order depending on the positive or negative placement of the items. Total each score. The higher scores indicate favorable attitudes. Conversely, the lower scores indicate unfavorable attitudes. Remember that a total score in the middle range does not necessarily indicate a neutral attitude since it can be arrived at in a number of different ways.

Advantages and Limitations of the Semantic Differential Scale

The semantic differential, as you can see, is really an expanded version of the adjective checklist, but allows the gathering of more detailed information. In responding to the adjective checklist, students are free to mark any or none of the adjectives. But in responding to the semantic differential, students react to each adjective as they mark each scale.

Advantages:	☐ **Express the intensity of their opinions, attitudes, and interests.**
	☐ **Provide more detailed information than checklists.**
Limitation:	☐ **Limited to assessment of a single concept.**

RANKING

Another procedure for obtaining student opinion is ranking: arranging items or activities in an order with respect to a common feature. In these examples, students are asked to rank various aspects of a course or a program of study on the basis of their relative merit.

Read through the list of learning activities. Rank them in numerical order, 1 for the most appealing, 6 for the least appealing.

Activity	**Ranking**
Demonstrations	________
Field trip	________
Gaming simulation	________
Group presentations	________
Guest speaker	________
Watching a film	________

Rank these courses on the basis of their relative helpfulness to your program of study. 1 is high and 6 is low.

Course	**Ranking**
Conducting	________
Ear training	________
Music history	________
Sight reading	________
18th century harmony	________
19th century harmony	________

Using the Ranking Format

Ranking is especially helpful when you want to find out the relative position of an item with respect to other items. When you ask students to rank items, you force them to decide what they would put first, second, third, and so on. This type of choice is not required of students using checklists and rating scales. The ranking format is also easy to set up—you just draw up a list of topics, activities or other items and ask students to rank them on a specified criterion.

The construction of ranking lists needs some guidelines. For a moment, assume the role of a social psychology student. Your instructor has just given you this ranking task.

Rank These Topics from the Most to the Least Interesting.

_____ Aggression	_____ Friendship formation	_____ Obedience
_____ Altruism	_____ Attitude change	_____ Communication
_____ Conformity	_____ Affiliation	_____ Social learning
_____ Leadership	_____ Crowding	_____ Sexual behavior
_____ Cooperation	_____ Decision making	_____ Language learning
_____ Competition	_____ Perspective	_____ Personality

Many students would be confused and perhaps angry at the instructor for putting them through this lengthy exercise. Do not ask students to rank more than about **10** items at a time.

Science students ranked the seven topics below on the basis of difficulty in understanding the application of principles. The instructor calculated the average of the rankings indicated for each topic (the higher number indicating greater difficulty).

Rank these topics according to the difficulty you had in understanding the scientific principles. (1 is low)

Nuclear fission	2.6
Nuclear fusion	3.1
Solar energy	2.4
Geothermal energy	1.4
Wind energy	1.7
Tidal energy	2.1
Hydro energy	1.8

Exercise 14.

A. Can you tell which topic the class finds most difficult?

______ Yes________ No

B. Can you tell how difficult students feel a given topic is?

______ Yes________ No

Here are the answers:

A. Yes, you can tell which topic students find the most difficult, in this case the topic having to do with nuclear fusion got an average ranking of 3.1.

B. No, you cannot say how difficult students felt any topic was, all you can say is that on the average, certain topics were ranked as more difficult than others. It could be that all of the subjects were relatively easy but that the subject of nuclear fusion was not quite as *easy* as the rest.

The point here is that the ranking format is effective to tell you how items stand in relation to others, but it does not give definitive information about the intensity of opinions, interests, and attitudes.

Turn to Exercise E on **gray sheet**, page 349. Refer to the list of questions you prepared on **gray sheet**, page 346. In developing a ranking format, be certain your instructions are clear and the items listed are understood to have separate meanings.

Ranking Format Advantages and Limitations

Advantages

- ☐ **It is easy to draw up a list of items for students to rank.**
- ☐ **You can find out how a given item stands in relation to each of the other items.**

Limitations

- ☐ **Ranking is difficult when more than ten items are included.**
- ☐ **Ranking doesn't give absolute data: It doesn't tell *how difficult, how interesting*, or *how helpful.***

Review of Fixed Response Formats

Format	Advantages	Limitations	Type of Data
Adjective Checklist	Easy to make.	Not as precise. Does not convert to numerical score.	Absolute
Behavior Checklist	Gives indication of how people respond or act.	Difficult to specify behaviors precisely. Does not convert to numerical score.	Absolute
Rating Scales General Likert	Allows a range of responses. Easy to get a numerical score. Easy to get information on a *wide variety* of specific issues.	Total score in the middle range difficult to interpret.	Absolute
Semantic Differential	Allows a range of responses. Gives a detailed profile on each concept.	Gives information on only a few concepts.	Absolute
Ranking	Gives precise inform-ation about relative standing of items.	Does not give any information about the intensity of attitudes, opinions, and interests.	Relative

III. REVIEW TEST ON FIXED RESPONSE FORMATS

SITUATION **For each of the situations below, indicate with a check mark which format is most appropriate.**	Behavior Checklist	Adjective Checklist	Likert Scale	Semantic Differential	Ranking
A. You know that students are very interested in 10 topics, but you want to get more information about their preferences.					
B. You want to find out if certain beliefs students have are reflected in what they do.					
C. You want a quick, overall impression of students' reactions to a guest speaker.					
D. You are interested in finding out the intensity of students' attitudes about various aspects of your course.					
E. You want detailed information about how strongly students feel regarding a single concept such as the desirability of take-home tests.					

Ranking would be best for situation **A**. Because you already know that students are interested in all of the topics, the only way to discriminate among them is to ask students to rank them. For situation **B**, a behavior checklist is the most appropriate format. An adjective checklist is good for situation **C**. It is easy to make and gives you an overall impression.

For **D**, a Likert scale is probably the best. The Likert is especially useful in a situation like this where you have a large number of issues you are concerned about. You simply write a positive or negative statement about each issue and ask students to show to what extent they agree or disagree.

For **E**, a semantic differential is probably the best format. You describe the one concept about which you are concerned at the top of the page and list the scales below. You might also use a Likert scale and present the students with a number of statements, each of which treats a single concept.

IV. OPEN RESPONSE FORMAT

In this part of the module you will practice writing *open* questions. An open question asks students to express themselves in their own words rather than select an answer from a fixed set of possibilities. Typical open questions for opinion, interest, and attitude questionnaires might be:

- ☐ What do you consider to be strengths of this course?
- ☐ In what ways might this course be improved?
- ☐ Students have various attitudes about the self-paced learning methods used in the course. What were your reactions?

Turn to **gray sheet**, page 346. Select any of the questions that interest you and add other questions you wish to explore for developing open-response questions. Write three open-response questions according to the instructions for Exercise F on **gray sheet**, page 350.

Guidelines for Writing Open Questions

The following guidelines will assist you to prepare well written open questions. Review your three questions according to each guideline.

Guideline 1: Avoid Leading Questions and Loaded Words or Phrases.

Pick the *better* worded question in *each* pair.

A. (1) ____ Are you against the proctors bossing students around too much? To what extent?

(2) ____ How would you describe the way the proctors are treating students?

B. (1) ____ To what extent do you dislike having too many films in class?

(2) ____ To what extent did the films shown in this class prompt your learning of the subject matter?

Answer **A.(1)** is a leading question. After all, too much of anything is usually undesirable. It also contains the loaded word *bosses*. It is wise to avoid using loaded words such as *bureaucratic* or *substandard* because they suggest an automatic feeling of approval or disapproval.

B.(2) is the better choice because **B.(1)** is a leading question and prompts a *dislike* reply.

Guideline 2: Be Specific; Define and Use Terms Carefully.

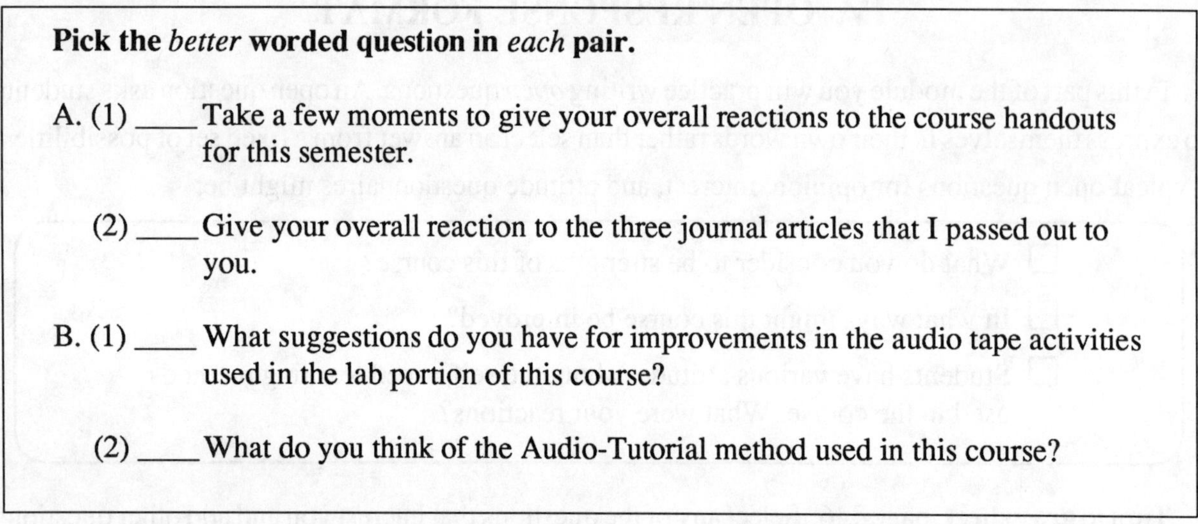

Pick the *better* worded question in *each* pair.

A. (1) ____ Take a few moments to give your overall reactions to the course handouts for this semester.

(2) ____ Give your overall reaction to the three journal articles that I passed out to you.

B. (1) ____ What suggestions do you have for improvements in the audio tape activities used in the lab portion of this course?

(2) ____ What do you think of the Audio-Tutorial method used in this course?

A.(2) is the better wording. It focuses specifically on the three journal articles. Students can respond more definitively when the question refers to a specific element.

B.(1) defines terms specifically so students are sure to know what they are to do. **B.(2)** is too broad, and responses may be too general.

Guideline 3: Counteract Social Desirability Bias by Asking Open Questions.

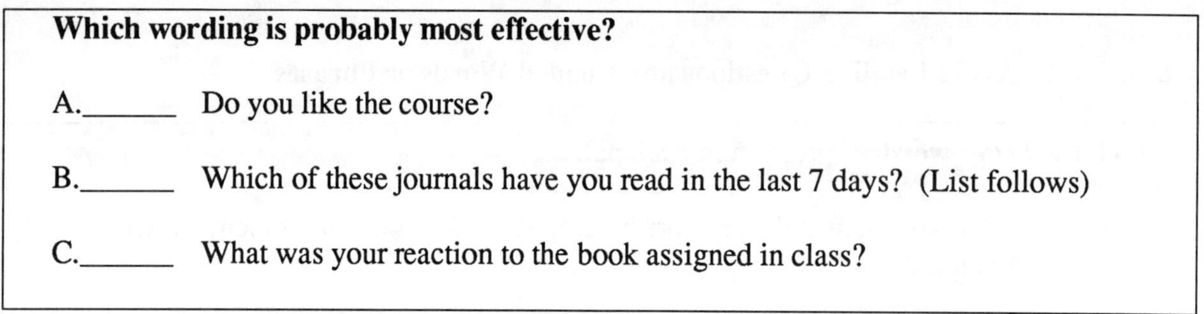

Which wording is probably most effective?

A.______ Do you like the course?

B.______ Which of these journals have you read in the last 7 days? (List follows)

C.______ What was your reaction to the book assigned in class?

Choice **C** is effective. It is a direct question with no *social acceptance* pressure.
Choice **A** is unacceptable. It may lead students to give an answer which would avoid criticism.
Choice **B** is a closed or limited question that presumes the student read some of the journals.

Students tend to tell instructors what they feel the instructor wants to hear. They will say they study more than they actually do or are more interested than they actually are. This tendency to give answers that command admiration or avoid criticism is the social desirability bias. To counteract this bias, it is helpful to word questions so that they are open and do not have value judgments attached to them. When this is done, the student will not feel the need to respond in order to meet assumed expectations.

Guideline 4: Encourage Criticism by Impersonal and Collaborative Wording.

Which question is preferable for encouraging student criticism?

A.______ Do you think my grading is fair?

B.______ Many students are quite properly concerned about being graded fairly. Do you feel you have been graded fairly in this class?

Question **B** is a preferable question because it is impersonal and non threatening. In the introduction students are told that it is perfectly proper to be concerned about being graded fairly. In **A** the use of the personal word *my* makes the question subjective. This is avoided in **B**.

Many students tend to say that everything is all right and present a rather bland facade because they feel any criticism offered would be taken as a personal affront by the instructor. This reservation on the part of students makes it difficult to get honest, constructive criticism. One way to counteract the problem is to word a question in an impersonal and collaborative manner.

Guideline 5: Avoid Response Prompting.

It is a good idea to start a questionnaire with non-directive questions that allow students to express themselves freely with confidence and a minimum of prompting. For example:

What aspects of this course did you find most relevant to your needs?

What is your reaction to having guest speakers in class?

What do you feel to be the value of student reports?

Comment on the various testing procedures used in this course.

What activities would you like to see given more emphasis in the course?

Finish this sentence, writing down the first thing that comes to your mind.
After participating in a discussion in this class, I . . .

These open questions get students to think about a specific topic with a minimum of prompting and encourage them to participate actively and develop a sense of empowerment.

Now turn to the **gray sheet**, page 350, to review the questions you have written and then complete Exercise G.

V. SUMMARY OUTLINE

I. FIXED RESPONSE FORMATS

Checklists: Students select words that best describe their reactions

Types: *Adjective checklist*
12-15 adjectives
Equal number of positive and negative adjectives
Behavior checklist
Specifies time periods
Names specific behavior

Advantage: Easy to make and use
Limitation: Does not show intensity of response

Rating Scales: Students rate levels of agreement with the statements

Types: *General:* Any number of rating points except 5
Likert: 5 point scale on several topics

Guidelines: Put only one concept in each concise statement
Use familiar words and phrases
Avoid proverbs and clichés
Have an equal number of positive and negative statements
Randomize the placement of pro and con statements
Watch how students respond to statements

Advantages: Shows intensity of response, gives numerical score
Limitation: Scores in the middle range difficult to interpret

Semantic Differential: Students rate a single concept on 7 point scales

Guideline: Randomly switch location of positive adjectives

Advantages: Gives detailed information and intensity of response
Limitation: Use of scale limited to single concepts

Ranking: Students rank items in order of preference

Advantages: Easy to prepare, gives *relative* importance of items
Limitations: Difficult to rank more than ten items
Ranking does not tell *how difficult* or *how interesting*

II. OPEN RESPONSE FORMAT GUIDELINES

Avoid leading questions and loaded words and phrases
Be specific and define terms carefully
Counteract social desirability bias
Encourage criticism by impersonal and collaborative wording
Avoid response prompting

REFERENCES AND RESOURCES

Aleamoni, Lawrence M. (Ed.) **Techniques for Evaluating and Improving Instruction**. San Francisco: Jossey-Bass Inc.,1987.

Braskamp, Larry A., D. C. Brandenburg, and J. C. Ory. **Evaluating Teaching Effectiveness.** Beverly Hills: Sage Publications, 1984.

Fuhrmann, B. S. and A. F. Grasha. **A Practical Handbook for College Teachers.** Boston: Little, Brown and Company, 1983.

Gronlund, N. E. and R. L. Linn. **Measurement and Evaluation in Teaching.** (6th ed.) New York: Macmillan, 1990.

Henerson, M. E., L. L. Morris, and C. T. Fitz-Gibbon. **How to Measure Attitudes**. Beverly Hills, CA: Sage Publications, 1987.

Hopkins, Kenneth D., Julian C. Stanley, and B.R. Hopkins. **Educational and Psychological Measurement and Evaluation.** (7th ed.) Englewood Cliffs, NJ: Prentice-Hall Inc., 1990.

Krathwohl, D. R., and others. **Taxonomy of Educational Objectives: Handbook II, Affective Domain.** New York: Longman, 1964.

McKeachie, W. J. **Teaching Tips: A Guidebook for the Beginning College Teacher**. (8th ed.) Lexington, MA: D.C. Heath and Company, 1986.

Osgood, C. E., G. J. Suci, and P.H. Tannenbaum. **The Measurement of Meaning.** Urbana: The University of Illinois Press, 1957.

Sax, Gilbert. **Principles of Educational and Psychological Measurement and Evaluation.** (3rd ed.) Belmont, CA: Wadsworth Publishing Company, 1989.

Seldin, P. **Changing Practices in Faculty Education: A Critical Assessment and Recommendations for Improvement**. San Francisco: Jossey-Bass Inc., 1984.

VI. APPLICATION EXERCISE

What are students' opinions, interests and attitudes regarding . . .

A. My course content. ***Do students . . .***

______ have enough say in course planning?

______ find the topics relevant? stimulating? poorly integrated? boring? repetitious?

______ find the content level suitable to their background? too difficult? too easy?

B. The instructional resources and activities in my course. ***Do students . . .***

______ learn more from lectures that are supplemented with visual materials than solely verbal presentations?

______ find hand-outs useful in studying?

______ feel free to ask for tutorial help when needed?

______ find the assigned learning activities either particularly helpful or difficult in mastering course objectives? (which activities or course objectives?)

C. The subject area. ***Do students . . .***

______ have any previous experience in the subject area?

______ want to take another course in the area?

______ freely choose to read articles and books in the area?

D. My teaching style. ***Do students . . .***

______ find my presentation well organized?

______ understand the language I use?

______ find the questions stimulating and challenging?

______ think I grade fairly?

E. Me as a person. ***Do students . . .***

______ show respect for me?

______ ask for individual help without hesitation?

______ find me open to criticism?

______ enjoy being around me?

F. Other:____

____

____

Exercise A.

Write your own adjective checklist here:

Directions: ____

____

____

Adjective list: ______________ ______________

______________ ______________

______________ ______________

______________ ______________

______________ ______________

______________ ______________

______________ ______________

______________ ______________

Exercise B.

Write your own behavior checklist here:

Directions: ____

____

____

Behaviors: ____

_______ ____

_______ ____

_______ ____

_______ ____

_______ ____

_______ ____

Exercise C.

Write your own rating scale questionnaire item below. Use a Likert scale of five rating points and include at least five statements.					
Show to what extent you agree or disagree with each of these statements by checking the appropriate columns. **STATEMENTS**					

Exercise D.

Use this form to lay out your own semantic differential scale. Fill in the blank to make the directions complete. Then write in appropriate adjectives.

Directions: Show how you feel about______________________________ by checking the appropriate blanks below.

(Adjectives) **(Adjectives)**

_______________: ___: ___: ___: ___: ___: ___: ___: _______________

_______________: ___: ___: ___: ___: ___: ___: ___: _______________

_______________: ___: ___: ___: ___: ___: ___: ___: _______________

_______________: ___: ___: ___: ___: ___: ___: ___: _______________

Exercise E.

Select an area that consists of items that may be ranked. Write the directions and list 10 items.

Directions:____

____

1.____________________
2.____________________
3.____________________
4.____________________
5.____________________
6.____________________
7.____________________
8.____________________
9.____________________
10.____________________

Exercise F.

On the lines below write *three* open questions to determine opinions, interests, or attitudes of your students. Select questions from the topics you checked or wrote in on the previous page.

1. ____________________

____

____

____

2. ____________________

____

____

____

3. ____________________

____

____

____

Exercise G.

Write a question with a non-directive opening about *lecturing* or an area of concern to you.

Index

O

P

Q

R

S

T

V

W